PRAISE FOR

THE PEACE THAT ALMOST WAS

The Peace That Almost Was is a thoroughly researched and engagingly written history of a crucial but mostly forgotten moment in American history, one that serves as a vivid reminder of how dangerous compromise can sometimes be.

—John Bicknell, author of *America 1844*

A truly neglected subject, too long overlooked, has now inspired a well-researched, evocatively recounted history. No one can possibly appreciate the drama that preceded and provoked the American Civil War without understanding the idea, and failure, of the Washington Peace Conference. The event and the author have finally met. The result is highly recommended.

—Harold Holzer, winner of the
Lincoln Prize

I most appreciate [Tooley's] insights into the roles that Christian ministers and churches played in the struggle between war and peace. Faith matters—and Tooley lifts up this often overlooked dimension of America's struggle for its soul.

—Ronald C. White Jr., author of
A. Lincoln: A Biography and *Lincoln's
Greatest Speech: The Second Inaugural*

Tooley brings to life a fascinating cast of characters, from politicians to ministers to socialites, who prayed for peace but could find no way to avert the sectional clash over slavery.

—Thomas S. Kidd, professor of
history, Baylor University

THE
PEACE
THAT ALMOST WAS

THE
PEACE
THAT ALMOST WAS

The Forgotten Story of the 1861 Washington Peace Conference
and the Final Attempt to Avert the Civil War

MARK TOOLEY

NELSON
BOOKS

An Imprint of Thomas Nelson

Published in Nashville, Tennessee, by Nelson Books, an imprint of Thomas Nelson. Nelson Books and Thomas Nelson are registered trademarks of HarperCollins Christian Publishing, Inc.

Interior designed by Mallory Perkins.

Thomas Nelson, Inc., titles may be purchased in bulk for educational, business, fund-raising, or sales promotional use. For information, please e-mail SpecialMarkets@ ThomasNelson.com.

Unless otherwise noted, Scripture quotations are taken from THE ENGLISH STANDARD VERSION. © 2001 by Crossway Bibles, a division of Good News Publishers. Scripture quotations marked KJV are from the KING JAMES VERSION.

Unless otherwise noted, images are from the Library of Congress's Prints and Photographs Division.

Library of Congress Cataloging-in-Publication Data

Library of Congress Cataloging-in-Publication Data
Tooley, Mark, 1965-
 The peace that almost was: the forgotten story of the 1861 Washington Peace Conference and the final attempt to avert the Civil War / Mark Tooley.
 pages cm
 Includes bibliographical references.
 ISBN 978-0-7180-2223-5
 1. Conference Convention (1861: Washington, D.C.) 2. United States—Politics and government—1857–1861. I. Title.
 E440.5.T66 2015
 320.97309'034—dc23
 2014038442

Printed in the United States of America

15 16 17 18 19 RRD 6 5 4 3 2 1

CONTENTS

INTRODUCTION

A house divided against itself cannot stand.

—Abraham Lincoln

The Civil War would kill more than 700,000 and leave wounds on the nation that took a century or more to heal. In February 1861 scores of America's leading statesmen frantically gathered at the storied Willard's Hotel in Washington, DC, to negotiate how to avoid disunion and war. Seven states had already seceded in reaction to Abraham Lincoln's election as president. Several more were poised to follow. Federal property in the South was being seized. On the day the Peace Conference began, the new Confederate government convened in Montgomery, Alabama.

The instigator and guiding force for the Peace Conference was former president John Tyler, referred to sometimes as "His Accidency" because he was America's first chief executive to gain office not by direct election but the death of his predecessor, William Henry Harrison. A patrician of noble bearing from an old Virginia family, the aging Tyler reemerged from a long retirement on his James River plantation to preside over the Peace Conference.

Tyler was accompanied by his vivacious and much younger wife, Julia, who was all too glad to return to the city where she had presided regally as First Lady when only in her early twenties. The social apex of her month in the nation's capital during the winter of 1861 was a lavish ball at the home of failed presidential candidate Stephen Douglas. More than four hundred of Washington's elite were there, including many peace commissioners, many of whom rushed over after a White House reception.

The Tylers had just missed their old friends Jefferson and Varina Davis, who had tearfully quit Washington only days before the Tylers' arrival. Senator Davis had resigned from the US Senate in solidarity with his departing Mississippi. Soon he would be president of the new Confederacy, with Varina as the South's new First Lady. The Davises had long lived next door to defeated presidential candidate Senator Stephen Douglas on a prestigious Washington street. The same street was home to Vice President John Breckinridge, another failed 1860 presidential candidate defeated by Lincoln, who would soon serve the Confederacy as a general. During that February of 1861 he presided over the US Senate as it received the Electoral College results electing Lincoln.

Presiding over Washington and the nation during the final tremulous weeks of his presidency, James Buchanan was a longtime friend to the Tylers and Davises, and to many others who were leaders in the unfolding drama at the Willard's Hotel. Buchanan had served his country since he was a young soldier in the War of 1812. He was deeply devoted to the Union while sympathetic to Southern determination to protect slavery. Now as that Union fractured, he was uncertain what power he had to sustain it, leaving both Unionists and Secessionists perpetually exasperated with him.

Buchanan was arguably the most experienced man ever to assume the presidency, having served as state legislator, US congressman, US senator, secretary of state, ambassador to both Russia and Britain, and a college president, plus his military service. But he was ill prepared for this national crisis, having declared at the advent of his presidency that the issue of slavery had been permanently settled by the US Supreme Court, whose Dred Scott ruling had declared all blacks, even when free, noncitizens.

Since Buchanan was a lifelong bachelor, his handsome niece Harriet Lane served as the country's First Lady. She was only in her twenties but socially confident, if deemed cold and reserved by some. She was friends with Julia Tyler and Varina Davis and virtually all other notables who were in or had just left Washington as the Peace Conference convened. It was she who artfully helped the president preside over his final lavish White House social entertainments, including the New Year's Day open house and the monthly levees of January and February. Typically thronging with Southerners and Buchanan's fellow Democrats, many of whom were now leaving town, suddenly the White House was filled with newly arriving Republicans, with whom Buchanan maintained a reserved cordiality.

The president's top military commander was the legendary Winfield Scott, the nation's only lieutenant general since George Washington. Scott had in fact been a general since his time as a dashing young commander in the War of 1812. Scott was now tall, fat, white haired, and—although unable to straddle a horse or even climb many stairs at age seventy-five—was still kingly in his bearing, his epaulets, sword, and medals gleaming. Born before the US Constitution was drafted, he had served every president since Thomas Jefferson. Although a Virginian, Scott was deeply loyal to the Union. Pragmatically unhopeful about the Peace Conference, he arranged for the military security of Washington as it prepared for Lincoln's inauguration.

To vividly illustrate the Union's strength, history, and durability, Scott had meticulously plotted a powerful military display for George Washington's birthday during the Peace Conference. In a plan originally hatched by a controversial, scandal-plagued New York Democratic congressman, the US Army and Marines would parade through Washington's streets both to inspire and intimidate. But at the last minute, President Buchanan felt obliged to consult ex-President Tyler, the Peace Conference president, as to whether the parade might offend Southern delegates. Tyler naturally replied in the affirmative. Even as military units donned their uniforms and equipment in the morning, the White House issued new orders rescinding their parade participation, disappointing gathered crowds and infuriating staunch Unionists. Characteristically, Buchanan was persuaded to change his mind later in the day, so US Army units were hastily reconfigured for their march through Washington, although it was too late for the marines.

Even the celebration logistics of Washington's birthday became a divisive and confused drama, illustrating the nation's predicament. In his opening address to the Peace Conference, Tyler had appealed to the patriotic valor of each state of the Union, particularly their role in the American Revolution. But now even the nation's founder and chief leader in that struggle could not be properly honored without acrimony, with all of the federal capital and nation to behold.

Each day of the Peace Conference opened with a prayer by a Washington clergyman. In fact, the convention met in what had been a venerable Presbyterian church where many great statesmen, including several presidents, had regularly worshipped. Its pastor had been the Reverend Phineas Gurley. Now US Senate chaplain, Gurley delivered the prayer on the Peace Conference's first day. As pastor of the newly created New York Avenue Presbyterian Church, he would soon become pastor and spiritual counselor to President Lincoln, especially during the agony of the death of Lincoln's beloved son, Willie. Gurley was an old-school Presbyterian who believed his role was to preach the gospel, not politics. This drew Lincoln to him. But even Gurley was glad to pray with and for the peace commissioners struggling to avoid national conflict.

During February 1861 Gurley had also led worship in the US Capitol, where worship services had convened since the very early days of the republic, when churches had not yet been built in the new city. Even President Jefferson had regularly attended. But worship at the Capitol, if a revered tradition, was no longer so necessary. Washington was now full of thriving churches whose spires punctuated the city's profile along the Potomac. St. John's Episcopal, across Lafayette Square from the White House, was the most prestigious of churches. Every president since Madison had worshipped there, and Lincoln would attend there on his first Sunday in Washington, escorted by his new secretary of state, William Seward.

The churches might have fostered greater national unity. Both the North and South worshipped the same God and read the same Bible, as Lincoln later famously recounted in his 1864 inaugural address. But instead, unable to agree on slavery, the churches had played a key role in the nation's tragically unfolding division. America's largest religious movement was Methodism, which originally was anti-slavery. But in 1844 the Methodist Episcopal Church agreed to divide into two denominations along sectional lines; Southern Methodism had decided that slavery had biblical merit, or at least could be tolerated. The Baptists shortly followed, as did the Presbyterians.

Statesmen and polemists for both the North and South were freely resorting to religious rhetoric in justification of their causes, for which the churches provided ample ammunition. Even in Washington, churches were divided, although Southern sympathizers would soon need to be careful. The Church of the Epiphany, just one block north of the Peace Conference's meeting at Willard's, had been Jefferson Davis's place of worship. It would be frequented by Edwin Stanton during the war. As President Buchanan's pro-Union attorney general, Stanton would negotiate with Tyler in the days before the Peace Conference, and would soon become Lincoln's fiercely competent war secretary. During the days of the Peace Conference, Washington's churches, or at least their clergy, publicly prayed and preached for national reconciliation, even if agreement over slavery was as impossible for the churches as it was for politicians.

The peace commissioners and other leaders of the drama in February 1861 were religiously devout to varying degrees. President Buchanan was a regular churchgoer, sometimes pronouncing the sermons "too long." He was considered by some overly sanctimonious. Tyler was a less observant Virginia Episcopalian who some considered inclined toward deism, but he became more religiously devout in his old age. His much younger wife would convert to Catholicism late in life. Winfield Scott was an ardent Episcopalian, even addressing a convention of the American Bible Society during Tyler's presidency. This required Tyler to assure a Jewish group that Scott was acting only in his private capacity. The leading Republican at the Peace Conference was Ohio's anti-slavery US Senator Salmon Chase, soon to be Lincoln's treasury secretary, and a devout Episcopalian. Chase's faith was likely increased by the tragic deaths by illness of all three of his wives, leaving him a permanent widower. Chase, like many ardent anti-slavery Americans, saw restricting the growth of slavery, if not eliminating it, as a religious imperative.

Later apologists for the Southern cause would try to insist that other sectional issues besides slavery were prime motivators behind the nation's crumbling in late 1860 and early 1861. For instance, tariffs benefited Northern industrialists at the expense of Southern agrarians. But the Peace Conference discussed slavery almost exclusively, and the proposed national compromises it ultimately endorsed dealt only with slavery. Congress would separately address tariff legislation in February 1861, with ascendant Republican Northerners now emboldened. Southern peace commissioners and others who sought to accommodate the South thought the tariff issue at that time provocative. But the Peace Conference did not formally address tariffs in its deliberations.

Nearly all of the Peace Conference was a desperate attempt to protect slavery and assuage Southern worries about Northern Republican encroachment on Southern political prerogatives. In December, Kentucky's Senator John Crittenden had become a national celebrity and near hero for championing constitutional amendments to protect slavery. Many thought these amendments could prevent disunion. Special committees in both houses of Congress, which included such Senate notables as Seward, Davis, and Douglas, examined the compromise package. But neither house would approve it. Peace commissioners sought to repackage the Crittenden ideas more palatably, hoping that the ongoing secession crisis and threat of war would intimidate otherwise recalcitrant Northerners and Southerners into compromise.

Meanwhile, the peace commissioners convened in a secret session from which reporters were barred, and for which there were not even formal minutes. As the commissioners met, the new president-elect was slowly meandering toward Washington in a train that crisscrossed the North. He carefully evaded public comment that would fully show his hand on the compromises being pondered at the Peace Conference and in Congress. His supporters insisted he and the Republican Party, faithful to their 1860 Chicago platform, were firmly committed to blocking any expansion of slavery into the West, even as they granted they had no power to touch slavery where it already existed. Adversaries thought Lincoln's relative silence irresponsible. His supporters thought him shrewd. But upon his arrival in Washington, DC, Lincoln engaged in two key moments of uninhibited confrontation between the old agrarian order of American slavery and the new emerging order of predominant Northern industrialism. The first was Lincoln's reception of the peace delegates soon after he arrived. The second was his later meeting with several key delegates when the compromise proposals seemed on the verge of collapse.

That evening an obliging slave passed a note to his startled master in the Peace Conference announcing Lincoln's arrival, in a vignette illustrating the irreconcilable differences between the old slave order and the new rule of a Free Soil Party. The delegates, despite their struggle, could not bridge this vast social and political chasm between the North and South. The Peace Conference, despite its failure to prevent disunion and civil war, was memorably the last hurrah of the nation's old guard. These aging statesmen had fought in the War of 1812 as young men, and had known Founders like Madison, Monroe, and Jefferson. Several of them were literally children of the Founders, who had for decades mediated and crafted compromises that kept the Union together, however precariously, delaying the final confrontation until the election of the first openly anti-slavery president in 1860. The Peace Conference and the ensuing upheaval it sought to prevent would quickly brush these men away. The path would be cleared for a revolutionary new generation who would lead the United States into a new era of industrialism and national growth, notably without slavery.

Here is the story of those very anxious weeks of February 1861, when that old guard tried its best to safeguard the nation and prevent the massive effusion of blood. But this would have to come at a price: perpetual protection for and even expansion of slavery. It was too much for the newly emerging anti-slavery majority.

ONE

CRISIS

The conqueror will walk at every step over smoldering ashes.

—John Tyler

About 60 of the 131 statesmen dispatched by their states to the Washington Peace Conference trooped into the assembly hall at Willard's Hotel in Washington, DC. It was noon on a chilly Monday, February 4, 1861. It had snowed late in the night, accumulating more than two inches, with the skies clearing by early afternoon. A hotel concessioner, targeting the peace commissioners, sold cockades, worn on the chest to demonstrate Union or Secession loyalty, "suitable for all political sentiments."[1]

A Washington newspaper pleadingly editorialized that morning:

We are sure we echo the consenting prayer of a great majority of our countrymen, who will mark the proceedings with a solicitude second to that which has attached to no similar meeting in our civil history.... We cannot doubt that every member will act with a deep and solemn sense of his responsibility in the sight of God and fellow-citizens throughout the whole land.[2]

Even with such prayers, the cold and snow perhaps added to the gloom in the nation's capital. Nearly every day since Abraham Lincoln's election four months earlier brought more reports of the Union's disintegration. Six Deep South states, starting with South Carolina in December, had already seceded, their congressional delegations having quit the US Congress. On that very day, February 4, their representatives convened in Montgomery, Alabama, as the Provisional Congress of the Confederate States of America. Federal facilities in the Deep South were seized by state authorities, excepting a few US Army installations like Fort Sumter, South Carolina, whose resistance would spark the war.

President James Buchanan dithered over resistance or acquiescence to the secession. In his final annual message to Congress in December, he faulted the unfolding crisis on the "long-continued and intemperate interference of the Northern people with the question of slavery." He further blamed the "incessant and violent agitation of the slavery question throughout the North for the last quarter of a century" for its "malign influence on the slaves and inspired them with vague notions of freedom." It had left no "sense of security . . . around the family altar," thanks to "apprehensions of servile insurrections," with "many a matron throughout the South . . . at night in dread of what may befall herself and children before the morning."[3]

The solution was "easy," Buchanan promised. All the American people must do to "settle the slavery question forever" was to leave the Southern slave states alone to "manage their domestic institutions in their own way." After all, he reasoned, "as sovereign States, they, and they alone, are responsible before God and the world for the slavery existing among them." He asserted that "the people of the North are not more responsible and have no more right to interfere than with similar institutions in Russia or in Brazil."[4]

Easy indeed. Buchanan warned Southern states they had no right to quit the Union, while professing he had no constitutional authority to hold them by force. His secretary of state, Lewis Cass of Michigan, resigned in December to protest Buchanan's inaction. The secretary of war, John Floyd of Virginia, was fired weeks later for suspiciously relocating US military resources to the South. Deep South members of the cabinet resigned in solidarity with their departing states.

On February 13, the Electoral College results of the presidential election were scheduled for ratification in a joint session of the US Congress. Some wondered if a sufficient congressional quorum would even be present. Others harbored dark fears of possibly violent plots to disrupt the ratification, over which pro-Southern Vice President John Breckenridge of Kentucky, one of Lincoln's presidential opponents, would preside.

In January Congress had rejected the "Crittenden Compromise." It came from aging Kentucky US Senator John Crittenden. Through constitutional amendments and congressional resolutions, it mandated that slavery could spread to new southern states in the West, in sync with the old Missouri Compromise of 1820. And it forbade congressional interference with the intrastate slave trade or any abolition of slavery by Congress, plus guaranteed federal reimbursement to owners of escaped slaves. President-elect Lincoln and his newly empowered Republican Party did not dispute slavery's legality where it was already existing, but they would not permit its spread, as their 1860 Chicago party platform stipulated.

Amid this brewing crisis, former president John Tyler, nearly age seventy-one, emerged from sixteen years of quiet retirement at his romantically named Sherwood Forest Virginia plantation on the James River, surging suddenly back into public life. On December 14, 1860, before South Carolina's secession, privately pondering the "lunacy which seems to have seized the North," he suggested to a Northern friend a "consultation" among border states, six free and six slave, as the "most interested in keeping the peace," and without whose agreement the "union is gone."[5]

A month later, on January 10, Tyler told his son that the "pressure on me for an opinion on the crisis leaves me no alternative." His public proposal would soon appear in a Richmond newspaper; he thought it would "strengthen our friends in the north." Published on January 17, and nationally publicized, Tyler's letter proposed a possible alternative to the "dissolution of that confederacy in the service of which so great a portion of my life has been passed." Virginia's legislature having already scheduled a state convention in February to ponder secession, to which he was himself elected, Tyler suggested the legislature also, in a final bid for "quiet and harmony," invite six free and six border slave states to negotiate preservation of the Union through "adjustment" of the Constitution. Absent such agreement, "peace and concord has become impossible," and the South should create its own new union, under the same Constitution, inviting all states to join it, "with the old flag flying over one and all."[6]

Virginia's legislature, the oldest elected assembly in the Western Hemisphere, expanded Tyler's idea. On January 19 it proposed a convention of all states to adjudicate their differences, lest disunion be "inevitable," and to "avert so dire a calamity" by making a "final effort to restore the Union and the Constitution, in the spirit in which they were established by the Fathers of the Republic." The Virginians commended the Crittenden Compromise, which protected "slavery of the African race" in the southwestern territories and the right of slave owners to transmit slaves across free territory, as a solution to the "unhappy controversy."[7]

Tyler was privately disappointed that the legislature had expanded his idea into an invitation to all states, which he feared would lead to Northern domination and gridlock. Northern and Southern diehards were exasperated and suspicious of Virginia's plea for reconciliation. A Richmond newspaper hyperbolically denounced the Virginia legislature's peace convention idea for supposedly suggesting that Virginia "submit to anti-slavery oppression" by the North. But a Cincinnati newspaper denied that Virginia's appeal "conceals some dark design of the Disunionists," asserting that it instead showed "perfect good faith." A Washington newspaper hailed the "ancient commonwealth" for trying to mediate "between the alienated sections of a common country."[8]

Hedging its bets, the Virginia legislature also affirmed that if reconciliation failed, Virginia would "unite her destinies with her sister slaveholding states." Firebrand legislator James Seddon was appointed to the Peace Conference with Tyler and three others who were more moderate. He successfully proposed that Virginia accept no restoration of the Union that didn't allow to "each section self-protecting power against any invasion of the Federal Union."[9]

As his ancient state's most prominent senior statesman, Tyler was quickly dispatched by the Virginia legislature to President Buchanan, bearing its peace proposal. He was to appeal in the interim for federal restraint toward the seceding states, "avoiding all acts calculated to produce a collision of arms."[10] On January 23, Tyler left for Washington, by way of Richmond. Mrs. Tyler noted he was "very unwell," heavily medicated with mercury and chalk, but he felt he "must go." She observed, the "excitement of convention always agrees with him." Mrs. Tyler expected Southern states to "stay" their secession out of respect to her husband, who was accompanied by their fourteen-year-old son playing the part of his courier with the White House.[11]

Tyler headed north along the route between Richmond and Washington, where hundreds of thousands from Northern and Southern armies would clash almost continuously for the next four years. From his rickety and likely not well-heated train on that winter afternoon, he could view from his window what would be some of the bloodiest battlefields in American history: Fredericksburg, Chancellorsville, the Wilderness, and Spotsylvania, among others. His warnings about the violent consequences of failure to conciliate the dividing sections, and his Virginia statesman's knowledge of war and geography, indicate he must have quietly pondered the possibility, even likelihood, that he was traveling through lands soon to be blood drenched and ruined.[12]

Tyler was committed to the Union, but his love began with his native Virginia, which he foresaw being especially ravaged by war. Four years earlier, he had given a speech commemorating the anniversary of English settlement at Jamestown, with Northern abolitionists probably in mind. He declared: "Political demagogues may revile and abuse, but they cannot detract from the high and lofty fame which belongs to this time-honored commonwealth."[13]

TYLER MEETS BUCHANAN

Upon Tyler's arrival in Washington, he sent a note requesting an immediate meeting with President Buchanan. The president readily invited him to the White House that evening. Tyler and Buchanan had known each other since Buchanan joined him in the US Senate in 1834. Tyler had even supported his earlier failed 1852 attempt for the Democratic presidential nomination. But Tyler had little warmth for Buchanan, once explaining, "he had none for me in my severe trials." Now explaining his health was "too delicate to make it prudent for me to encounter the night air" of a cold January, Tyler instead visited Buchanan the next morning for ninety minutes.[14]

Buchanan received his predecessor cordially. Nearly age seventy, just a year younger than Tyler, he was desperate for national conciliation, having served in public office nearly a half century as Pennsylvania state legislator, US congressman, US senator, minister to Russia under Andrew Jackson, minister to Britain under President Franklin Pierce, and US secretary of state under President James Polk. He came from modest means, literally born in a log cabin, with a Scots-Irish immigrant farmer for a father. Buchanan began politically as an antiwar Federalist and later became a Democrat. The last War of 1812 veteran to sit in the White House, and the last US president born in the eighteenth century, he had overcome his war skepticism to serve in the defense of Baltimore against the British in 1814—the battle that would inspire Francis Scott Key's "Star Spangled Banner."

In 1834, when Buchanan was a rising politician, he was alarmed by the implications for his career when his sister married a Virginia slave owner. Buchanan purchased two of their slaves for manumission, although Pennsylvania law kept the adult woman bound to Buchanan for seven years and the five-year-old girl until age twenty-eight.[15] In 1836 he had warned his fellow US senators, "touch this issue of slavery seriously . . . and the Union is from that moment dissolved." He explained that Pennsylvanians "are all opposed to slavery in the abstract" but would never violate Southern rights.[16]

In an 1844 US Senate speech, Buchanan argued that annexing Texas as a slave state would facilitate gradual emancipation by drawing slaves from throughout the South and ultimately funneling them into Mexico, where they could attain "social equality." He faulted the "mad interference" of abolitionists for interrupting public opinion's trend toward gradual emancipation.[17]

Fussy, gossipy, obsessed with detail, sometimes irritable, ever ambitious, and often eager to please, Buchanan reputedly was derided in private by President Jackson as "Miss Nancy." He was a lifelong bachelor whose First Lady during his presidency was his attractive and coldly proper young niece, the very devoted Harriet Lane, whom he had adopted after her parents' death, and with whom he maintained a sometimes tense but still solid social partnership.

Seen as sanctimonious, Buchanan was sarcastically called "the Pride of the Christian World" or "Old Gurley," after his sometime Presbyterian pastor and US Senate Chaplain Phineas Gurley.[18] Late in his presidency he reportedly conferred with a New York Presbyterian minister about "regeneration, atonement, repentance, and faith," after which he indicated he had "much of the experience which you describe." He promised to formally "unite" with Presbyterianism after retirement, to avoid charges of hypocrisy, lest he seem to profess religion only for political gain.[19]

Buchanan preferred to be known as "the Old Public Functionary," signifying his years of public service and multiplicity of offices. Loyal to the Union he had served so long, he was long partial to Southern concerns and, like nearly all his presidential predecessors, never publicly criticized slavery. He had precipitously acclaimed the US Supreme Court's 1857 Dred Scott decision, which was announced right after his inauguration, and which denied any citizen rights even to free blacks, as permanently settling the slavery question.

As the nation crumbled over slavery, Buchanan nonchalantly insisted to all during his final months in office that he slept soundly. But some noticed that his hair had grown pure white. He was a tall, large bellied figure dressed formally in black, his head chronically tossed to one side. Reserved and with few close friends, he was still sociable, had female admirers, deployed warmth and charm when necessary, and could be physically demonstrative. He and his diligent niece tried with some success to cohere Washington socially even as it fractured politically. Their final New Year's Day reception, open nearly to all, had been mostly a success, even if many Southern notables were noticeably absent. Some attenders wore cockades of competing loyalties, and some defiant women ignored the offered hand of President Buchanan "with an effort at display of lofty disdain."[20]

Buchanan's monthly levee a couple of weeks later was pronounced "elegant" but singularly unique. Most of his fellow Democrats were observed absent, while newly arrived Northern Republicans proliferated, offering him "many words of patriotism and kindness," which the president naturally, if nervously, appreciated.[21] A Georgia newspaper more caustically portrayed Buchanan's reception as "thinly attended" and including "few congratulations," as his visitors were mainly his formerly "bitterest opponents." It warned the president: "Save me from my friends."[22]

Buchanan was always a careful party loyalist who had fought his way upward politically from obscurity. But Tyler, on the other hand, was a self-assured, patrician political maverick born into Virginia aristocracy. He was confident he spoke for his commonwealth at the hour of its peril. On the morning of Thursday, January 24, at the White House, his own former residence, he assured Buchanan that Virginians were "almost universally inclined to peace and reconciliation" and urged his sharing with Congress Virginia's plea for the "status quo."[23]

President Buchanan readily agreed to transmit to Congress Virginia's appeal for a peace summit of the states, which he "hailed with great satisfaction." But he complained that seceding Southern states had "not treated him properly" by "seizing unprotected arsenals and forts, and thus perpetrating useless acts of *bravado*, which had quite as well been let alone." Tyler admitted these acts were meant to "fret and irritate the Northern mind, that he could see in them only the necessary results of popular excitement which, after all, worked no mischief in the end if harmony between the States was once more restored."[24]

Tyler met with Buchanan a second time the following day, and Buchanan approvingly reviewed the text of the presidential message to Congress. Tyler personally watched with satisfaction as Virginia's appeal for peace was presented to the US Senate, where it was received politely but without formal response. New York Republican Senator William Seward, soon to be Lincoln's secretary of state, approached him to shake hands, with a "timidity he could not disguise," Mrs. Tyler recalled.[25] Buchanan's message stressed the urgency of ensuring the "slaveholding states adequate guarantees for the security of their rights" and commended to Congress Virginia's plea for a pledge to avoid force. Trusting that "Virginia's mediation" under the "Providence of God" would "perpetuate the Union," he declared with optimistic bravado: "I am one of those who will never despair of the Republic."[26]

Tyler sent notes from his customary lodging at Brown's Hotel on Pennsylvania Avenue, firmly asking for explanations from Buchanan about a US military supply ship's rumored dispatch to the South. Buchanan assured him it was "an errand of mercy and relief." A Richmond newspaper approvingly reported Tyler was "looking well" and "quite determined to see that the rights of Virginia are maintained." After a week, Tyler left Washington, satisfied his dramatic mission of peace had at least somewhat succeeded, although a Georgia newspaper inferred it was "not entirely successful," however "kindly" the president may have received him. He would return for the Peace Conference one week later.[27]

Ominously, Tyler had warned of failure's bleak consequences in his first public proposal of the Peace Conference:

> The conqueror will walk at every step over smoldering ashes and beneath crumbling columns. States once proud and independent will

no longer exist and the glory of the Union will have departed forever. Ruin and desolation will everywhere prevail, and the victor's brow, instead of a wreath of glorious evergreen such as a patriot wears, will be encircled with withered and faded leaves endeared with the blood of the child and its mother and the father and the son. The picture is too horrible and revolting to be dwelt upon.[28]

Unheeding of Virginia's appeal, none of the seven seceded states (Texas ratified secession during the convention on February 23) agreed to attend the Peace Conference, nor did three strongly Republican Midwestern free states.[29] But fourteen free states and seven slave states sent representatives. Arkansas ignored the invitation, while California and Oregon were too distant to consider in time. New York's governor responded:

The great mass of the people of this state, and of the entire North, are actuated by an earnest desire that no honorable effort should be left untried to maintain, by peaceful means, the American Union as it has existed for almost a century; and especially to encourage every exertion made toward an adjustment of existing differences by the loyal states.[30]

Some avid Republicans were reluctant for their states to participate in the Peace Conference, perceiving it would undermine Lincoln's presidential options. Massachusetts US Senator Charles Sumner was a strong slavery opponent who had been famously thrashed with a cane on the Senate floor by a pro-slavery congressman in 1856, while Senator Crittenden was blocked by a Southern colleague from intervening. Sumner denounced congressmen from his state who were urging participation in the Peace Conference. Congressman Charles Francis Adams, son of President John Quincy Adams and grandson of John Adams, rebuffed the admonishment, prompting a supportive Washington newspaper to say the "son of such fathers cannot do wrong in a moment of gloom like the present."[31]

Sharing Sumner's concern, the strongly Republican, pro-Lincoln states of Michigan, Minnesota, and Wisconsin refused to send delegates. They were populated by the New England Puritan diaspora, strongly anti-slavery, but not as wedded as the East Coast to trade with the cotton South. Minnesota had voted for Lincoln by almost two to one, and Republicans had fifty-nine out of sixty-three state legislative seats. A St. Paul newspaper editor decreed: "Before this rampant fever of disunion will at all abate, THERE MUST BE BLOOD LETTING!" State legislators resolved: "It is not expedient to compromise when the only basis is for the protection of slavery."[32]

A Michigan US senator urged his state to appoint stalwart representatives to "prevent compromise." The state's other US senator similarly had urged the dispatch of "stiff-backed men." But the state legislature declined to acknowledge the Peace Conference, by a far narrower margin than Minnesota. Wisconsin's governor had intoned, "secession is revolution: revolution is war: War against the government . . . is treason." The state legislature was two to one Republican, but each house narrowly approved sending delegates to the Peace Conference. However, they could not agree on the terms, so none were sent.[33]

Most solidly Republican states warily sent representatives to hinder appeasement of the slave states. Even then there were intra-Republican Party objections. Vermont US Senator Solomon Foot snarled to his own state's delegates that the Peace Conference was "a fraud, a trick, a deception—a device of traitors and conspirators again to cheat the North and gain time to ripen their conspiracy."[34]

The Delegates at Willard Hall

Later recalled as the "Old Gentlemen's Convention," the nearly unprecedented gathering included scores of elder statesmen, including six former cabinet members, nineteen ex-governors, fourteen former US senators, fifty former US representatives, twelve state supreme court justices, plus of course former president Tyler. Four fifths of them were lawyers. Eleven had served with Lincoln in Congress, including five Southerners.[35]

A New York newspaper hailed the peace gathering as "one of the most dignified assemblages of men ever gathered together in this country." A Washington newspaper approvingly observed that representatives were "not chosen by popular election or party favor" but only for "fitness for the high trust." The states had provided the "sagest of their citizens, if not in every case their oldest," exemplifying experience, wisdom, dignity, and strength of character."[36]

One Washington newspaper offered an overview of some Peace Conference delegates. Illinois sent Judge Stephen Logan, a "strong, warm, personal friend of Mr. Lincoln," and former governor John Wood, a "strong, anti-compromise Republican." New York sent James Wadsworth, "a wealthy gentleman from the western part of the state"; former lieutenant governor Addison Gardiner, a Democrat with "high reputation"; the "eminent lawyer" Greene Bronson, a "strong national Democrat"; and merchant William Dodge, an "ultra Lincoln man." Also from New York came Democrat congressman-elect and financier Erastus Corning; wealthy, newly appointed, pro-Lincoln US Senator William Evarts; Republican lawyer David Field, who was "anxious for public position"; and fellow Republican lawyer William Noyes.

Ohio, the newspaper reported, sent former US senator and governor Salmon Chase, "one of the bright shining lights of the Republican Party" of the "ultra school" and "avowed enemy of slavery." Along with Chase came Ohio's own Thomas Ewing, US Treasury secretary (under Presidents Harrison and Tyler) and an "old line Whig" hoping to influence Lincoln toward "whiggery"; and former congressman William Groesbeck.

Pennsylvania dispatched former US Treasury secretary (under President Zachary Taylor) William Meredith; former governor James Pollock; and Congressman David Wilmot, author of the famed proviso attempting to ban slavery in former Mexican territory. New Hampshire sent former congressman Amos Tuck.

New Jersey sent its governor, Charles Olden, a "moral and upright gentleman" of "conservative sentiment"; former US senator and US Navy Commodore Robert Stockton, a War of 1812 veteran and, unmentioned by the newspaper, grandson of a Declaration of Independence signer Richard Stockton. He was accompanied by wealthy former governor Rodman Price; and former governor Peter Vroom.

Rhode Island sent its chief justice, Samuel Ames; former governor William Hoppin; and Alexander Duncan, "one of the wealthiest men in the state."

Kentucky was represented by former US Treasury secretary (under President Franklin Pierce) James Guthrie, whose retirement was devoted to "railroad enterprises" and "enjoyment of domestic and social intercourse"; former congressman James Clay, son of the legendary late US senator Henry Clay; former governor and US postmaster (under Presidents Harrison and Tyler) Charles Wickliffe; and former vice presidential candidate, Indian fighter, and War of 1812 veteran William Butler.

From Virginia there were George Summers, a "distinguished literateur" and former state legislator; former judge John Brockenbrough, one of Virginia's "most distinguished jurists"; former US senator and US minister to France (under Presidents Taylor and Pierce) William Rives, who "ranks high as lawyer, minister and statesman."[37]

The newspaper later reported on Wednesday, February 6, that "new delegations are arriving daily," with a "multitude of preliminaries" required before they addressed the "only question upon where there bids fair to be any considerable difference of opinion—the territorial slavery question." It hoped that by a week from Saturday there would be a "settlement" that was "disposed of with much unanimity." The delegates continued to arrive at the meeting hall of Willard's Hotel, which "like a parasitic plant, had gradually surrounded and taken in an old church, which became known as Willard Hall," as one peace commissioner described.[38]

Tyler had likely been in this hall before. It had been until very recently the F Street Presbyterian Church, where many Washington luminaries including Presidents John Quincy Adams, Franklin Pierce, and Buchanan had sometimes worshipped. Buchanan had maintained a pew near the pulpit, attending church without an overcoat even in cold weather. He attended typically with his secretary, since his niece and First Lady, Harriet Lane, worshipped at St. John's Episcopal Church. After the benediction, he hurriedly strode down the aisle as the congregation respectfully stood. Often a congressman's wife would exclaim to him, "Good sermon, Mr. President!" to which he invariably responded, "Too long, Madam, too long."[39]

The congregation was founded in 1807 originally as a Reformed congregation, but became Presbyterian in the 1820s. Rev. Phineas Gurley, who would open an early Peace Conference session with prayer, pastored the church starting in 1854, merging it with another Presbyterian congregation in 1859. He would authorize the building of a new sanctuary a few blocks away that would be New York Avenue Presbyterian, where the president and First Lady Mary Lincoln would worship regularly for four years.

Gurley was a Princeton Seminary graduate and Old School Presbyterian committed to traditional doctrine and mostly avoiding politics. He had agreed to come to Washington to help a church "struggling against the tide of error and ungodliness then prevailing in the nation's capital." He condemned profanity, which he sarcastically surmised had become one of the "most important qualifications for office," while also deriding extreme partisanship by politicians and the press as "iniquitous and shameful in the extreme." The venerable old F Street Presbyterian Church was sold in 1859 for $12,500 to Willard's Hotel, which used it for concerts and balls. One report claimed it could seat eight hundred.[40]

In the 1840s the church had added a Greek Temple–style portico with Doric columns to the new facade of the brick sanctuary. The portico measured sixty by one hundred feet. By 1861, "Willard Hall" was connected to the backside of an expansive and increasingly prominent hotel that filled nearly a city block and fronted on Pennsylvania Avenue. It was one block from the White House and, at the front, within view of the US Capitol, whose uncompleted dome and construction cranes loomed overhead.

Willard Hall's interior had the high ornamented ceiling of worship space, high paned windows with blinds, chandeliers overhead, a front altar space flanked by pilasters, and two front doors to F Street behind the portico's columns. The interior also had a side exit into the main body of the hotel. During the Peace Conference the City of Washington posted police at all entrances to bar intruders, and the mayor loaned a full-length portrait of George Washington to add decorum to the hall, about which delegates were "very agreeably surprised." One newspaper suggested the city also loan its portraits of Andrew Jackson and Henry Clay, other icons of national union. The mayor, acknowledging the generous hotel owners' "highly creditable public spirit," noted that the hall was sufficiently spacious "yet not affording surplus room enough to permit the body to be incommoded and annoyed by a great mass of spectators, as the halls of Congress unfortunately are."[41]

Spectators and reporters were banned from the start, to the chagrin of some Northern representatives. A New York newspaper reported, "citizens are indignant that the meetings should be held in a small hall with closed doors," making it more of a "dark lantern convention than one to where deliberations the largest publicity should be given."[42]

A Vermont newspaper was more approving, saying secret sessions would permit "greater freedom in the expression of opinions" but are "distasteful to the sensation papers and the body of reporters at Washington, and they are tempted to retaliate by disparaging the convention and otherwise exciting ill-will towards it." It predicted "false and perverted news" about secret events at Willard's.[43]

The hotel dated to 1816, formed out of six houses built at Pennsylvania Avenue and Seventeenth Street. Henry Willard, later joined by his brothers, procured the property in 1847, streamlining the structures into a four-story edifice that stretched back to F Street. Their view of the White House was long since blocked by the US Treasury Department's very imposing new classically columned edifice. Forty-seven years earlier in

1814, according to legend, British officers had watched the incineration of the White House from F Street, at Rhodes Tavern, which still stood across the street from Willard Hall. More than a few old Washingtonians remembered the British destruction of their city's public buildings and wondered about even more disastrous results if mediation of the current national crisis failed.

The Peace Conference and subsequent war began Washington's greatest growth spurt to date. And Willard's Hotel became the city's chief political and social beehive, teeming with peace commissioners. Not long after the Peace Conference, as civil war ensued, writer Nathaniel Hawthorne stayed at Willard's. He wrote that the building "may much more justly be called the center of Washington and the Union, than either the Capitol, the White House, or the State Department," as "everybody may be seen here." He noted approvingly that in Willard's highly social milieu "you adopt the universal habit, and call for a mint julep," or other beverage, as the "conviviality of Washington sets in at an early hour," and "never terminates at any hour." He also noticed a "constant atmosphere of cigar smoke," which formed a "more sympathetic medium, in which men meet more closely and talk more frankly than in any other air."[44]

British journalist William Howard Russell stayed at Willard's only weeks after the Peace Conference, and intriguingly found it a "huge caravanserei" with "every form of speech and every accent under which the English language can be recognized" resounding down long corridors in "tones of expostulation, anger or gratification." So-called senator-hunters prowled the hallways, aspiring supplicants found "fresh confidence" in the barroom, and ladies of the party in power were objects of "irresistible attraction."[45]

A few years later, at the height of the war, New York diarist George Templeton Strong was less beguiled by Willard's, denouncing it as "absolutely worse than ever; crowded, dirty, and insufferable," beset by loud, leaking, and vaporous steam pipes, at least in his room. Of Washington and its famed hotel, he proclaimed: "Beelzebub surely reigns there, and Willard's Hotel is his temple."[46]

Lincoln's private secretary, John Hay, recalled Willard's and Washington's hotel atmosphere in general as "littered with a mixture of dirt, scraps of paper, cigar stumps and discarded envelopes, and the whole is embroidered with an irregular arabesque of expectoration." Yet Hay would regularly dine for years at Willard's even while living in the White House.[47]

In early 1861, amid national crisis, the Willard brothers quickly offered Willard Hall to the Peace Conference without charge, including the lighting, patriotically hoping their facilities would be "sanctified by restoring peace to the Union."[48] They were also savvy businessmen. The gathering placed a national spotlight on Willard's Hotel, where many if not all the delegates would reside. Fifty US congressmen were living at Willard's as of December 1860, and during the Peace Conference its profits grew to almost $1,200 daily. Lodging and food at Willard's cost $55 to $60 per week. Peace Commissioner Daniel Barringer, a Unionist US congressman from North Carolina, approvingly wrote his wife of Willard's great convenience: "The Conference of the Commissioners is held in a large concert hall attached to this building and my room is within ten steps of it under the same roof."[49]

Meeting in a former sanctuary like Willard Hall would have seemed familiar to nearly all the Peace Conference delegates. They served as statesmen in an era when often only churches offered sufficiently large and dignified space for important gatherings. Tyler was himself an aristocratic Episcopalian from Tidewater, Virginia, no doubt comfortable in a Greek Revival–style church turned hotel conference room. He was baptized and reared at venerable Westover Episcopal Church in his native Charles City, Virginia, along the James River. The parish dated to 1613, and the sanctuary to 1730. Tyler was baptized there, and a portrait of the old parson who baptized him was said to have hung at Tyler's Sherwood Forest estate until relocated to Richmond, where it was destroyed by fire at the Civil War's end. In 1847 then ex-President Tyler was noted as among the "most regular attendants and supporters of the Church" at Westover. Two years later he was elected to the church's vestry.[50]

TYLER: CONVENTION PRESIDENT

Tyler's personal faith was largely unarticulated and perhaps rationalistic, similar to Virginia's Founding-era icons like his father's college roommate, Thomas Jefferson, as well as James Madison and James Monroe, whom he had known. But he may have become more devout in later years, even during his time at the Peace Conference. As a US senator in the 1830s, Tyler observed that the "variableness in the things of the world [is] designed by the Creator for the happiness of His creatures." Two decades later, in old age with ailments, he was "convinced that all is wisely ordered by Providence." Later, after illness, he remarked, "Nothing but the kind providence of our Heavenly Father could have saved me." He later confided to his Episcopal clergy a "bright faith in the Christian religion." As president, Tyler purchased a pew at St. John's Episcopal Church near the White House, which he left for use in perpetuity for future presidents.[51]

Tyler shared with the Founders a deep commitment to religious liberty and church-state separation. He was a student and disciple of President Madison's cousin, Episcopal bishop James Madison, who for more than thirty years presided over Tyler's alma mater, William and Mary College at Williamsburg, Virginia. Tyler thought of him as a "second father" and "strikingly impressive" as teacher and mentor, perhaps more for Madison's views on republican virtue and American exceptionalism than for theology.[52]

That patriotic commitment likely informed Tyler's zeal for the Peace Conference as a last-ditch attempt to salvage the Union. Born in 1790 during George Washington's presidency, he was literally a son of the Founding generation. His father was thrice Virginia's governor, and a friend of Monroe and Patrick Henry. He entertained his children at their twelve-hundred-acre estate near Williamsburg with stories of his service in the American Revolution.

Tyler was first elected to the Virginia legislature at age twenty-one. Later serving as governor of and US senator from Virginia, the younger

Tyler followed after his father politically until breaking with President Andrew Jackson and most Democrats over Jackson's threat of force against South Carolina's attempt to "nullify" US tariff law. He was the Whig vice presidential candidate in 1840, and quickly became the first "accidental" president when William Henry Harrison died from pneumonia in 1841, after only days in office.

Derided famously as "His Accidency" and even "His Fraudulency" by snarling critics, Tyler antagonized his fellow Whigs by opposing their tariff policies and frustrating Henry Clay's presidential ambitions, while ruining his own chances for re-nomination. As a man without a political party, he pursued nationalist goals, annexing Texas into the Union and settling a Maine border dispute with British Canada.

Several prominent officials of his administration and a New York US congressman were killed in a warship accident on the Potomac River. The USS *Princeton*'s captain, Robert Stockton, who was not considered at fault for his ship's disaster, was later peace commissioner of New Jersey. Tyler, a recent widower, comforted and eventually married the deceased congressman's fainting daughter, Julia Gardiner. She was thirty years younger than he, and a Presbyterian who would convert to Catholicism in her later years after his death. Always precocious, she had moved to Washington after she scandalized proper society in New York by appearing in the stylish advertisement of a clothing store. Tyler called her the "most beautiful woman of her age and the most accomplished." She was attractive, intelligent, and queenly as First Lady, riding a carriage with many fine horses, receiving visitors in the White House while enthroned on a raised platform, wearing three feathers in her hair, and clad in purple velvet. Ambitious for her husband and herself, she was the first First Lady to dance publicly in the White House, and may have introduced "Hail to the Chief" as the presidential anthem. She was the first First Lady photographed in office, authorized the sale of lithograph prints of herself labeled "The President's Bride," tried to manage her media coverage, and hosted huge champagne-soaked White House galas that perturbed some religiously devout critics. After leaving office, she publicly rebutted aristocratic English women who appealed to America's ladies to work against slavery.[53]

Tyler fathered seven children with his young, second wife, his last at age seventy in 1860, in quiet retirement and political exile at his Sherwood Forest estate near Williamsburg, Virginia. He brought his considerable virile and robust energies to his sudden political return in 1861, especially at the Peace Conference. Thin and tall, he had been described over the years as "charming," "bewitching," "cultivated," well-read, eloquent, "fine-looking," and resembling an ancient bust of the Roman statesman Cicero, with high forehead and Roman nose. A visiting Charles Dickens, typically critical, had found him pleasantly "agreeable." Tyler was also considered vain. Although he pleaded "severe indisposition" and "every possible personal inconvenience" upon his appointment by Virginia, likely he was energized by his return to the national arena.[54]

Like virtually everybody else, Tyler was privately exasperated after meeting at the White House with Buchanan, who "obviously is to throw all responsibility off his shoulders."[55] The president solicitously visited the ex-president at his suite at Brown's Indian Queen Hotel, which Tyler shared with his wife, twelve-year-old son, and baby girl, and which often became a sort of court thronged with his admirers. "We are very handsomely accommodated here, private parlors, etc.," Mrs. Tyler reported with satisfaction. Tyler had been sworn in as president at the Indian Queen in 1841, so perhaps it was a place of reassuring memories. A young Congressman Abraham Lincoln had also lived there in 1847. Brown's was about eight blocks from Willard's, closer to the Capitol. Perhaps Tyler wanted some distance between himself and the other delegates, or more proximity to Congress. Like other hotels, Brown's hosted regular dancing parties, creating a socially rambunctious atmosphere that may have appealed to the still relatively young, very sociable Mrs. Tyler.[56]

Most other peace commissioners seem to have stayed at Willard's, including reportedly the whole delegations from Vermont, Massachusetts, New York, New Jersey, Pennsylvania, and Ohio. Some delegates stayed at the National Hotel at Sixth Street and Pennsylvania Avenue. Three of Virginia's five delegates, including Tyler, were at Brown's, across the street from the National, as was the whole Missouri delegation.[57] More than two dozen congressmen and several senators lived at the National Hotel, but its reputation had never fully recovered from an 1857 epidemic that sickened thirty people, including then president-elect Buchanan, whose nephew later died from the hotel illness—an intestinal malady attributed to sewer gas. Mary Todd Lincoln told her husband they would not stay there upon their arrival for his inauguration.[58]

From his perch at Brown's, Tyler respectfully challenged Buchanan on reports of the US Navy reinforcing Fort Sumter in Charleston, which the South saw as a provocation. More sternly he cited to the president reports that Fort Monroe in Tyler's own Virginia had swiveled some of its artillery to face inland, "when Virginia is making every possible effort to redeem and save the Union," only to have cannons "leveled at her bosom." Buchanan promised to investigate.[59]

Tyler respectfully intoned to Buchanan his hope that his administration "might close amid the rejoicings of a great people." A New Hampshire newspaper supposed that, had Tyler been a "man of any wit," that comment actually would have been a "cruel hit," as Americans were instead rejoicing over the administration's end.[60]

Buchanan was even weaker than the usual lame duck, and with Lincoln's arrival and inauguration still weeks away, Washington had a power vacuum. It's possible that Tyler saw his brief window to fill it. He was the only one of four living former presidents to step forward in a major way during this crisis, although Franklin Pierce, fourteen years younger than Tyler, privately said he would also attend the Peace Conference if his health allowed. Former president Millard Fillmore visited Washington during the conference to urge conciliation, but seems to have had little impact.[61]

A critic scornfully likened Tyler to a "tottering, ashen ruin," more "cordially despised than any other president." But friendlier visitors were gratified by his hearty appearance, "even under the weight of so many years." Several newspapers called him the "same slim, tall-looking, high bred Virginia gentleman," whose "striking features" evinced a "high degree of mental activity," and whose "prominent nose" indicated "intellectual superiority." Others noted his "animal vigor," his "keen and gentle eyes," and "well preserved" appearance showing "great age with remarkable grace."[62]

Tyler would turn seventy-one in the month following the Peace Conference. His much younger wife, herself going on age forty-one, admired his zealous activity now that he was back in the saddle, saying he was "in a stronger condition to bear up than for many a day, and looks well." She noted he went to bed "upon a dose of hydrargum," a sedative, perhaps reflecting his heightened state of anxiety, but heroically performing as "they are all looking to him in the settlement of the vexed question." Indeed, she observed, "his superiority over everybody else is felt and admitted by all." And she noted his hotel table was "loaded with correspondence from every quarter."

Always intensely politically interested, Mrs. Tyler wondered if she were eyewitness to the "last days of the republic," while denying any interest in Washington's "gay entertainments" and preferring the "doings of the convention, which has for me the most intense interest." Presumably channeling her husband, she expected that the South and border states had little hope of saving the Union, thanks to "mischief" by "black Republicans," or abolitionists, and General Scott's "absurd and high-handed" gathering of troops in Washington to "overawe" Virginia and Maryland.[63]

Reverend Gurley returned to his very familiar, former regular place of worship on February 5, to pray before the Peace Conference on its second day. Commissioners had agreed that each day thereafter, a Washington clergy would start their session with prayer. Before Gurley's invocation the delegates had already quickly and unanimously elected Tyler president of the convention, perhaps aided by the absence of some Northern Republican-dominated delegations who were still traveling. His election must have not surprised him, as he was immediately able to deliver a stirring oration summoning his audience to reconciliation, patriotic fervor, and national unity. Over the course of his career he had always championed national expansion and greatness, minimizing slavery as an issue.[64]

Tyler and Slavery

Like many highborn Southerners, especially from Virginia and the upper South, Tyler opposed slavery in the abstract. But he believed advocating abolition would be "political suicide," sometimes wishfully suggesting it would fade away naturally. He was a US congressman during the 1820 crisis over Missouri's admission as a slave state, when he advocated that slavery's expansion over wider territory would diffuse the slave population, making eventual emancipation more feasible, as it had been in the Northern states. "You advance the interest and secure the safety of one-half of this extended republic: you ameliorate the condition of the slave, and you add much to his prospects of emancipation, and the total extinction of slavery," Tyler had suggested. In later years, he insisted that temperate climate "assuredly" would eventually eradicate slavery, starting in the upper South, including Virginia.[65]

In an 1835 speech as US senator, Tyler condemned abolitionists as "libelers of the South" who defamed slaveholders as "demons in the shape of men." He accused them of fomenting slave insurrection, warning, "unexpected evil is now upon us; it has invaded our fire sides, and under our roofs is sharpening the dagger of midnight assassination, and exciting cruelty and bloodshed."[66]

Unlike most other southerners, Tyler opposed a "gag rule" on antislavery petitions when he was a US senator in the 1830s, fearing that petitions would only encourage abolitionists. And he publicly supported colonization of freed slaves in Africa, while admitting it may be an unattainable "dream." Apparently offended by slave auctions, he proposed banning the slave trade in Washington, DC, and he supported punishment for cruelty to slaves while opposing a ban on slavery in the nation's capital outright.[67]

He was an ex-president during debates over the great Compromise of 1850, when he strongly supported Senators Daniel Webster and Henry Clay in their cobbling together omnibus legislation over slavery to forestall disunion. This irked both Southern and Northern firebrands. Tyler's strongest condemnation was aimed at abolitionists, who deserved the "deepest curses of the patriot for having put in jeopardy the noblest and fairest fabric of government the world ever saw."[68]

Tyler owned "plenty of slaves," he said—several hundred slaves throughout his life, perhaps about seventy at one time, about a dozen of whom were house servants, three of them living in the main house. A Northern visitor described slaves at Tyler's Sherwood Forest on the James River as living in a childlike "minority that never terminates" but "uniformly cheerful and happy." Slaves facilitated Tyler's aristocratic equipage, which included a splashy carriage with liveried coachmen in white pantaloons, and a dashing blue riverboat, *Pocahontas*, with blue-and-white-uniformed oarsmen with straw hats and shirt collars decorated by a braided bow and arrow, representing Tyler's Robin Hood theme, of course. Tyler's mother-in-law thought this regal showiness in "bad taste," but her daughter relished it.[69]

"They are a strange set, are they not?" Mrs. Tyler once exclaimed to her mother, describing their own slaves as "generally kind and happy and don't want to have anything to do with poor white people."[70] Naturally relieved when fiery abolitionist John Brown's 1859 attempt to ignite armed slavery revolt from Harpers Ferry, Virginia, (now West Virginia) failed, she celebrated his hanging as the "miserable consequence of his shameful outrage." In the Tylers' native Charles County, blacks outnumbered whites by two to one, making the prospect of an uprising terrifying and the idea of emancipation politically outrageous.[71]

Regarding slaves as the "most important article of Southern property," then Congressman Tyler had tried to sell a woman slave to finance his new career as US senator in 1827. While president, abolitionist critics alleged Tyler had fathered slave children, which Tyler's defenders stoutly denied. Abolitionists also condemned the presence of Tyler's slaves in the White House.[72]

During the heated 1860 presidential campaign, when Northern and Southern Democrats split, he endorsed Southern Democrat Vice President John Breckinridge. "I fear that the great Republic has seen its last days," he worried, while stressing that defeating Lincoln and the Republicans was the "great matter."[73] Briefly he pondered his own possible return as the Democrats' presidential candidate, his wife believing he had "outlived the abuse of his enemies," but he soon abandoned the idea. He had previously recognized he was the "last of the Virginia presidents," as the South lost demographically to the North, compelling reliance on sympathetic Northern Democrats like President Buchanan.[74]

Political controversy entered the Tylers' Sherwood Forest parlor in 1860 when a local Episcopal clergyman, a Unionist, denounced Virginia's governor for overreacting to John Brown's raid the year before to bestir anti-abolitionist sentiment. Another neighbor present exploded by denouncing "clergymen coming from the pulpit to make themselves Sunday evening politicians," prompting Mrs. Tyler later to commend his "spirit and independence," with which her husband did not disagree.[75]

During the 1860 campaign Tyler denounced Northern abolitionists, while he pledged to defend the South, "live or die, survive or perish." After Lincoln's election he pronounced the nation had "fallen on evil times," with "madness" and demagoguery prevailing over statesmanship. He quiescently left to "others younger than myself the settlement of existing disputes," suggesting that under the current "degeneracy" peaceful separation might be preferable to Union and strife. He predicted that Virginia would never permit her "blacks to be cribbed and confined" within the present limits that Northerners demanded, which would ensure a future race war. Virginia and the South must have "expansion," if not within the Union, then looking to Latin America or the Caribbean as "ultimate reservations of the African race."[76]

In a January 1861 public letter, Tyler explained: "The man who would talk of cultivating the rice and cotton fields and sugar plantations of the South with free white labor, denies to himself the light of experience and observation." He added: "Asia and Africa have to be resorted to for laborers, while the Caucasian of Europe flees, as from pestilence, the rays of a burning sun, and becomes the cultivator of the cereals, or turns herdsman amid the snows of the North." Northern demands for no more slave states, he warned, would create a situation amid a growing black population that "cannot be contemplated by any Southern man with any absolute composure." Of his own Virginia, Tyler declared: "Her destiny good or evil is with the South."[77]

But at the Peace Conference, on February 5, 1861, Tyler was far more conciliatory. Lincoln was now elected, and the country's future in doubt. Modestly professing to have forgotten parliamentary rules, Tyler rejected making "personal considerations" when the "country is in danger," accepting his duty in the "work of reconciliation and adjustment." What "our Godlike fathers created, we have to preserve," Tyler insisted. "They built up through their patriotism monuments that eternalized their names." His audience had a task no less grand, he said, "quite as full of glory and immortality." They had to "snatch from ruin a great and glorious confederation, to preserve the government and reinvigorate the Constitution." If successful, their children's children would "rise up and call them blessed."

"I confess myself to be ambitious of sharing in the glory of accomplishing this grand and magnificent result," Tyler admitted. "To have our names enrolled in the Capitol, to be respected by future generations with grateful applause. This is an honor higher than the mountains, more enduring than monumental alabaster."

Tyler poetically sounded the roll call of the states represented there in Willard Hall, recalling their glory in America's War for Independence and in creating a republic seventy years previous. He cited the grandson of a Declaration of Independence signer present in the New Jersey delegation. Admitting the absence of several states, he expressed hope their "hearts are with us in the great work we have to do."

Their ancestors had probably committed a "blunder" by not requiring a new constitutional convention every fifty years or so, Tyler lamented, as what worked for five million was not now fit for thirty million. But "patriotism" could yet surmount the present difficulties, he hoped, by "triumph over party." What is party, he pointedly asked at his conclusion, "when compared to the task of rescuing ones country from danger so that one long, loud shout of joy and gladness will resound throughout the land?"[78]

According to a Richmond newspaper, the "deep and earnest patriotism evinced by the speaker melted the stoutest heart, and as he finished each member seemed to rise simultaneously to his feet, and moved towards the venerable speaker with words of peace and good will." Tyler was congratulated by "most" of the state delegations.

A delegate from Ohio, that state's former governor and US senator, told Tyler he was "particularly gratified," the newspaper pronounced, and that the states "were ready to follow where Virginia led, as she pursued only the path of virtue and honor." He was Salmon Chase, an anti-slavery Republican who would soon famously serve as Lincoln's treasury secretary.[79]

A Washington newspaper spoke for many in hailing Tyler's speech as "one of the most affecting and eloquent efforts of the kind ever spoken in the country." A New York newspaper declared: "The hopes of the Union men are high tonight."[80] A month earlier, Tyler's son, John Tyler Jr., had reportedly told a crowd in Norfolk, Virginia, with his own vehemence: "Let the Union go to hell."[81] His father was prepared to accept that outcome but still hoped and worked to avoid it.

Meanwhile, days later, Northern Peace Commissioner William Fessenden, a US senator whom Lincoln would describe as "a Radical without the petulant and vicious forgetfulness of many Radicals," privately predicted the Peace Conference would accomplish nothing. Fessenden himself promised not to "yield one particle of that great idea of human liberty, which lies at the foundation of our institutions, and without which they must inevitably fail."

On the US Senate floor, Fessenden warned, "If the time ever does come . . . when it will be necessary to use force in order to execute the laws of the United States under the Constitution anywhere and everywhere within what is properly the United States, I am perfectly ready to do it, but I trust we shall have no such necessity." He added, "I trust we shall be ready to meet all our responsibilities like men."[82]

More hopefully, a Vermont newspaper editorialized about the Peace Conference: "Every Christian, every reasonable and patriotic man must hope that, with due regard to essential principles, some plan may be suggested for the peaceful rescue of the nation from the perils evidently arising out [of] a now rampant secessionism."[83]

With more determined optimism, a Washington newspaper declared that the peace commissioners would reach compromise by at least a two-thirds vote that majorities of Northern and Southern voters would then "instantly" accept, with Southerners overthrowing Secessionist "revolutionary leaders" who were suppressing self-government. And the newspaper firmly predicted: "The Peace Congress will make such a settlement, and under its happy influence six months will find every seceded state restored to its allegiance to the Union, by the exertions of the Unionists within its own limits only."[84]

Guided by cautious realism, a New York newspaper predicted that even with all the "master minds of the country" now gathered, "no voice is loud enough, no patriotism deep and broad enough, no spirit self-sacrificing enough to recall the seceding states back to the fraternal fold of the Union." Instead, there should be "earnest prayer" for at least "saving the border states."[85]

Abolitionist William Lloyd Garrison had been at war with the "slave power" for thirty years through his Boston-based newspaper the *Liberator*. He denounced Virginia's "crafty policy" of summoning a Peace Conference, which was a "snare and mockery." He warned: "Trojans! Beware the wooden horse!"[86]

Of Tyler, a Georgia newspaper reported he was "now doing a good service to the country," having made a "poor President, but he appears to be a capital ex-President."[87] But whether Tyler, as president of the

Peace Conference, was in fact such an effective former chief executive would become highly debated over the next several weeks, as both the North and South watched and debated the proceedings at Willard Hall in Washington, DC.

TWO

THE FEDERAL CITY

People are catching at straws as a relief to their pressing anxieties, and look to the Peace Commissioners as if they possessed some divine power to restore order and harmony.

—Julia Gardiner Tyler

Few aspects of official life in Washington, DC, were untouched by the swelling national storm that the Peace Conference delegates were desperately striving to defuse. Even a George Washington birthday parade became controversial, when in normal times it would have been a unifying pageant in the federal city, closing local businesses and drawing festive crowds into the streets.

A Philadelphia newspaper thought celebrating the nation's Founding Father deserved "pious reverence," as the "hour of the nation's peril was as dark as was Israel's when Saul summoned the specter at Endor; but the priceless legacy of wisdom embodied in . . . the Father of his Country will . . . soften and guide the extremes of passion that rule this hour." Surely the public would support the "most liberal program" to honor him.[1]

But the hypersensitive President Buchanan made his second voyage to President Tyler's suite at Brown's Hotel, to inquire whether the martial display of parading federal troops in the birthday commemoration might ruffle the "susceptibilities" of peace commissioners.[2]

When Tyler unsurprisingly replied yes, despite his own admiration for General Washington, Buchanan tried to cancel at the last minute what was already well along in plans, provoking loud complaint from assembling Washingtonians and visitors. US Army commander Lieutenant General Winfield Scott didn't hear from Buchanan until breakfast the morning of the parade that federal troops should not participate. Many of them were already early in line on the parade route. At about 10:30 A.M., horses were unharnessed and soldiers silently withdrew, while spectators, according to Northern newspapers, were unsparing in condemning compliance with "southern threats."[3]

"Astonishment was depicted upon the face of officers and men," a New York newspaper reported. After Tyler's involvement became known, this "astonishment of the officers was turned to rage," the paper asserted, adding, "It may well be imagined what were the feelings of Gen. Scott." Thousands along the parade route, already "weary of waiting," then "universally expressed towards the President" a "feeling of condemnation."[4]

Much of the anticipating crowd was at Fourteenth Street and Pennsylvania Avenue, around the Willard's Hotel, where many federal troops were expected to assemble. Their absence provoked "no little disappointment." Starting at 11:00 A.M., companies of local Washington, DC, militia, many of them only recently formed, marched under "brilliant sunshine and clean streets." President Buchanan's niece, the elegant and carefully reserved Harriet Lane who served as First Lady for her bachelor uncle, was observed watching the parading militia from a White House window. Although commended for their colorful uniforms and good spirit, making a "fine appearance" and maneuvering "exceedingly well," the militia presumably lacked the full panache of the absent regular US Army troops and US Marines.[5]

New York Democratic congressman Daniel Sickles personally rushed to the War Department to complain about the awkward absence of federal forces. "Mr. President, there are ten thousand people out on the streets of Washington today to see the parade which was announced," Sickles exclaimed. "I have just heard that it has been countermanded, and the report is exciting great indignation. I come to ask if it is true, and if so whether the parade may yet be carried out."[6]

The ever sensitive president then reversed course again, urging that federal troops reassemble for a late version of the parade.[7] Sickles had first proposed his resolution for a resplendent George Washington's birthday celebration in the US House of Representatives earlier in the month. He had doubtless intended it both as a paean to Unionism and martial intimidation to Secessionists. A Virginia congressman had sarcastically suggested that Washington also be honored as "slaveholder," while another, from the North, riposted that Washington likewise had been an emancipator.[8]

Sickles, a charming rascal, was already infamous for having shot his wife's lover, the prosecutor son of Francis Scott Key, in the light of day across the street from the White House only several years before. Edwin Stanton, now President Buchanan's US attorney general, and later President Lincoln's secretary of war, had triumphantly gained acquittal for his client with the first successful legal appeal to temporary insanity. Reputedly Sickles's escape from conviction had pleased President Buchanan and much of official Washington. Sickles had served in the US legation in London when Buchanan was US minister there, exciting scandal by bringing a New York prostitute to London instead of his wife. Buchanan sent him home, but more over policy differences than personal scandal. Sickles, although also exasperated by Buchanan, supported him for the presidency. Later he would become a US Army general, losing a leg at Gettysburg.[9]

Doubtless the indecisive Buchanan was hard-pressed to resist the very aggressive Sickles's insistent demands for a full military display. As a Philadelphia newspaper drily observed, the president changed his mind, "in accordance with his usual custom." Scott was instructed to hastily mobilize what forces he could for a delayed 3:00 P.M. march on

Pennsylvania Avenue. Likely both peeved and delighted by the day's reversals, Scott was joined by Buchanan and the war secretary outside the White House to review the parading US Army troops, which the New York newspaper reported were "very imposing, and the subsequent drill of the battery, cavalry, and sappers and miners corps was exceedingly interesting and skillful." The US Marines could not be summoned in time for the parade; they were at their barracks two miles away. But the pounding thud of field batteries, firing thirty-four gun salutes in honor of General Washington, ricocheted throughout the city, foreshadowing the artillery sounds that would become more familiar to Washingtonians over the next four years.[10]

Even if delayed, such display of federal military force with flags flying, choreographed by General Scott, must have encouraged Washington's Unionists and irritated more than a few sensitive Peace Conference delegates, likely Tyler chief among them. That evening, celebration of Washington's birthday continued with military balls, full of "good looking men," and ladies with "no lack of partners for the dance," a Washington newspaper reported. Not to enjoy one's self "would argue an overly fastidious disposition indeed, so everybody did enter upon the pleasures of the occasion with zest." A gala hosted by the Federal Rifles Militia continued until breakfast.[11]

Earlier in the day the streets had filled with vendors selling inexpensive pig's feet and gingerbread to the many country people in town for the day, whose carriages and wagons clogged the streets, sometimes to the detriment of parading troops. Boy vendors carried large placards upon their chests announcing their availability to sing "New Union Songs." The capital's streets were festooned with flags and pro-Union banners. One such banner was strung across Pennsylvania Avenue by a restaurant, declaring: "The Union, Now and Forever." Others exclaimed, "God save the Union," and "We are for the Union." It was reported that the "avenue was gay from one end to the other with the Stars and Stripes."[12]

A Washington newspaper rhapsodized that the "mild and beautiful" day was "in perfect harmony with the feelings of the people, not clouded nor yet too bright," a "happy mingling" of the changing season, indicating that the "winter of discontent is past," with a "glorious summer of peace and prosperity and reunited brotherhood" ahead. After all, the people were "out in their holiday attire," while the "stars and stripes waved in the breeze."[13]

But the parade episode further undermined Buchanan's already diminished authority. He had been "severely censured" for complying with "desires of Virginia Secessionists," as one Northern newspaper asserted. It noted Buchanan's turnabout only "incensed Secessionists, without appeasing the Union men."[14] Such vacillation perhaps further encouraged Tyler to exert his own authority. The president sent Tyler a note of apology that day, explaining he had reversed his parade order after realizing a newspaper, without his knowledge, had advertised it that morning. The War Department had regarded the celebration of a national anniversary merely a "matter of course." He pleaded that canceling federal participation would have been "impossible" without giving "serious offense to the tens of thousands of people who have assembled to witness the parade."[15]

GENERAL SCOTT'S DISPLEASURE

At nearly age seventy-five, General Winfield Scott had been a national hero for nearly a half century. Scott had little patience for Buchanan's indecision, over the parade or much else. And likely Scott had little faith in the Peace Conference. He was already focused on securing the city for the Electoral College vote tabulation on February 14 and Lincoln's March 4 inauguration, with whatever followed. Although he was a native Virginian who had attended the College of William and Mary only a few years before Tyler, Scott was a firm anti-slavery Unionist. He was also fearless, even now in old age when he was too aged and immense to mount a horse, or even climb many stairs, although still resplendent in his uniform. Tall, broad, and white haired, he was regal in his gold epaulets and braid, with a plumed great hat whose feathers scraped the floor when he bowed. It was said that Scott by himself could form a military parade.

Scott had become a general when still only in his twenties during the War of 1812, making him one of the longest serving generals in US history, and the only three-star officer since George Washington. He had served under every president since Thomas Jefferson, having become general-in-chief in 1841 under Tyler. And he had himself been the Whig presidential candidate in 1852, after he secured glory in his almost faultless campaign to capture Mexico City against superior forces during the late war with Mexico. After his electoral defeat, his reputation was such that he seamlessly returned to military command. He quickly moved his headquarters from New York to Washington as the secession crisis unfolded.

There was bad blood between Scott and Tyler that dated back twenty years. President Tyler had declined the general's counsel, viewing him as a political foe, and even prohibited his travel as army commander if Tyler perceived political implications. Scott would go on to say that Tyler had "committed the grossest tergiversation in politics" during his presidency, having "brought into market and bartered for support" all office patronage. "To the honor of the country, Mr. Tyler was allowed to lapse into a private station," Scott harrumphed, undoubtedly displeased later by Tyler's sudden 1861 political reemergence.

In January 1861, newspapers published excerpts from Scott's thoughts on the sectional divisions that he composed the previous year during the election campaign. In them, he esoterically suggested that a "lesser evil" may be to divide the country into four regional confederacies. He warned against any Southern "act of rashness" that would particularly involve seizing federal forts, whose defenses he urged bolstering. And he hoped that with firmness and moderation from the president, the "danger of secession may be made to pass away without one conflict of arms, one execution, or one arrest for treason." Somewhat disingenuously, he declared he would stay away from the presidential election out of a "sense of propriety" as a soldier, while still announcing his "sympathies" were with the Constitutional Union Party, whose candidate, John Bell, was supported by Southern pro-Union moderates.[16]

A GROWING CAPITAL

The city that General Scott was now determined to defend had more than 75,000 people as of the 1860 census, of whom nearly 3,200 were slaves and more than 11,000 free blacks. Despite legal restrictions on free blacks, some were prosperous, including Scott's landlord. The landlord was owner of I Street's popular Wormley's Hotel, which even snobby British novelist Anthony Trollope commended to fellow English visitors, and where he found himself "greatly in luck" to reside, at least compared to the city's other lodgings.[17]

Washington in that era was often commonly derided as swampy, backward, and uncivilized. Trollope sniffed that the city was a "ragged, unfinished collection of unbuilt broad streets," most "ungainly," and the "most presumptuous in its pretensions." It was a "straggling congregation of buildings in a wilderness" whose "design is grand," but falls far short of the vision and is "therefore a melancholy place," even in winter, when "abuzz with Congress in session."[18]

But Washington had its beauty. Congressional wife Sara Pryor romantically recalled Washington of that time as a near Eden:

I remember Washington only as a garden of delights, over which the spring trailed an early robe of green, thickly embroidered with gems of amethyst and ruby, pearl and sapphire. The crocuses, hyacinths, tulips, and snowdrops made haste to bloom before the snows had fairly melted. The trees donned their diaphanous veils of green earlier in the White House grounds, the lawn of the Smithsonian Institution, and the gentle slopes around the Capitol, than anywhere in less distinguished localities. To walk through these incense-laden grounds, to traverse the avenue of blossoming crab-apples, was pure pleasure. The shaded avenues were delightful long lanes, where one was sure to meet friends, and where no law of etiquette forbade a pause in the public street for a few words of kindly inquiry, or a bit of gossip, or the development of some plan for future meetings.[19]

Mrs. Pryor also admitted Washington's "discomforts" as the "cold, the ice-laden streets in winter; the whirlwinds of dust and driving rains of spring; the swift-coming fierceness of summer heat; the rapid atmospheric changes which would give us all these extremes in one week, or even one day, until it became the part of prudence never to sally forth on any expedition without 'a fan, an overcoat, and an umbrella.'"[20]

Likely the peace commissioners would see only the budding crocuses among these "delights" at most, and much more of the "discomforts" before their wintry work in Washington ended. But they did experience the city's easy sociability, which included a sophisticated social life of statesmen, diplomats and their wives, elegant hotels like Willard's, many stately homes, and several magnificent government buildings that had no equal in the nation. Even Trollope admitted that Washington's "six principal buildings" exhibited a "certain amount of success."[21]

There was the White House, of course, which survived its burning by the British invaders of 1812, sporting coats of white paint ever since. Trollope granted it was a "handsome mansion fitted for the chief officer of a great republic," even if there were "private houses in London considerably larger." He regretted it was built on "marshy ground" and "very unhealthy," leaving its residents subject to "fever and ague." Yet the president "must make the most of the residence which the nation has prepared for him."[22]

Next to it on the eastern side was the sprawling US Treasury Department, still very much under construction. Trollope, impressed with its grand row of Doric columns, called it "perhaps the prettiest thing in the city."[23] It occupied much of a city block, obscuring the Willard Hotel's sight of the presidential mansion. Washington's original city planner, Pierre Charles L'Enfant, had intended a clear view between the White House and the US Capitol, but President Andrew Jackson was said to have defiantly insisted otherwise, legendarily planting his cane in the ground where the new Treasury headquarters would go.

The Capitol, parts of which also survived British flames, was easily becoming the city's most imposing monument. Even Trollope grudgingly admitted that it "commands attention" and had not "disgraced the city."[24] It had doubled in size and length in the previous decade. The addition of new wings housed new expanded chambers for the Senate and House of Representatives. Now a stunning new dome was rising from the base, its construction cranes looming overhead. Jefferson Davis had promoted and managed the Capitol's expansion as US senator from Mississippi and as war secretary under President Pierce. Now he was becoming president of the new Southern Confederacy. During his involvement with the expansion he had ironically desired a great legislative temple to emblemize American unity and greatness. Davis had vetoed adorning the female statue representing freedom that was to crown the dome with a liberty cap, which was worn by freed slaves in antiquity. Instead, she would receive a headdress of feathers.

Mrs. Pryor likely spoke for many when she recalled that "my heart would swell within me at every glimpse of the Capitol; from the moment it rose like a white cloud above the smoke and mists, as I stood on the deck of the steamboat (having run up from my dinner to salute Mount Vernon), to the time when I was wont to watch from my window for the sunset, that I might catch the moment when a point on the unfinished dome glowed like a blazing star after the sun had really gone down. No matter whether suns rose or set, there was the star of our country, the star of our hearts and hopes."[25]

Another great building in the city was the redbrick, turreted Smithsonian castle, which was a museum space funded by bequest from a wealthy Scotsman who never saw America. Trollope discerned its style as "bastard Gothic" but "not ugly," and whose lectures and museums were, it was suggested to him, not popular with Washingtonians.[26]

Within sight of the Smithsonian was the uncompleted obelisk intended to honor George Washington. Marble and stones, some inscribed by donor organizations, lay about the grounds awaiting their eventual assembly next to the marsh that stretched to the Potomac. Trollope imagined that the completed tower, which he thought unlikely, could never be "graceful," and was overall, like the city itself, "vast, pretentious, bold, boastful . . . but still in its infancy."[27]

To the west near the Potomac River was the US Navy Observatory, a domed window into the heavens long managed by a distinguished naval officer who would soon join the Confederacy, Matthew Fontaine Maury. He was also a friend to former president Tyler, who had originally appointed him to manage the observatory. Upon arrival in Washington, Tyler confided to Maury in a "long talk" his questions about the future of the Union. Maury afterward described Tyler as "full of Virginia abstractions" on the "right of secession in the Constitution," with Maury assuring him that "no parchment provision would stand."[28] The observatory would become a favorite evening spot for President Lincoln on sleepless nights with clear skies.

There was the columned and marble Patent Building, where designs and models of the nation's new inventions were displayed, along with lavish gifts from foreign potentates for America's president. Trollope called it "massive and grand, and, if the streets round it were finished, would be imposing." But he dismissively found the displays within "no better than a large toy shop."[29]

Across from it was the similarly classical and imposing US Post Office headquarters, which Trollope hailed as a "very graceful building," and "creditable to any city," though surrounded by "mud and sloughs of despond," presumably, he opined, to spare "over tasked officials" from a "crowd of callers."[30] Later in the year General Scott would plan that several of these sturdy edifices would serve as final fortresses of military defense in case of enemy attack. They would also function as military hospitals and bivouacs. To the south Washington Arsenal at Greenleaf Point sat where the Anacostia River enters the Potomac. Farther up the

Anacostia was the US Navy Yard and, just north of it, the US Marine barracks.

Hovering over the city across the Potomac on the Arlington Heights was the neoclassical, columned mansion of the late George Washington Parke Custis, grandson of Martha Washington and adopted son of President Washington. As Trollope observed its view, the city's "white stones of the big buildings when the sun gleams on them, showing the distant row of columns, seem to tell something of great endeavor and achieved success."[31] The mansion now belonged to Custis's son-in-law, US Army Colonel Robert E. Lee, who was himself debating how he would choose if the Peace Conference failed.

Within view of the Lee-Custis Mansion were the spires of the many churches that dotted the city. The most distinguished in appearance, and probably also in social standing, were Episcopal. St. John's was designed by Benjamin Latrobe, who also designed much of the US Capitol. It sat across from the White House and dated to President James Madison, who sometimes attended, as did all other presidents since. Just three blocks east of the White House, on G Street, was Church of the Epiphany, where Jefferson Davis had attended during his Washington years, and where Stanton as war secretary would worship, taking Davis's pew. Reverend Gurley's newly constructed brick and steepled New York Avenue Presbyterian Church was just a few blocks north of it, nearly within sight of the White House looking down the avenue. Trinity Episcopal, with its Gothic spires, was at Third and C Streets, within sight of the Capitol.

Although crisscrossed by many theoretically grand avenues, Washington's only paved, cobblestone streets were Pennsylvania Avenue and parts of Seventh Street. An often fetid canal ran east to west, south of the White House toward the Capitol. The train station was on the south side of Pennsylvania Avenue, not very far from Brown's Hotel where John Tyler was headquartered. The city's old Center Market, the main grocery for Washingtonians, was also close by, likewise on the avenue's south side. The market site was first selected by George Washington, and was now a busy, disheveled hive of "old wooden sheds" with "low, soiled, whitewashed, weather-beaten walls, with the green moss growing over the shingled roof and hanging from the eaves."[32]

Although undistinguished in appearance, the city's main market was "abundantly supplied with the finest game and fish from the Eastern Shore of Maryland and Virginia, and the waters of the Potomac," including brant, ruddy duck, canvasback duck, sora, oysters, and terrapin. Oysters, "to be opened at a moment's notice, were planted on the cellar floors, and fed with salt water, and the cellars . . . were protected from invasion by the large terrapins kept there—a most efficient police force, crawling about with their outstretched necks and wicked eyes."[33]

West of the market, south of the avenue and Willard's, was a disreputable hodgepodge of saloons, gambling dens, and houses of ill repute that would soon grow in popularity when the city filled with soldiers. That neighborhood was predictably crime infested and often untamed by the city's limited police force.

"Pennsylvania Avenue is positively a disgrace to Christendom," one newspaper editorialized in 1859. "It abounds with sinks of iniquity, where human crime is as coolly planned as in a robber's cave." The city administration was praised for suppressing "rowdyism" but implored to challenge the spreading "gambling evil."[34]

Eastward across Fourteenth Street from Willard's on Pennsylvania Avenue was newspaper row, where one scribe then called Washington a "great, little, splendid, mean, extravagant, poverty-stricken barrack. . . . The one and only absolutely certain thing is the absence of anything permanent." He surmised it had a "Monument that will never be finished; a Capitol that is to have a dome; a Scientific Institute which does nothing but report the rise and fall of the thermometer." His judgment was unduly sarcastic, but he accurately understood that its "destiny is that of the Union," to be the "greatest capital of the world," or a biblical "wasteland."[35]

Despite the apocalyptic talk, Washington's cultural, social, and economic life continued, and perhaps even began to accelerate under the pressure of the national crisis. During the days of the Peace Conference, the renowned Boston-born Shakespearian actress Charlotte Cushman appeared at the Washington Theater as Queen Catherine in Shakespeare's *Henry VIII*. Despite the great expense of her appearance to the theater owner, theatergoers were promised no increase in the admission price.[36] The resulting audience was "immense," and the "wonderful power of her rendition of this striking Shakespearian character kept the large assemblage spell-bound."[37]

While in town Cushman also performed in another play called *The Stranger* and a comedy called *Simpson & Co.*, prompting a newspaper to hail the chance to see her in both drama and comedy on the same night as "one much to be made of."[38] Her audience was mostly ladies, and "not a few bright eyes were dimmed with tears." Leading congressmen insisted she also perform *Hamlet*, as she was scheduled soon to retire from the stage.[39]

During the Peace Conference, evening military concerts were given, featuring "amateur" singers and the US Marine Band, with several companies of DC local militia present. There were songs by a female duet, including "The Lonely Bird" and "Joy, Joy, Freedom Today," with a chorus singing "The Rock Beside the Sea." The band performed a piece from Verdi's *Il Trovatore*. An "immense" crowd gathered, with the "ladies of Washington" presenting a new set of flags to the militia, and with New York Democratic congressman John Cochrane offering the oratory after the militia paraded on stage. "Let us as a nation and a people stop the tide of fanaticism that is sweeping us to destruction," he cried. "Let us grant to all sections of our land the inalienable and immutable rights which the Constitution grants, preserve the equality it proclaims, and respect the immortal principles of liberty and justice, which it embodies.[40]

There were also lectures at the Smithsonian Institution during February 1861, including one on Japanese and Chinese culture.[41] Another focused on Francis Bacon and philosophy, as part of a series by Congregationalist Reverend John Lord of Hartford Seminary in Connecticut, who additionally lectured on Michelangelo, Oliver Cromwell, Christopher Columbus, and Madame de Staël, the French woman of letters. Citing "unfavorable weather" and the "distracted condition of the public mind," the Smithsonian noted lower than usual attendance that month.[42] Board members of the Smithsonian included a bipartisan mix of congressmen, including US Senator and 1860 presidential candidate Stephen Douglas, who had earlier been Lincoln's famous debate opponent.[43]

Compared to the Smithsonian, there was better attendance at the city's churches, which were reported to be largely full on Sundays. The clergy preached on spiritual themes and mostly avoided politics. On Ash Wednesday, Lent was diligently explained in one newspaper as the start of the Lenten season for Catholics, Episcopalians, and Lutherans, "in commemoration of the last days of our Savior." Supply and demand for fish during the Lenten season was increasing at the Center Market.[44] The churches were central in offering charity to the city's many poor and transient. The English Lutheran Church operated a Good Samaritan Soup House, expanding its hours from three days a week to every day in February 1861, receiving on one Saturday 275 "applicants."[45]

On the second Sunday of February, Reverend Gurley preached on Christ's atonement in the US Capitol, where worship services regularly convened. A Lutheran pastor at his church expounded on the Eucharist. At the Southern Methodist Church (Methodist Episcopal Church, South) there was a sermon on the power of salvation. At Grace Episcopal Church, the sermon, drawn from the book of Daniel, drew an "analogy from the tree of Daniel's vision," urging prayers that "though the branches of our own national tree may be topped and its leaves and fruit stripped, its roots may not be disturbed."[46]

The following Sunday, at the Methodist Protestant Church, the preacher likened present times to the book of Jeremiah, attributing national prosperity to God's favor and recalling George Washington's prayers. "Politicians may make light of the troubles of the times and scorn the remedy proposed, but our beloved country is in danger," he warned. "Are thirty million souls of no importance? Great God, save thy people and save quickly," he pleaded, offering "fervent" prayers for the Peace Conference, state conventions, and others in authority.[47]

Amid prayers for divine deliverance, the anxiety of national crisis took its personal toll. A fifty-one-year-old US Navy captain shot himself at home, with his family downstairs, his "mind having been greatly troubled with the sad condition of the country for two months past."[48] Public fistfights were not uncommon. An Illinois congressman repeatedly struck a *Chicago Tribune* reporter until onlookers intervened in the lobby of the National Hotel, the former displeased over coverage of him by the latter regarding "national troubles."[49]

THE CLOSE OF A PRESIDENCY

More happily, during the Peace Conference that February, President Buchanan hosted the closing reception of the social season, and presumably his presidency. It attracted to the White House an "immense crowd" whose "locomotion soon became impossible." Buchanan looked "hale and well, and seemed to feel relieved that he was drawing near to a rest from his wearing cares and labors." Cabinet secretaries, foreign diplomats, and US military officers attended, including aged but still actively in command US Army General John Wool, a War of 1812 veteran who was also a peace commissioner from New York. There were several US senators, including Ohio's John Sherman, whose brother William would soon become a celebrated general and whose stepfather was Ohio Peace Commissioner Thomas Ewing. Both "Dixie" and "Yankee Doodle" were performed, reflective of Buchanan's chronic desire to please and conciliate, creating an "exceedingly pleasant" evening.[50]

Buchanan was the nation's first lifelong bachelor president (others had been widowers) and presided over Washington's official social life with "republican simplicity." His niece Harriet Lane, who was "very handsome, fair, and blue-eyed," as Sara Pryor observed, was "very affable and agreeable, in an unemotional way" in her time as First Lady. Self-contained, dignified, and predictable, with "exquisite taste," she was admired but not popular, lacking "magnetism" and spontaneous charm.

"Always courteous, always in place, silent whenever it was possible to be silent, watchful, and careful, she made no enemies, was betrayed into no entangling alliances, and was involved in no contretemps of any kind."[51] Lane must have had tremendous discipline to have held steady as the city and nation fractured so quickly.

More spontaneous, and fully availing herself of Washington public life, was former First Lady Julia Tyler, who appreciated the faster pace and increased attention in Washington after years at their Virginia plantation. Expenses were tight during a month's stay at Brown's Hotel, as the state was barely covering her husband's travel costs, and hers not at all. "Wherever I went the first position was accorded me," she gushed, perhaps benefiting from a city enduring a bachelor president, and nostalgic for a glamorous presidential wife. The hotel owner's wife generously loaned her a fine carriage for her excursions.

Mrs. Tyler appreciated the newfound respect now accorded her husband after a long political exile, which also restored her own prominence. She recounted that a North Carolina peace delegate had told her: "President Tyler has had the great happiness accorded him of living to see himself fully appreciated. All party feelings have faded away, and his old enemies are among his warmest friends."[52] Kentucky Peace Commissioner James Clay, son of the great Henry Clay, paid her homage, echoing her father's charm of earlier years, even though the elder Clay had been a political nemesis.

"You ought to hear all the compliments that are heaped upon me," Mrs. Tyler told her New York mother with glee. "Of course I haven't changed a bit, except to improve, etc." She wasn't yet sure she would have occasion to wear the box of clothing her mother had sent her, being exhausted no less than her husband from the exhilarating press of business. There was an invitation to a massive gala at the home of failed 1860 Democratic presidential candidate US Senator Stephen Douglas, but she wasn't certain they could accept.[53]

Of course, they did accept, and it was likely chief among Mrs. Tyler's pleasures that February 1861, once again to stand in the social and political spotlight before Washington's elite, and in the home of Lincoln's longtime political adversary who was also a steadfast Unionist. "At Douglas's ball it was as much our own reception as theirs; we were bowing and courtseying and shaking hands incessantly," she fondly recalled of the unforgettable evening.[54] Four hundred office holders and other notables jammed into the Douglas mansion, including Tyler's fellow peace commissioners and many wives. One guest pronounced that Mrs. Douglas was a "fine woman" and "plays the agreeable hostess in admirable style."[55]

Mrs. Tyler boasted to her mother that she had been "paraded" about at the party by the "handsomest man here," Kentucky's governor, prominent Peace Delegate Charles Morehead. He resembled her father in every way, she happily reported, not knowing he would later that year, after war began, face Northern imprisonment for perceived Secessionist sympathy. "I suppose I may conclude I looked quite well," she further surmised, perhaps wearing the clothing her mother had sent from New York after all. Meanwhile, her husband had playfully identified a woman who was his wife's "old friend" as the "handsomest person in the room." They were "all the time surrounded" by the "throng," and Mrs. Tyler was clearly energized by her triumphant return to Washington's social whirlwind. "People turned up and recalled themselves to me that I certainly never expected to have met again," she noted. She also passed along word that previous social attempts in Washington that winter had failed, so the energy of the Peace Conference had made the Douglas soirée uniquely successful. "People are catching at straws as a relief to their pressing anxieties, and look to the Peace Commissioners as if they possessed some divine power to restore order and harmony," Mrs. Tyler concluded, not inaccurately.[56]

Young Henry Adams was also at the Douglas party, with nearly everyone else of official Washington, and was more cynical. He was the son of Congressman Charles Francis Adams, and himself a future historian. Referring to Mrs. Douglas's "crush ball last night," Adams described the "wildest collection of people I ever saw." Compared to the president's receptions, of which there was one earlier that evening, it was "beyond all description promiscuous." Stephen Douglas was a "beast" and "drunkard" who was "ruined as a public man." But his wife was "as usual, handsome 'splendidly null,'" who "stood and shook hands with all of her guests, and smiled and smiled."

Adams observed that a "crowd of admiring devotees surrounded the ancient buffer [John] Tyler," along with the similarly aged Senator Crittenden. "Ye Gods, what are we, when mortals no bigger, no, not so big as ourselves, are looked up to as though their thunder struck from the real original Olympus." Tyler was merely an "old Virginia politician, of whom by rights, no one ought ever have heard, reappearing in the ancient ceremony's of his forgotten grave political and social and men look up at him as they would at Solomon, if he could be made the subject of resurrection."

Unsurprisingly, Adams was also cynical about the Peace Conference. "Like most meetings of this sort, I suppose they will potter ahead until no one feels any more interest in them, and then they may die," he surmised, although adding the meeting may at least "gain time" for the Secessionists to implode and the Union to prevail.[57] Presumably young Adams thought more favorably about the "grand entertainment" at his father's house two nights after the Douglas party, as the Massachusetts peace commissioners had been invited.[58] Ohio US Senator Thomas Corwin had hosted a party for peace delegates on February 11, while Delegate Reverdy Johnson, a former US senator from Maryland, had hosted a party on February 1.[59]

The Douglas gala would be among the last great social events in pre-war Washington that were non-partisan and inclusive of personages from all regions. Weeks before, many of the leading Southern notables in government who had dominated the city's political and social arenas had already departed Washington, many of them forever. Most exceptionally among them was US Senator Jefferson Davis of Mississippi, whose emotion-choked good-bye speech in the Senate chamber in January had precipitated tears both from colleagues and gallery spectators, from friend and foe. In December he had served on the US Senate's Committee of thirteen senators that struggled unsuccessfully to find compromise, along with Douglas, William Seward, and Crittenden. This left Davis crestfallen but thereafter resolute about secession.[60]

DAVIS'S FAREWELL

On a chilly January 21, Davis was the last of five Southern senators who bid formal farewell that day. The wife of Davis's Alabama colleague recalled that "the blood within me congealed" as she sat in the gallery among emotive, handkerchief-waving women, remembering:

> Men wept and embraced each other mournfully. . . . Scarcely a member of that Senatorial body but was pale with the terrible significance of the hour. There was everywhere a feeling of suspense, as if, visibly, the Government structure was tottering; nor was there a patriot on either side who did not deplore and whiten before the evil that brooded so low over the nation.[61]

Davis had resisted secession. He was a longtime senator, congressman, war secretary, West Point graduate, and wounded soldier who had served heroically in the Mexican-American War, and whose first wife, now deceased, had been the daughter of ardently pro-Union eventual president Zachary Taylor. Now his young, vivacious second wife, Varina, was tensely seated in the Senate gallery, having dispatched a servant at 7:00 A.M. to reserve her seat. She later recalled that her husband, in his anxiety, had suffered a disabling attack of neuralgia, rising from his bed that morning after a week of "suffering with an aching head," compounding his already "unutterable grief."

Still wracked by pain, Davis explained to the Senate that the South was "to be deprived in the Union of the rights which our fathers bequeathed to us," having heard "proclaimed the theory that all men are created free and equal, and this made the basis of an attack upon her social institutions; and the sacred Declaration of Independence has been invoked to maintain the position of the equality of the races."

Davis insisted the Declaration's assertion of equality had "no reference to the slave," and the Constitution likewise for blacks had "not put upon the footing of equality with white men—not even upon that of paupers and convicts; but, so far as representation was concerned, were discriminated against as a lower caste, only to be represented in the numerical proportion of three fifths." He cited the "principles upon which our Government was founded; and when you deny them, and when you deny to us the right to withdraw from a Government which thus perverted threatens to be destructive of our rights, we but tread in the path of our fathers when we proclaim our independence, and take the hazard."

Expressing hope to his Northern colleagues for "peaceful relations with you, though we must part," he warned the "reverse may bring disaster on every portion of the country; and if you will have it thus, we will invoke the God of our fathers, who delivered them from the power of the lion, to protect us from the ravages of the bear; and thus, putting our trust in God and in our own firm hearts and strong arms, we will vindicate the right as best we may." Davis forgave any offense to him by his colleagues during "points of collision" and offered "apology for any pain which, in heat of discussion, I have inflicted."[62]

Having listened "spellbound," Davis's colleagues surrounded him for handshakes. He had appeared "firm and manly" but still "pale and evidently suffering." Davis pronounced it the "saddest day of his life," and recalled his words were "leaves torn from the book of fate." The next day he left Washington with Varina, "tortured" and "grief-stricken."[63]

Varina mourned no less than her husband as they left the city where they had lived across fifteen years. She remained "warmly attached" to the city evidently even more than he, according to her seamstress, Elizabeth Keckley, a free black woman. Late in 1860, after Lincoln's election, Varina claimed she would not socialize with Republicans, while also avoiding Secessionists and their "blathering." She told her husband, as the national crisis worsened, "Everybody is scared," including President Buchanan, of whom she remained fond even as her husband dismissed his "weakness" and "perfidious" stance toward South Carolina over Fort Sumter. She in fact "love[d] the dear old man and would like forget that I do," giving him slippers for Christmas 1860, telling the president she hoped "they may sometime remind you of the great regard with which I shall ever remain faithfully your friend." Before leaving Washington, she would visit the White House, without her husband, for a final good-bye to Buchanan.

On New Year's Day 1861, Varina complained: "This town is like some kind of mausoleum, comparatively, no one visiting, no dinners or parties—just a sullen gloom impending over all things." She confided in Keckley, an ex-slave who had purchased her own freedom years earlier through her successful seamstress work in the city, that she dreaded returning south, imploring Keckley to go with her. Keckley would instead work for and become a confidante to First Lady Mary Todd Lincoln.[64]

Varina and her husband left Washington before the Tylers' arrival for the Peace Conference, tearfully hosting friends for the last time, while closing their rented Washington house on I Street and leaving with their three small children, a parrot, and a dog.[65] But later, as Confederate First Lady in Richmond, Varina befriended Julia Tyler, whom she called her "beautiful stepmother." During the war, Varina's sister would marry John Tyler's grandson by his first wife, cementing family ties.[66]

Despite her earlier anti-Republican claim, Varina sustained ties until the end in Washington, even with anti-slavery Northern politicos and their families. This included the sister of future Lincoln cabinet member Montgomery Blair, Lizzie Blair Lee, who recounted that Varina "was sad enough now that the time is come to leave all her friends." At a Christmas season party, Davis had asked Lee if she would go south to "fight" against Davis, prompting Lee to declare she would not let Davis "break any bonds" between them, drawing applause from onlooking partiers.[67]

Several years earlier Varina had, characteristically, enjoyed a dinner with Northern anti-slavery senators William Seward and Solomon Foot, who would later fiercely denounce the Peace Conference for trying to appease the South, but whom she had found "pleasant."[68] She actually liked Seward, never forgetting that he had dispatched a sleigh to deliver her friend in a snowstorm while Varina recovered from a difficult childbirth. When she once asked him if he really believed his anti-slavery rhetoric, Seward smilingly claimed, in typical fashion, that it was only for votes, which left her wondering if he was teasing her.[69]

"PRECONCEIVED HARMONY"

Such social friendships across regional and political divisions were now being torn asunder. But they found brief respite, or at least were intended to, when President Buchanan hosted the Peace Conference delegates shortly after their arrival. After meeting briefly on the morning of February 7, their third day, they proceeded at noon to the White House. Reporters were excluded, a New York newspaper noted, because "some of the members, fearing that their constituents would learn through the press what they said to Old Buck, and what he said to them, insisted that the interview should be in secret." They remained with Buchanan "but a short time."[70]

A Washington newspaper reported Buchanan's reception of the delegates in the White House East Room as a "friendly conversation."[71] Mrs. Pryor would hail this East Room "with its ornate chandeliers, fluted pillars, and floriated carpet" as an "audience chamber fit for a king."[72] But behind the cordial veneer that day there were of course complexities. "We marched to the Executive Mansion with the solemnity of a funeral procession," recalled Vermont Peace Commissioner Lucius Chittenden, a banker and state legislator, as well as outspoken anti-slavery Unionist. He would serve as registrar of the US Treasury in the Lincoln administration under Ohio Peace Commissioner Salmon Chase, who became treasury secretary.

Chittenden remembered Buchanan as "advanced in years, shaken in body, and uncertain in mind," showing "every symptom of an old man worn out by worry." Although not doubting his loyalty to the country, Chittenden thought the president unsettled by "anxiety," greeting each peace commissioner with "effusion" and "uncontrollable emotion." Urging "compromise and concession," Chittenden thought it "very painful to watch him throw his arms around the neck of one stranger after another, and, with streaming eyes, beg of him to yield anything to save his country from 'bloody, fratricidal war,'" a phrase Buchanan kept repeating. Chittenden was irritated that the president had "not one word of condemnation" for secession, instead viewing the South as the "injured party" meriting "apology" from the North.

Buchanan urged the peace commissioners to support constitutional amendments that the South desired for protecting slavery. The often suspicious Chittenden suspected that this suggestion implied Buchanan's earlier "consultation" with Southern peace commissioners. When a Northern commissioner suggested the presidential election had already "pronounced judgment," Southern commissioners distracted the conversation, Chittenden described, since the Northerner's point disrupted the "preconceived harmony" of the White House visit.

Afterward, a Northern commissioner sarcastically likened Buchanan's stance toward the Constitution to a bull breeder, willing to cede the whole body in order to retain the one essential part for his business. "This call upon the President produced an impression very different from that anticipated by those who brought it about," Chittenden surmised. Instead of persuasion toward concessions, Northern commissioners instead saw a president "broken in mind and body" and incapable of confronting the national crisis. "Months of debate could not have united the northern delegates so firmly as the insensible influence of this formal call," Chittenden asserted.

That evening, nearly all Republican peace commissioners met in caucus, electing Salmon Chase as their chair. Ohio's governor had appointed Chase a delegate without consulting him. Chase wanted to decline, expecting that even on the all-Republican Ohio delegation he'd be alone in resisting the "surrender of our principles" and rejecting another "Border State Compromise." Instead, he had told Lincoln that he favored "inauguration first—adjustment afterwards." A Cincinnati paper had opposed Chase's appointment because he "has declared himself in advance as opposed to all and any compromise."[73]

Under Chase's leadership, the Republican peace commissioners agreed to act in unison throughout the Peace Conference and to invite "all loyal Democrats" into their group. Thereafter, as Chittenden remembered, the Republicans at Willard Hall were a "compactly united body."[74]

After the White House visit, the peace commissioners went to the Capitol for courtesy visits with Congress. "The strictest precautions are taken to keep the doings of the convention from the public eye," a Washington newspaper reported, "to prevent outside pressure, particularly from the other Congress which meets at the other end of Pennsylvania Avenue."[75]

In the coming weeks there would be more parties for the peace commissioners, and more receptions, concerts, theater productions, and excursions about the rough-hewn but still grand capital city. But there would chiefly be somber and sometimes tense sessions in the former church that was now Willard Hall. Across many wintry days, the steam pipes about them sizzled trying to keep the high-ceilinged hall reasonably warm, and the gas-powered chandeliers above exuded a constant glow and hum while some of the nation's most renowned statesmen toiled to save their country.

THREE
OPENING DEBATE

War! Civil War! is impending over us. It must be averted! Who does not know that such a war, among such a
people, must be, if it comes, a war of extermination?

—Kentucky Peace Commissioner James Guthrie

The Peace Conference's first day on February 4, 1861, was opened with fifty-eight-year-old former US congressman and former Kentucky governor Charles Slaughter Morehead as initial chair. Later that year he would be arrested for disloyalty to the Union, at the urging of Lincoln's Kentucky friends. He would remain incarcerated at a US Army fort in Boston Harbor for several months, confined with nine men in a ten-by-twenty-foot room. After his release he would flee to Canada and Mexico for the war's duration.

The bewhiskered, stately appearing Morehead, whom Mrs. Tyler hailed as the "handsomest man," was an old political friend of former president John Tyler. Tyler would also be denounced as a traitor after his own election to the Confederate Congress, and would become permanent Peace Conference president, elected on the second day. For many of the men in Willard Hall over the coming days, although many had been friends or at least associates for decades, it would be their last time together before irretrievably divided by war.[1]

Morehead quickly nominated that first day an even older colleague as succeeding temporary chair, with unanimous acclamation. Seventy-seven-year-old, blind, and enfeebled John C. Wright from Ohio had served with Tyler in the US House of Representatives in the 1820s and was the oldest member of the Peace Conference, having been born four years before the US Constitution. A former journalist and Ohio Supreme Court judge, he was widely and highly venerated. His younger and more politically militant Ohio colleague, Salmon Chase, escorted him to the front dais.

"We have assembled as friends, as brothers, each, I doubt not, animated by the most friendly sentiments," Wright assured his attentive audience. He also told that he favored "justice to all sections of the Union," and favored any constitutional amendments giving the "government permanence, strength, and stability, as will tend to secure to any state, or any number of states, the quiet and unmolested enjoyment of their rights."

Wright declared that his confidence in Republican institutions had increased every year of a "life which has been protracted beyond the term usually allotted to man," a life "now drawing to a close, and I hope, when it ends, I may leave the Government more firmly established in the affections of my countrymen than it ever was before." Almost delivering a benediction, he closed: "I pray God that He will be with us during our deliberations, and that He may guide them to a happy and wise conclusion."[2]

In nine days, Wright would be dead—the Peace Conference's only death—not living to see any happy conclusion for his country's crisis.

On that first day, most of the delegations from eleven states were present of the twenty-one who would eventually arrive. "Their appearance was grave and their deportment extremely sedate," observed one colleague.[3] Twelve delegates of the eventual 132 were seventy or older, thirty-four were at least sixty, and seventy-four were fifty or over. Only six were under forty, prompting abolitionist editor Horace Greeley to mock them as "political fossils, who would not have been again disinterred but for the shock . . . [of] the secession movement."[4]

Former New Jersey governor Rodman Price, a Democrat, bald, mustached, and relatively young at age fifty-four, motioned that reporters waiting outside be allowed in to cover their proceedings. "When my country is in danger, my political robes hang loosely on my shoulders," he once had professed. His wide-ranging political life had included Mexican War naval service and participation in California's formative state convention, before returning to New Jersey.[5]

Virginia's Southern firebrand former US congressman James Seddon immediately objected. "In the present excited condition of the country, I can see how much harm might result from that publicity," he warned. Frail, skinny, intense, sometimes wearing a skull cap that accentuated his ascetic image, he was likely the most zealously partial to the South's concerns of any Peace Conference commissioner. He was described by a Richmond newspaper as a "Democrat of the [John] Calhoun school." He would serve as Confederate war secretary for three years.[6]

A Vermont colleague at the Peace Conference, Lucius Chittenden, grudgingly admitted Seddon was the "most powerful debater of the conference; skillful, adroit, cunning," and having a tremendous "hatred of all forms of northern life," from New England statesmen to the "sheep that fed upon her hillsides." Seddon's physical appearance was called "extraordinary," marked by the "pallor of his face, his narrow chest, sunken eyes, and attenuated frame," accompanied by a voice "husky at first" but clearing with "excitement of debate, in which he became eloquent." Not obliged to pay even lip service to slavery's evils, he instead insisted on slavery's "moral beauties" and equally on "the North's humiliation." From Chittenden's suspicious New Englander Republican's view, Seddon was the "soul of the plot the Peace Conference was intended to execute," by which he evidently meant the breakup of the Union.[7]

Seddon was likely more militant than most of his fellow Virginians because he had maintained property and slaves in Louisiana for twenty-five years, in the state where he had first traveled to escape Virginia's winters for reasons of health. He would years later counsel that slaves and land, especially in the Deep South, were a far "more secure" investment than stocks and bonds. Later he built his own plantation, Sabot Hill, west of Richmond, Virginia, while still often traveling to oversee his Louisiana holdings. His Virginia home included a well-stocked library and was a place of literature, music, and culture for his large family amid much entertaining. Seddon had married a Virginia heiress in 1845 at newly built St. Paul's Episcopal Church in Richmond, which later became known as the "Cathedral of the Confederacy." Jefferson Davis and Robert E. Lee would worship there with Seddon during the war, although he was himself Presbyterian. Seddon's wedding was in fact the new church's first such ceremony. Jefferson Davis would later famously worship at St. Paul's on a Sunday in 1865 when he received urgent word from General Lee at the front to evacuate Richmond immediately. Mrs. Seddon would later serve as the very proficient organist at Old Hebron Presbyterian Church near their plantation. Seddon and his bride socialized with John Tyler, who found him a promising young man. Jefferson Davis's wife, Varina, called Mrs. Seddon "very handsome." Earlier in their marriage the Seddons resided in a Richmond mansion that later became Jefferson Davis's home as the "White House of the Confederacy," and where the Davises endured personal tragedy when their young son fell to his death off the back porch.[8]

As a US congressman, Seddon had opposed the Compromise of 1850, believing it "perilous ground to every true Southern man." As always emphatic, he declared of the legislative omnibus that US Senator Henry Clay orchestrated to forestall disunion: "I eschew the thing in thought, heart and deed as much as any honest man may." He would later declare disbelief that the North was "so mad and besotted as in the face of this united and determined opposition in the South to subvert the union and destroy at once their own prosperity and all the glorious prospects of the confederacy; If they are then disunion is inevitable." After John Brown's

1859 raid on Harpers Ferry, he privately surmised that the South should "scheme" for separation if necessary.[9]

A subordinate at the Confederate War Department would describe Seddon during the war as "gaunt and emaciated, with long struggling hair, mingled gray and black," looking like a "dead man galvanized into muscular animation." He had sunken eyes, and the "hue of a man who had been in his grave a full month," and "much afflicted with neuralgia," which he contracted in the 1850s. But he was also recalled as an "orator" with "fine education," full of intelligence and force, as he would demonstrate throughout the Peace Conference.[10]

"If our deliberations are to attain the successful conclusion we so much desire, it certainly is the course of wisdom that we should follow the illustrious example of the framers of the present Constitution, and sit with closed doors," Seddon argued persuasively at Willard Hall that first day. The delegates rejected any outside observers, as they repeatedly would throughout the convention.[11] Vermont's Chittenden would sarcastically recall that Seddon had "assumed the duties of managing director of the conference."[12]

Former Kentucky governor Charles Wickliffe was the seventy-two-year-old former US postmaster general under President Tyler who had been Tyler's roommate during their even earlier congressional years together. Two days later at the conference he would partially echo Seddon, when the issue of reporters at the conference reemerged. "In my judgment, secrecy is absolutely indispensable to successful action here," he insisted. "I do not wish to be precluded from abandoning a position to-morrow, if I see cause for it, which I have taken to-day." He warned that if the proceedings got into the newspapers, "when a member is understood to have committed himself to a particular proposition, or any special course of policy, that pride of opinion, which we all possess, will render any change of policy on his part difficult, if not impossible," making persuasion and compromise difficult.

Pointing out they had "all come here with an earnest desire to harmonize our conflicting opinions . . . and save the union," Wickliffe was adamant that, after the South and North had spoken of each other in "severe terms," conciliation now depended on "mutual concessions, by confessing our sins to each other, and endeavoring to live harmoniously together in future."[13]

Hard core Republican delegations from Vermont, Connecticut, and Iowa were more open to public transparency. They took their seats next day, some complaining of "self-appointed managers" who had already organized most of the convention rules. Mostly the Republicans initially "contented themselves by looking on, without any interference with the harmony of the proceedings," one recalled. Tyler, despite his own well-known Southern partiality, was unanimously elected president on the second day. On the third day, fourteen state delegations were present, with Illinois, Kansas, Missouri, New York, Tennessee, Massachusetts, and Maine still yet to arrive.[14]

A Vermont newspaper lamented that too many die-hard Republicans believed that "accomplishment of any good" at the Peace Conference was impossible without unsavory "sacrifice of principle," confusing it with "sacrifice of opinion," which was essential and admirable. It noted the slow progress and granted, "it is not a favorable omen that the arch-traitor John Tyler is president of the convention. But we shall see what we shall see."[15]

"A Complete Record"

Over the first several days, some Republican commissioners decided they should "take a more active part," making motions for a recording secretary and an official stenographer, which were defeated. Vermont's Chittenden, a relative youngster in this setting at only age thirty-six, relished "casting the first firebrand into the inflammable materials of the conference" by announcing he would take detailed notes for reporting to his state. "Then there was trouble," he recalled, "and great confusion," as about a dozen Southerners each tried to speak simultaneously.

Chittenden claimed one delegate demanded his censure, and another his expulsion. President Tyler, "whose discretion never deserted him," announced that the group could not control any individual member's communication with his constituents. So the "storm passed, and the skies were clear again," Chittenden perceived.[16]

Chittenden proceeded to take his own thorough minutes, which he published three years later. Originally he had in mind that the Peace Conference would craft constitutional amendments, and the country would need a "knowledge of the motives." Clearly modeling himself on James Madison, with the consequences no less serious, he tried to heed the "example of the illustrious reporter" of the Constitutional Convention of 1787. Even if his notes lacked Madison's "beauty and felicity," they were "not less full and accurate."[17]

The rules of the Peace Conference were popularly perceived as "rigid and formal," especially by Northerners frustrated by its closed doors. A Cleveland newspaper reported with some amazement and likely exaggeration that delegates were "precluded from reading newspapers or pamphlets, or crossing the hall while any one is speaking, and all rise when the President [Tyler] passed out."[18]

From nearly the start, there was no evasion about what the Peace Conference urgently sought to avert. "We have come from the North and the South, from the East and the West, to see whether our wisdom can devise some means to avert the dangers which threaten to destroy this noble Republic, founded by the wisdom and patriotism of our ancestors," orated sixty-eight-year-old former US Treasury secretary James Guthrie of Kentucky, who had served under President Pierce.

In what a New York newspaper called a "powerful and patriotic speech," Guthrie painted a gloomy picture of what would happen if the Peace Conference failed. "The storm is threatening," he observed, and the "the horizon is covered with dark and portentous clouds," with each section "arrayed against section, and already seven of our sister states have separated from us and are proceeding to establish an independent Confederation." He became more vehement: "War! Civil War! is impending over us. It must be averted! Who does not know that such a war, among such a people, must be, if it comes, a war of extermination."[19]

In a similarly urgent spirit, Seddon warned against deferring the convention's main work to a committee, as Guthrie had proposed, when the work "ought to commence now" and be "accomplished speedily." After all, he reminded his fellow delegates, "events are on the wing," and "already in my state the delegates are elected to a convention, which is to meet next week, to consider the subject which now engrosses the minds of the American people."[20]

But the work centered on the resolutions originating from Virginia that had launched the Peace Conference. As Guthrie urged, it was referred to a Committee on Resolutions composed of one member from each state delegation, which would deliberate for a week, chaired by Guthrie. Meanwhile on the fourth day, February 7, New York, Illinois, and Tennessee arrived, and the convention adjourned after only an hour to walk to the White House for their brief meeting with an emotive President Buchanan.[21]

The next day, Friday, February 8, the new Resolutions Committee demurred on providing an update. Guthrie explained that they preferred Monday; it was a pattern of delay that would indicate difficulties among the committee's discordant members. But Seddon objected, insisting on a Saturday meeting and report, which was agreed. On Saturday, the Maine delegation appeared, with several members from Massachusetts. Kentucky's forty-three-year-old former US congressman James Clay, previously US ambassador to Portugal, shared with his colleagues Unionist resolutions from Connecticut Democrats, "expressing an anxious desire for the settlement of the difficult questions now before the country." He didn't know why these Connecticut people had contacted him as a Kentuckian, although he guessed they recalled his late father, US Senator Henry Clay, as the "Great Compromiser" who was central to maintaining the Union, culminating with the Great Compromise of 1850.[22]

James Clay and his famous family embodied the divisions in the nation and within the Peace Conference. His father had been abstractly anti-slavery, favoring gradual emancipation and overseas colonization, while still owning slaves. The son had purchased his father's Ashland estate outside Lexington, Kentucky, with help from his wealthy wife. He lavishly rebuilt and redecorated its mansion, and disclaimed interest in slave labor. But in the 1850s he was purchasing slaves as apparent investments. He had become a Democrat after the collapse of his father's Whig Party in the 1850s because it was the "only party this day in existence worthy by its nationality and its principles to wield the destinies of a great and free people." And he campaigned for James Buchanan in the 1856 presidential election, for which Buchanan sought to reward him with an ambassadorial post to Prussia, which he refused. Instead, Clay was elected to Congress by Kentucky as a Democrat, even as his brother became a Republican, foreshadowing even more tragic Clay family fractures during the war.[23]

The Clays were just one of many great American families represented at the Peace Conference whose fates were inextricably bound with the nation. Seddon, himself the scion of Virginia gentry, must have been frustrated with others when the Resolutions Committee announced on Monday, February 11, that it still had not even a preliminary report, prompting adjournment until Wednesday. But on that day, after the conference convened at noon, the committee's chair, Guthrie, offered regrets. He insisted that the committee had "labored diligently" during "protracted sessions," but now could not report until Friday. He assured his colleagues that the committee was "fully impressed with the necessity of immediate action," since Congress would have little time to act on any proposals. So the conference adjourned, scheduled to reconvene Friday, February 15, until Tyler summoned them in special session on Thursday to appreciate the "act of Divine Providence" in "removing from the sphere of his earthly labors one of the most valued commissioners in attendance," referring to the death that day of the aged John Wright, who had died after an illness of six or eight days.[24]

Wright's son had accompanied his frail father to Washington and served the Peace Conference as one of its secretaries. He informed the delegates that his father's last words had been of saving the Union. Wright had even asked his son, in a final act, to read to him "sections in the Constitution in regard to counting the votes," perhaps reflecting concern about the Electoral College vote scheduled in Congress the next day. After hearing the constitutional passage, Wright poignantly "terminated his knowledge on earth."

Before the sullen but surely not shocked delegates, Salmon Chase offered his already carefully prepared formal eulogy for his Ohio colleague, whom the "mysterious ways of Divine Providence" had summoned when the "prudence and patriotism of his counsels seemed most needed." Wright was recalled as an orphan who began with little in life "save his own energies and God's blessing," rising rapidly in business and politics, becoming a congressional associate and friend to his legendary contemporaries Henry Clay and Daniel Webster. He had left a "tranquil retirement" to represent his state at the Peace Conference. Chase hoped Wright's death foreshadowed national reconciliation:

God grant that the clouds which now darken over us may speedily disperse, and that rough generous counsels and patriotic labors, guided by that good Providence which directed our fathers in its original formation, the Union of our states may be more than ever firmly cemented and established.[25]

A flood of additional effusive eulogies followed spontaneously, with Charles Wickliffe of Kentucky and William Rives of Virginia both remembering having entered Congress with Wright thirty-seven years previously, where in the US Capitol "there were giants in those days." Rives suggested Wright's sudden death "seems to me to exalt—in some degree to canonize—our labors," as a "manifestation of the visible hand of God among us." Doubtless everyone in Willard Hall that day, Rives was certain, would gladly lay down their own life to follow Wright if by so doing they could "restore peace and harmony to this glorious Republic of ours."

Dramatically, Wright himself then reappeared in Willard Hall as his casket was ushered in, preceded by Rev. Charles Hall of nearby Church of the Epiphany, who read the "impressive service of the Episcopal Church." Then a funeral cortege took Wright to the Baltimore and Ohio Railroad depot for the return home to Ohio. Hall would later officiate at the funeral for General Robert E. Lee's daughter and at President Lincoln's funeral, among many, many others in the war years ahead.[26]

Wright's quickly appointed successor was controversial former Ohio attorney general Christopher Wolcott. He was thirty-seven years younger than Wright, and unlike his moderate predecessor, a staunch anti-slavery Republican skeptical of conciliating the South. The Republican-controlled Ohio state senate barely approved Wolcott's nomination, with six Republicans voting against him. A Cincinnati newspaper denounced his appointment since he was "against all compromise, and will go to Washington determined to prevent the peace conference agreeing to any compromise," complaining that "such a man [has] a bad look." Since Wolcott was nominated right after president-elect Lincoln's departure from Ohio's capital, the newspaper hoped Wolcott's selection was not "at the suggestion of Mr. Lincoln," and lamented that Ohio's governor had "made no reputation by the appointment."[27]

But another Cincinnati newspaper sarcastically mocked Wolcott's critics. "Mr. Wolcott is shockingly unfitted" for the Peace Conference, it bemusedly surmised, since he was only age thirty-five, when at least age seventy or a "miraculous resurrection from the political tomb" was the proper qualification. After all, Wolcott was a "living man, which is irreverent to the antiquities of the Conference," plus he was "strong and plucky," which was a "monstrous unfitness for a place where cowardice is patriotism." He also likely was "demented" with "fanatical" devotion to the Constitution and supremacy of law, "when any patriot can see that the true way to save the Union is to allow any pack of fools to kick it over, and then have the old political midwives reconstruct it." Of course some "immaculate" Republicans had voted against him, true to their "neutral instincts," while Democrats naturally voted against him, predictably, not wanting any delegate who affirmed the "rights and dignity of the people of Ohio."[28]

A Nashville newspaper denounced Wolcott for essentially having defended "negro-stealing" as Ohio's attorney general, by not arresting the "thieves" under fugitive slave laws. He was also noted as "notorious as a mourner over the fate of John Brown," who had famously died in Harpers Ferry, Virginia, two years before while trying to inspire a slave revolt.[29] Salmon Chase of course privately welcomed Wolcott's addition to the Ohio delegation and the political shift in his preferred direction of non-accommodation. Likely Chase agreed when one sardonic friend told him: "Among so many very old gentlemen such an actuary as Mr. Wright would tell us, the chances are that every sixty days will improve the quality of the convention."[30]

SALMON P. CHASE

The fifty-two-year-old Chase was the ascendant voice among Peace Conference die-hard Republicans. Originally from Vermont, the nephew of a US senator, Chase lost his father while a boy and was sent to live with his "tyrannical" and "often very harsh and severe" Ohio uncle who was an Episcopal bishop—the first in Ohio—and also a presiding bishop of the denomination. Doubtless his ambition, discipline, courage, learning, and nearly lifelong religious piety were owed to this uncle, along with his internal anxiety. The bishop practiced and preached a very exacting form of frontier Christianity with little patience for softness or ambiguity.[31]

Chase was a student at Dartmouth College back in Vermont when there was a spiritual revival on the campus that touched Chase deeply: "It has pleased God in his infinite mercy to bring me . . . to the foot of the cross and to find acceptance through the blood of His dear Son." Ignoring his uncle's counsel to enter the clergy, Chase instead heeded his older brother's counsel against becoming just one more "hypocritical" reverend and instead to become a "conscientious and moral lawyer."[32]

As a young Cincinnati lawyer, Chase was active in the Young Men's Temperance Society, the Young Men's Bible Association, and the American Sunday School Union. He superintended the Sunday school at his local Episcopal congregation. After an illness he determined to "try to do more for God than I had before done, to live a more godly life, and to be more instant in prayer, and more abundant in good works." His wedding to his first wife was conducted by the famed Congregationalist preacher Lyman Beecher, but his bride died only twenty months later. This prompted both grief and his guilt for not engaging her more spiritually, fearing that she may not have "died in the faith." His second wife, whom he married four years later, was more religiously devout, and Chase relished, "We are in a common dependence on the Savior and in a common hope of immortal life." Devastatingly, his second wife died six years later, after Chase had already lost three of four daughters. "The Lord hath dealt very bitterly with me," he grieved. But he was confident this time: "She died trusting in Jesus." Chase married again a year later, but his third wife died six years later, following the death of one of their two daughters. He was relieved that his third wife was "safe in the bosom of her God and Savior" but mourned: "What a vale of misery this world is." He had consoled his dying third wife with words that doubtless applied to him: God "will not suffer those who trust in Him through Christ to be utterly cast down."[33]

Chase's lifelong walk with death strengthened his faith and drove him more furiously into his legal and political career, especially as a proponent of reforming religious and social causes. He remained devoted to his two surviving daughters. One of them, Kate, would herself become a prominent figure in Washington social and political life during the Civil War. Chase first came to the nation's capital at age eighteen to start a school but ended up clerking with US Attorney General William Wirt under President John Quincy Adams. He often worshipped with the Wirts at St. John's Episcopal Church, where presidents and other prominent Washingtonians often attended. "I confess I desire to be distinguished but I desire more to be useful," he resolved at the time. He helped a Quaker petition Congress for gradually abolishing slavery in Washington—a perennial hot-button cause for Congress and the nation—in what he would momentously recall as his "first anti-slavery work."[34]

In his early years Chase had supported the conventional cause of colonizing freed slaves in Africa, extolling it in 1834 as a "sure powerful mode of extending civilization and Christianity to that great, but as yet barbarous, continent." Two years later he was energized to defend a Cincinnati abolitionist newspaper publisher continuously threatened by mobs. The publisher persuaded Chase that the "Slave Power" was the "great enemy of freedom of speech, freedom of the press and freedom of the person." A large man, Chase physically blocked a mob from entering the boarding house of the threatened abolitionist publisher, although not yet himself "technically an abolitionist." Chase went on shortly to legally represent an escaped slave, arguing in court that "all men are born 'equally free.'"[35]

In 1845 Chase was honored by black churches in Cincinnati, who presented him with a sterling silver pitcher purchased with donations by black parishioners, in "gratitude towards you . . . for your remembrance of our brethren in bonds as bound with them and also for your zealous and disinterested advocacy of the rights and privileges of all classes of your fellow-citizens, irrespective of clime, color or condition . . . and obloquy and reproach," as the presenting black clergyman fulsomely explained. The preacher exclaimed that when Chase was "called from earthly labors" he would be welcomed with the "plaudit from the lips of Him who came on earth to open the prison doors and undo the heavy burdens, of 'Well done, thou good and faithful servant, enter into the joys of thy Lord.'"[36]

Chase was emotionally impressed by the honors and applause of his black audience. Citing Ohio's Black Laws excluding blacks from legal equality in access to education, the courtroom, and voting, he vowed to struggle on until the "colored man and white man are equal before the law," as "true democracy makes no enquiry about the color of the skin or the place of nativity." Indeed, he would persevere until "every vestige of oppression shall be erased from the statute book" and until our "broad and glorious land" no longer beholds the "foot print of a single slave."[37]

Chase was originally a Whig with hopes that the party could be turned anti-slavery, but quit the party after slave-owning John Tyler became president. Chase became a founder of the Free Soil Party and was appointed in 1848 to the US Senate, where he opposed conciliatory legislation like the Compromise of 1850 and the Kansas-Nebraska Act. Unlike hard-core abolitionists, he did not believe the Constitution affirmed slavery, and he favored political pragmatism to the point of dispiriting and sometimes inspiring distrust among his allies about his personal ambition, which was intense. "My best years have been devoted, in no wild or fanatical spirit I hope, to the advancement of the anti-slavery cause," he said in 1858.[38]

A chief theme for Chase across the decades was to divorce the federal government from protecting slavery, whether by fugitive slave laws or the spread of slavery to the West. He wrote in 1856 that, at least in aspiration, "the faith and practice of the national government is on the side of freedom." And he made clear, at least in private correspondence, "There is no spot on earth in which I would sanction slavery . . . without consideration of the color or origin of the slave . . . which day may God and men of a divine spirit speed!"[39]

Declaring he could not support religious tests for public office, Chase rejected the surging Know-Nothing movement of the 1850s that sought to marginalize immigrants and Catholics. He became Ohio's first Republican governor in 1855, establishing a reforming record. Failing to gain traction as a presidential candidate at the 1860 Republican convention, he was reappointed to the US Senate, from which he would soon resign to serve as Lincoln's treasury secretary. He had enthusiastically congratulated Lincoln upon his election: "The object of my wishes and labors for nineteen years is accomplished in the overthrow of the Slave Power," noting that the new era allowed "for the establishment of the policy of freedom."[40]

Formal, dignified, diffident, fastidiously dressed, tall, physically imposing, and nearsighted, Chase could be off-putting. An associate noted Chase knew "little of human nature" and although "profoundly versed in man, he was profoundly ignorant of men." He did not drink or dance and did not form friendships easily, although he had many admirers. He was also privately emotional and warm with intimates, especially his family, chiefly his two surviving daughters, all the more precious to him after losing four other children.[41]

Chase was also a very shrewd, calculating politician. After the 1860 Republican victory, he suggested federal compensation for owners of fugitive slaves, which was "infinitely better for all-than disunion." Yet he also warned against premature conciliation with the South that would needlessly surrender political capital: "Let the word pass from the head of the column before the Republicans move . . . the simple watchword—Inauguration first—adjustment afterwards." A premature compromise could precipitate "disruption of the Republican Party," he told Lincoln. Agreeing with Chase, other steadfast Republicans primarily saw the Peace Conference as purchasing needed time until Lincoln was installed and the border states deterred from secession.[42]

Suspicious Southerners and others were not oblivious to the strategy of some Republicans to play out the clock. A New York newspaper reported on February 7 that Republicans hoped to protract the Peace Conference and other proceedings until after Lincoln's March 4 inauguration, so that Lincoln could creditably present his own propositions for conciliation. Meanwhile, some Southern delegates were "indignant" over the parade of federal troops every morning up and down Pennsylvania Avenue outside Willard's Hotel by order of General Winfield Scott, a display they saw as federal intimidation. Doubtless Scott simply saw the show of force as deterring any brewing threats to the impending Electoral College presidential count and the presidential inauguration. The general himself was receiving threatening letters, which reportedly prompted his move from his quarters "uptown" to the more centrally located and presumably more secure National Hotel on Pennsylvania Avenue.[43]

Initially Chase was embarrassed to be appointed to represent Ohio at the Peace Conference. The delegation was nearly all cautious Republicans who favored determined negotiation with the South, especially Chase's old political nemesis, the conservative Whig Thomas Ewing. But Chase agreed to serve, believing he could advocate his views in that forum. He also hoped to better position himself for a role in the Lincoln administration, from which he believed Senator William Seward and other more moderate Republicans were striving to exclude him. After Wright's death, Chase welcomed Wolcott to the Peace Conference as a needed ally, but he was still outvoted on his own Ohio delegation.

"HARMONIOUS" PROGRESSION

Salmon Chase was elected to the Senate in 1860 but chose to focus on the Peace Conference. Other delegates chose differently. Five of Maine's seven delegates who were members of Congress remained primarily on Capitol Hill, including Senator William Fessenden. Iowa's Senator James Grimes thought along the same lines, letting his delegation be guided by his colleague Senator James Harlan and two members of the US House of Representatives.[44]

Meanwhile, the Resolutions Committee moved ahead in its own deliberations, although somewhat delayed by late arriving delegations from Massachusetts and Maine. Led by Kentucky's Guthrie, its members included Virginia's Seddon, Ohio's Ewing, Iowa's Senator Harlan, and Indiana's Caleb Smith. While the plenary council of the Peace Conference was meeting sometimes only a few hours or less per day, the committee was toiling long hours, often until 10:00 P.M. and sometimes until midnight. Largely they were crafting constitutional protections for slavery that would mollify border states and hopefully tempt Deep South seceding states to reconsider, in a similar way to the Crittenden Compromise. The stickiest points touched on the territories; Republicans had already pledged against any expansion of slavery there. A New York newspaper pessimistically reported that the committee's composition was unlikely to be "harmonious," as a "clear majority" opposed "any adjustment" satisfactory to the South.[45]

But a Washington newspaper claimed on February 9 that overall, the Peace Conference had been "very harmonious." Both Northerners and Southerners who had been previously "indisposed" to concessions had since "modified their views" affirming the "substantial rights of the South," and empowering Southern Unionists to "overthrow the spirit of disunion." If the Resolutions Committee failed, it was reported, the Maryland delegation would propose a National Convention, "transferring the whole question direct to the people." Yet the newspaper expected the Peace Conference to settle on compromises by a "large majority vote from both sections."[46]

Resolute among Republicans on the committee was Francis Crowninshield of Massachusetts, scion of a famous Boston family, who emphasized to his committee colleagues that his own state had committed no offenses against the Constitution. Rather, as a New York newspaper reported him saying, the state had endured "obnoxious" and "unconstitutional" laws, by which he certainly meant the Fugitive Slave Act, which brought "humiliation" on Massachusetts. He pointed out that his state's authorities had enforced these repellant laws even when federal authorities were too "weak" to do so, so that the "majesty of even a contemptible law might be vindicated." His delegation had no proposals for the Peace Conference, he said, but was willing to hear from others. Many Republicans, likely including Crowninshield and most of his Massachusetts colleagues, suspected that the emerging compromise was partly calculated to divide the Republican Party. A New York paper quipped that the "compromise feeling" among Republicans resembled "mild cases" of scarlet fever, with in some cases the fever having "struck inwardly."[47]

A Georgia newspaper reported on February 10 that the Union men at the Peace Conference were insisting that compromise was possible, while Disunionists from the North and South opposed any "conciliation" and were doing "all in their power to check the hopeful feelings of their associates." Republicans were trying to retrieve their party members who had "wandered out of the sectional fold," while Secessionists were advocating the "most extreme Southern demands."[48]

A Baltimore newspaper the same day described the Peace Conference progressing "most harmoniously" toward a possibly "almost unanimous agreement," with the Resolutions Committee combining the Crittenden Compromise with various border state proposals. Virginia's delegation were "disposed to yield to the voice of the people," especially since their state's recent election of a Unionist majority to the state convention considering secession. Maryland's Peace Commissioner Reverdy Johnson was a Resolutions Committee member and staunch Unionist who the previous month had addressed a rambunctious and sometimes angrily disrupted rally of ten thousand Unionists in Baltimore. He predicted that most of the key Ohio delegation would support the final compromise.[49]

Johnson, age sixty-four, was a former Democratic US senator of the 1840s who later served as US attorney general under President Zachary Taylor. A famed lawyer, he feared the fractious impact of slavery's expansion into new territory after the Mexican War, but represented the slave-owning defendant in the infamous Dred Scott case. He would later represent accused Lincoln assassination conspirator Mary Surratt, a fellow Marylander.

Having freed his own slaves, which he inherited from his father, Johnson had declared while in the US Senate: "I believe and have ever believed since I was capable of thought, that slavery is a great affliction to any country where it prevails and, so believing, I can never vote for any measure calculated to enlarge its area, or to render more permanent its duration." He granted that in some climates for agriculture slave labor may be, for the master, the "most valuable species of labor, though this I greatly doubt." He observed that in his own Maryland slavery was the "very dearest species of labor" and "admits of no comparison with the labor of freemen." He ominously forecast that if the "laws of population shall not be changed by Providence, or man's nature shall not be changed, it is an institution, sooner or later, pregnant with fearful peril."[50]

Yet Johnson opposed specifically restricting slavery's spread westward as unconstitutional, while admitting that with continued Northern expansion westward "slavery would no longer be permitted to exist in the South." He earnestly wished "that no African had ever been brought to this country, but that our land was exclusively peopled by freemen." And though he thought "slavery was a great evil," it still was an entrenched "domestic institution, in some respects mutually advantageous" for slaves and masters. He faulted Northerners for corrupting freed slaves, compelling Maryland to curtail the rights of owners to emancipate.[51]

Johnson was ever cordial and courtly, even if a fierce debater. After his former colleague Massachusetts US Senator Charles Sumner was caned nearly to death in the Senate chamber by an enraged Southern opponent, Johnson sent Sumner his "kindest remembrance" and "highest regard for him as a friend, though differing with him on the exciting question of the day."[52]

Recalled by a contemporary as "round bodied, solidly, almost sturdily, built, just such a physical mold as indicated perfect health," Johnson had "capacity for work and endurance, without the risk of a breakdown, of all the toils and strains of the most active life at the trial table." The "dome of his head was its most striking feature, so lofty, so symmetrically rounded, that it seemed to tower above all others, as the dome of St. Peter's minimizes all other designs." In 1842, when in his midforties, Johnson lost one eye in an accident with a revolver, likely explaining why he posed for pictures in careful profile.[53]

Although a reluctant Democrat, Johnson strongly supported Stephen Douglas in the 1860 presidential election, as Lincoln was "reeking with the grossest heresies of political abolitionism." At a Douglas rally in Boston, he cited slavery as the "sole cause of peril disturbing the fraternal feeling which our fathers entertained" while affirming its constitutional protections. He would repeatedly denounce the "mischievous heresy of secession."[54]

That September, in distant California, Johnson soaringly described the Union's fate in cosmological terms:

Unless God, for our sins, specially interposes for our punishment, our Union will, must be perpetual. It is too crowded with blessings to us and to mankind: it has too deep a seat in the honest American heart; it is too strongly supported by the remembrance of the patriotic sufferings and wisdom of an ancestry, the greatest that ever blessed a people; it is too vital to the cause of freedom, humanity and religion, to yield to the schemes of crazed enthusiasts, fanatical sentimentalists, or the plotting of disappointed political aspirants. It will, I trust in Heaven, stand forever a glorious monument of an age of men having no parallel in the world's history, daily working out the glorious problem, which it has so far happily solved—man's capacity for self-government.

With evangelistic fervor, Johnson promised that "under the Providence of Heaven . . . we will forever be joint heirs of a freedom baptized in patriotic blood, secured by a Constitution almost the work of inspired wisdom, and of a country prodigally adapted to every human heart."[55]

Four months later, in January, Johnson brandished his decades' worth of courtroom debate experience at a massive pro-Union rally in Baltimore, after secession by South Carolina and several other states. He mocked South Carolina as "that gallant state of vast pretensions but little power, though, apparently in her own conceit, able to meet the world in arms." He was unabashed in his rejection of states rights arguments, insisting the "offending citizen cannot rely, as a defense, on state power" but is responsible "to the United States alone," to which he owes "his paramount allegiance." He insisted the Constitution is not "fatally impotent." And he unequivocally warned that "if the state places herself between the United States and the offending citizen and attempts to shield him by force of arms, it is she who declares war upon the United States, not the United States upon her." Unlike others seeking conciliation, Johnson urged federal reinforcement of Fort Sumter no matter the consequence. With his unmistakable Unionist colors fully unfurled, Johnson was shortly afterward appointed to the Peace Conference by Maryland's governor.[56]

Thanks to his intense skills as jurist and debater, Johnson was known as "the Trimmer" for his expertise at seeking political compromise. Despite his own political deal making, during the Peace Conference he was quoted saying the political "stench of Washington is such that the man in the moon holds his nose as he goes over it."[57]

New Jersey's Peace Commissioner Frederick Frelinghuysen was a Republican lawyer who worked for railroad interests. He reportedly heard from leading New York bankers and Wall Street brokers that absent a political settlement, credit would be withheld from the new administration. The story was presumably calculated to scare Northern delegates but largely failed to do so, and the claim about a lack of credit for the federal government during the impending war turned out to be spectacularly incorrect, thanks to the exertions of Treasury Secretary Salmon Chase.[58]

Among financial issues, debate over a new tariff bill also affected the Peace Conference; the Morrill Tariff Bill would increase tariff protection for Northern industry, at the South's expense. On February 16 a New York newspaper reported the bill had "done more to engender a bad feeling among members of the Peace Conference than anything else," as it "even overshadows the slavery in territories question." The new tariff was passed in Congress only a few days later, with so many Southern senators having already left with their seceding states.[59]

Of course, much reporting and consequent national impressions about the Peace Conference were based on "rumors." A Cleveland newspaper admittedly cited hearsay to a report that the "debate today in the Peace Conference was of an exciting character among the Northern and southern extremists," as they once again discussed admitting reporters.[60]

The same Cleveland newspaper on February 14 speculated the Peace Conference might assent to the Crittenden Compromise's guarantee that slaves may be taken through free states. It noted approvingly that Ohio's Salmon Chase had intimated this would "soon be the means of closing the Convention." The newspaper shared a pessimistic prediction: "We predict an early explosion of the Peace Convention; an immediate pouncing upon all the Federal property in the Southern States, and a civil war along the whole line of our Southern free borders."[61]

With Congress's impending adjournment and the presidential inauguration fast approaching, and absent any substantive reports of progress from Willard Hall, such pessimism was growing around the nation. "The last Congress has now almost completed its cession, yet a basis of compromise is apparently as far from being adopted as when it first met in December last," noted a Louisiana newspaper. It further explained the lack of hope for conciliation:

> Despairing of obtaining anything from Congress, the border States, under the lead of Virginia, inaugurated a Peace Conference, which is likely to adjourn without even proposing anything at all; or if it should offer a compromise which would require the Black Republicans to yield in the slightest their principles, there is no chance of its ever being adopted. On the contrary, the Black Republicans have not changed in the least in their arrogant and hostile attitude towards the Southern States. They are building war steamers, contracting for men and money, and making the necessary preparations to subjugate the seceding states after the inauguration of Mr. Lincoln, who indicated very clearly in a speech the other day at Indianapolis on his way to Washington, that he considers it his duty to retake the forts and collect the revenue in the States which have declared their independence.[62]

With equal pessimism, a Massachusetts newspaper on February 19 surmised the Peace Conference would "accomplish nothing," just as both houses of Congress had failed with their compromise efforts through the House's committee of thirty-three and the Senate's committee of thirteen, which the newspaper likened to the Peace Conference's Resolutions Committee of twenty-one. It predicted the delegates, having the "gift of gab," would talk for at least two weeks after receiving the committee's report, by which time Lincoln would be inaugurated, and the Union "will be saved without their assistance." John Tyler, as the elderly and long-retired "distinguished" conference president, was referred to sarcastically as "fresh from the people."[63]

Tyler was likely indifferent to such sarcasm. A polished and proficient parliamentarian, he crisply opened the Peace Conference on Friday, February 15, with a few items of esoteric business. They included an invitation to visit the Washington, DC, studio of Horatio Stone, the famed sculptor whose work was in the US Capitol; an offer of passes for peace commissioners to visit the floor of the US House of Representatives; and an offer of flags ostensibly from the original Constitutional Convention. These items were placed on a table in Willard Hall for delegates to peruse as they pleased.[64]

Indiana Delegate Godlove Orth derided the "perverted and distorted" coverage of the Peace Conference by New York newspapers and proposed that reporters be allowed passes to their proceedings with hopes of facilitating more accurate reporting. Wickliffe of Kentucky objected, complaining that reporters in the gallery would only ensure more and longer "speech-making," with resulting coverage that would still be distorted. "I do not care what the newspapers say of us," he claimed. "Some of them assail us as a convention of compromisers—as belonging to the sandstone stratum of politics."[65]

In a rare moment of levity and wit for the Peace Conference and for Salmon Chase, the Ohio delegate reposted that sandstone stratum was the helpful "formation which supports all others." Wickliffe cleverly replied that he hoped the convention would be the "stratum which supports and preserves the Union and the country," for which secrecy and avoidance of speeches for "outside consumption or personal reputation" should be avoided. The delegates voted down the proposal for allowing reporters.[66]

Rumors continued to swirl outside the Peace Conference's closed sessions. A Nashville newspaper reported with some accuracy on February 15 that the long awaited Resolutions Committee had agreed upon a plan from Maryland's Reverdy Johnson that echoed the Crittenden Compromise. "If these dispatches be true we presume that the Conference will adopt this plan, their being a majority of Northern votes in the Conference; and then there will be a secession from the Conference on the part of some of the Southern delegates," the newspaper opined, citing the Tennessee legislature's preference for a national convention and consultation with seceded states.

Due to the "secrecy imposed upon the members of the Conference by themselves," the Nashville newspaper admitted its lack of definitive reporting on the thoughts and behavior of Tennessee's delegates at the Peace Conference. But it suggested that if "all the slaveholding States had first met together and agreed among themselves upon a plan of adjustment there would have been more probability of a speedy issue of their consultation."[67]

The seeming gridlock in the Resolutions Committee was naturally concerning to the convention's president, who likely grew pessimistic at this point. Tyler's wife revealingly wrote her mother on February 13 about the likely absence of a happy resolution, obviously based on her husband's observations to her:

> All is suspense, from the President down. The New York and Massachusetts delegation will no doubt perform all the mischief they can; and it may be, will defeat this patriotic effort at pacification. But whether it succeeds or not, Virginia will have sustained her reputation, and in the latter event will retire with dignity from the field to join without loss of time her more Southern sisters; the rest of the slave Border States will follow her lead, and very likely she will be able to draw off, which would be glorious, a couple of Northern States. It is to be hoped that this state of suspense, which is bringing disaster to trade everywhere, will soon be removed in one way or another.[68]

THE RESULTS OF THE RESOLUTIONS COMMITTEE

Finally, on February 15, Kentucky's James Guthrie unveiled the Resolutions Committee's long deliberated proposals for the Peace Conference. He admitted that it had taken many "protracted sessions," without unanimity, but with a majority believing they could offer "peace to the country." They were constitutional amendments protecting the expansion of slavery under the old Missouri Compromise south of latitude 36°30', stipulating that the United States may not acquire new territory without three-fourths approval from the US Senate. The amendments prohibited Congress from interfering with slavery in Washington, DC, without Maryland's consent, and prohibited any Congressional authority over slavery in states where it existed. They protected state enforcement of fugitive slave laws, reiterating the ban on international importation of slaves. Any changes to these amendments would be prohibited without unanimous approval of the states. Federal reimbursement of escaped slaves would be mandated when the law could not be enforced.

Sixty-eight-year-old former Connecticut governor and former US senator Roger Baldwin immediately offered a minority report to these constitutional proposals. He was grandson of the famed Declaration of Independence co-drafter and Constitution signer Roger Sherman. He was also a celebrated jurist who, appealing to the "claims of humanity and justice," had successfully litigated on behalf of African slaves who famously seized their Spanish slave ship, Amistad. In 1841, thanks to Baldwin's exertions, the US Supreme Court historically ruled that the Africans, as victims of illegal slave trading, were free, which led to their return to Africa.

Baldwin had told the Supreme Court some twenty years before the Peace Conference that the Amistad case presented "for the first time, the question whether that government, which was established for the promotion of justice, which was founded on the great principles of the Revolution, as proclaimed in the Declaration of Independence, can, consistently with the genius of our institutions, become a party to proceedings for the enslavement of human beings cast upon our shores, and found in the condition of freemen within the territorial limits of a free and sovereign state." The answer to this question, he said, would reveal America's "national character in the eyes of the whole civilized world."

And it would also answer "questions of power on the part of the government of the United States, which are regarded with anxiety and alarm by a large portion of our citizens."[69]

Former president John Quincy Adams had partnered with Baldwin in defense of the Amistad Africans before the Supreme Court. Adams said, "The rights of my clients to their lives and liberties have already been defended by my learned friend and colleague in so able and complete a manner as leaves me scarcely anything to say, and I feel that such justice has been done to their interests, that any fault or imperfection of mine will merely be attributed to its true cause."[70]

The Amistad case was the high-water mark of Baldwin's career, but not his first involvement with opposing slavery. His father had officered an anti-slavery society dating back to the Constitution; Baldwin was reared predisposed toward emancipation. As a young New Haven lawyer with a "strong faculty for order" and a "complete control of good English," he had been urgently alerted by the local seizure of a supposed fugitive slave reputedly owned by the Kentucky statesman Henry Clay. Baldwin intervened to ensure the alleged escaped slave's release and freedom, years later meeting the appreciative free black man at his Boston barbershop. Such cases enraged much of the South, with perceived non-enforcement of fugitive slave laws in Northern states. Baldwin had also publicly supported a black pastor's unpopular effort to launch a school for black children at his church.[71]

As a US senator, Baldwin opposed the Mexican War as a pretext for expanding slavery and opposed the Compromise of 1850, especially its fugitive slave law enhancement. Baldwin's oratory, which he had deployed for decades in courtrooms, legislatures, and now at the Peace Conference, "was not often impassioned" but "dignified, logical, clear, and convincing, addressed to the intellect rather than to the sympathies." It had been feared earlier in his career that "he was too up right and puritanical in his style of character to be a popular candidate" for public office, which his electoral success rebutted. His reserve, reticence, and seeming coldness masked an inner warmth revealed to his intimates and in his love for animals.[72]

So unsurprisingly, Baldwin was reticent about religion. He assured his pastor he had "great respect for Christianity" but "felt an utter inability to express his personal feelings" on religion and asked his friends "to judge of them by his course of life." After twenty years of association, his pastor believed Baldwin was a Christian, not relying "on his own righteousness for acceptance with God" but believing in the "Gospel which reveals salvation by Christ alone, the Lamb of God that taketh away the sin of the world." The pastor cited Baldwin's having "stood by his sick and dying child, and directed him to Christ, and exhorted him to put his trust in Christ."[73]

Baldwin's eulogist recalled only four years later that "there was no part of Governor Baldwin's public life, in which he gave more anxious, arduous, and exhausting labor to his country than during the brief period when he was a member of the Peace Congress," when the "air seemed full of the elements of revolution and anarchy." Like other Northerners, he feared plots to prevent the Electoral College count or even to assassinate president-elect Lincoln. Baldwin adamantly fought any concessions entailing the "triumph of slavery over freedom" or "utterly hostile to the spirit and design of the Constitution and the Union." Among those delegates against all such concessions, he was unmovably "among the firmest and strongest."[74]

Those same principles of justice that his grandfather had helped articulate in the nation's founding documents were now at stake at the Peace Conference, as it deliberated the nation's future. Baldwin acknowledged that their failure might lead to a "permanent dissolution of the Union." The minority report he presented urged acceptance of a proposal from Kentucky's legislature calling for a national convention of all states to discuss possible constitutional amendments. Baldwin was sufficiently realistic to know his minority report likely could not prevail. But he hoped it could at least neutralize the unsavory accommodations of slavery that much of the Peace Conference seemed determined to rat-ify. From the Resolutions Committee, sixty-six-year-old New York legal reformer and anti-slavery Democrat David Field also offered his com-plete dissent from the majority but said he would offer his own views later. He was joined by Crowninshield of Massachusetts.[75]

Virginia's Seddon also objected to the majority report, offering his own proposal based on Virginia's resolutions. It endorsed but supple-mented the Crittenden Compromise, stipulating the right of slave owners to transport slaves through free states, and preventing Congress from taxing slaves at rates higher than for land. Seddon's proposal supported procuring reimbursement of escaped slaves from jurisdictions that failed to apprehend them, prohibiting any future Constitutional amendment allowing congressional interference with slavery, and prohibiting voting rights or elective office to any person of the "African race." It urged the repeal of state laws hindering fugitive slave enforcement. Seddon also wanted US Senate actions subject to approval by majorities from both slave and free states, and recognition of any state's right to withdraw from the Union.[76]

Adding to the growing list of proposals was one from Wickliffe of Kentucky, who cited the "excitement and alarm" among the slaveholding states across decades, regarding "personal liberty" laws in free states that sought to minimize or evade fugitive slave laws, such as granting trial by jury to escaped slaves. His resolution urged all free states to abrogate these laws as unconstitutional. Ohio's Chase, professing to speak for his state, and in keeping with Republican preference for delay, complained that the Peace Conference was called on too "short notice" before the presidential inauguration and should adjourn until April 4.[77]

Before adjourning that action-filled Friday, President Tyler declared the next business item would be the proposed substitution of Baldwin's minority report for Guthrie's majority report. The Peace Conference, now finally with action items before it, adjourned until noon the next day.

Meanwhile, the nation began to react to the Peace Conference's first definitive proposals for consideration, which immediately leaked out and were telegraphed nationwide, if incompletely, despite official policies of secrecy. A Nashville newspaper surmised that if the majority report had been unanimous then all sections might be prone to accede to it. "But we imagine, if the telegraph fairly and fully states the report, that it was not unanimous, and that it will lead to warm debate in the Convention," and it "may follow that the action of the Convention may not fully accomplish its object." It hoped the telegraph "imperfect in its report, as it not infrequently is," so that most if not all states would "perpetuate the government on the principles of justice and equality." The newspaper regretted that "slavery agitation" was smothering the "patriotic impulses of the American people, and operate constantly as a blight upon true American statesmanship, and foster the fungus growth of demagogues and mischief makers." It had thought the Peace Conference a "fitting occasion to settle this mischievous question, and to banish it forever from American politics to release the American mind from the curse of its agitation, and once more inaugurate a feeling of universal confraternity, and thus bring back our erring friends in the South into the old cherished Union of the fathers of the Republic." And it warned that a "class of agitators and mischief makers on both sides . . . must be deprived of their occupation before the settlement can be made final, and the public mind of the nation released from the despotism of agitation and fanaticism."[78]

A Cleveland newspaper reported that within the Resolutions Committee, North Carolina's Judge Ruffin and Missouri's Alexander Doniphan were among Southerners who had refused to support it, effectively siding with Virginia's Seddon. "An intelligent member of the Conference informs me that their proceeding may be terminated any day, but cannot continue more than three or four days longer," a reporter related. He even claimed that Mrs. Tyler had already left, with her husband expecting soon to follow, evidently realizing that the majority report had "no chance of adoption by the present Congress." It was reported that President Buchanan had just dined with the Resolutions Committee on the night of their report, along with ten other peace commissioners. There was a "friendly interchange of views on the questions now agitating the country," according to a Washington newspaper, and "everything passed off in a most harmonious manner," supposedly. Separately they were also entertained by War Secretary Joseph Holt.[79]

A Richmond newspaper noted that the Peace Conference majority report from the Resolutions Committee offered "no guarantees of power" for the South. "It secures peace only so long as we have a majority in power—but we have no such majority and never can," the newspaper warned, also predicting the proposals had no chance for passing Congress. Its "only value" was that the Virginia secession convention could "wrangle over it" until Lincoln was in office.[80]

Such negative prognostications aside, the watching nation was probably more ambivalent as it awaited further word on the debates and final votes in Willard Hall.

FOUR

THE CLERGY
AND CHURCHES

> God, in His merciful providence had afforded another op-
> portunity for counsel, for pause, for appeal to Him for as-
> sistance before letting loose upon the land the direst
> scourge which He permits to visit a people—civil war.
>
> —Rev. Phineas Gurley

Rev. Charles Henry Hall of the Episcopal Church of the Epiphany had led the Peace Conference's funeral for Judge Wright. He also was one of at least twelve Washington, DC, clergy who opened the convention on one of eighteen days when prayer was recorded in the journal. These clergy's stories and churches illustrate the state of religion in 1861 America, especially in the nation's capital, where the clergy, as public men of education and status, held political influence and were commonly incorporated into affairs of state. Religion, and especially its understanding of the Bible as it related to slavery, was central to the impending conflict that the Peace Conference strove to avoid.

Kentucky's Charles Wickliffe proposed opening each day with prayer; the "clergymen of the city of Washington be requested to perform that service."[1]

Nearly all of these dozen clergy who appeared at the Peace Conference were mostly nonpolitical in their sermons and ministry. Yet nearly all had famous and powerful men in their congregations, whom they influenced. They also operated socially at venues where members of Congress and the cabinet, as well as the president, would appear. All had views about the Union and slavery, and their denominations each struggled deeply with those issues, some of them having already long since divided over them. At the Peace Conference, all the clergy prayed for peace and national unity. Not least of them was Reverend Hall, a Georgian who strove to remain loyal to the Union even after his native state had just seceded.

The easy exchange of clergy at the Peace Conference even as the nation crumbled illustrated an underlying religious collaboration across denominations. Washington's clergy and churches had long loaned one another sanctuary space during renovations or natural disasters, besides cooperating in helping the city's needy or even evangelistic revivals. A Catholic priest good-naturedly contributed toward a neighboring Presbyterian church's building fund, with a smile specifying it was for the sidewalk, since he couldn't fund a Protestant sanctuary. Reverend Hall, in an 1864 sermon to his diocese, wondered if denominations couldn't "separate the metaphysical question from their ideas of churchly life, and each holding on its grounds of relative worth to their profound convictions, could unite with one Church Catholic and Apostolic, as brothers in deed and in truth; that in place of us here, a few men holding our banner for certain ideas of unity, we should gather in one grand assembly the sweet persuasive eloquence of our Arminian Methodists, the skill and majestic subtlety in grace of our Calvinist denominations, the practical self-denying humility of many of the followers of the Vatican, and behold our idea of unity realized in practical effect?"[2]

Hall's Church of the Epiphany on G Street was only two blocks away from Willard Hall on F Street. The church congregation dated to 1842, first meeting in a public lecture hall south of Pennsylvania Avenue, then constructing its gothic sanctuary in 1843 and 1844. It was the fourth Episcopal congregation in the city and created especially to appeal to lower-income Washingtonians who couldn't afford the often-high pew rental fees at the other churches. St. John's Episcopal Church near the White House, dating to 1816 and frequent worship place for presidents, was only four blocks away. Most of Epiphany's first members had come from St. John's with its rector's blessings. When a donor contributed the G Street property for the new sanctuary, the proximity to St. John's created some initial tensions. Pews seating four people sold between $50 and $150, less than half the original prices years before at St. John's. Nearby were F Street Presbyterian Church in what would later become Willard Hall, Second Presbyterian on the site of what later became New York Avenue Presbyterian Church, and Foundry Methodist Church.[3]

By the time of the Peace Conference there were forty-three white churches in Washington and nine black churches.[4] Reverend Hall became the new rector at Epiphany in 1856, coming from a church near Charleston, South Carolina. He was then a thirty-six-year-old widower, who would marry again shortly after coming to Epiphany. He had attended Yale, where he "renounced Presbyterian doctrine" despite his mother's "strict Presbyterian faith." Afterward he attended an Episcopal seminary in New York and served churches in New York, including chaplaincy at the US military academy at West Point, where doubtless he met many of the future protagonists on both sides of the Civil War. Although a native Georgian and strong Democrat, he was a staunch Unionist. He was described as having "fine literary taste and great beauty of diction," a "man of athletic build and energy," at home everywhere, broad-minded, tolerant, and sympathetic, yet loyal to his own convictions, a "lover of the outdoors," and someone who "loved life and people." Hall was a low church Episcopalian.[5]

Shortly before the Peace Conference, the previously unadorned Epiphany Church added a new "lofty" bell tower, whose bell would eventually be melted down for Civil War military use. There were also stained glass windows added for more than $1,000, along with a gas chandelier and other light fixtures. A new organ was installed that was comparable in size to the city's St. Patrick's Catholic Church, performing with the choir Rossini's oratorio *Moses in Egypt* as a fund-raiser to retire church debt.

New sets of pews were sold for between $80 and $230, with the first offered to US Senator Jefferson Davis and his wife, Varina. The church supported a mission church in the somewhat dangerous neighborhood south of Pennsylvania Avenue, and also an Epiphany Church Home to extend "relief to the sick and the poor, the ignorant and the destitute," which included help for orphans, the unemployed, and youth "tempted to form idle or dissolute habits." By the time of the Peace Conference, this home had been consolidated with the social welfare ministry of Washington's other Episcopal churches.[6]

During the years before the Civil War, Epiphany Church had a small number of black communicants, and its services included baptizing and marrying blacks. In 1857 the church had a segregated black Sunday school with forty students and six teachers.[7]

In 1860, Reverend Hall joined the Episcopal Bishop of Minnesota to meet with a Southern federal official on behalf of Indian tribes, during which the official predicted Southern secession. Reputedly Hall angrily responded: "If you go out of the Union, it will be because God has permitted you to be stone blind, and slavery will be doomed. It will be a righteous retribution. We have married men and women at the altar, and have separated them on the auction block, and Christian men have not dared to call it a sin.[8]

Early in the war, Church of the Epiphany became a regular worship spot for many Union soldiers, including the president's mounted guard. Military chaplains sometimes preached from the pulpit. Soldiers served as the choir.[9] When the war began, Reverend Hall offered to "go his way quietly" if the church disapproved of a Southern clergyman. If asked to remain he promised to avoid politics and preach "Jesus Christ and Him crucified." But politics were hard to avoid altogether in such times. Jefferson and Varina Davis had asked that a plaque mark their pew after their departure for the South, which Hall honored, but the plate was soon and unsurprisingly stolen after Davis became president of the Confederacy. Like some other Washington clergy, Hall tried to demur from saying prayers during worship for Union battle victories, not wanting to further divide his congregation, but he finally agreed at his bishop's request. The neighborhood around Church of the Epiphany included Southern sympathizers, and Hall tried to uphold his pledge to avoid unnecessary controversy. One adamantly pro-Union young Episcopal deacon who also worked at the US Navy Department during the war found Hall's policy of avoidance unacceptable, successfully asking the bishop for his own transfer to St. John's Episcopal Church. "The events of the present week render it impossible for me to retain my place at the Navy Department and continue to assist the Rector at the Parish of the Epiphany," the young deacon explained in early July 1862. "I must cease to have any connection to him," meaning Hall. During 1862 Epiphany was one of eleven churches in the city converted to hospital use for wounded soldiers, to which the vestry "cheerfully" agreed. During those months of the "Epiphany Hospital," the congregation worshipped at nearby Foundry Methodist Church or Willard Hall, until regaining its own sanctuary in early 1863.[10]

Before closing as a hospital in 1862, Church of the Epiphany hosted a large official funeral for a prominent Union general, with a full military procession arrayed outside the church and President Lincoln among the mourners. Weddings continued at the church during the war, including one attracting a "throng of fashionable carriages" for an army officer and the niece of President Zachary Taylor.[11]

After he became war secretary, Edwin Stanton reputedly expressed concern that Hall was a Southern sympathizer, prompting Hall to hurry to Stanton's office, where he reportedly exclaimed: "Mr. Stanton, I am a Southern man. I am a Southern sympathizer, and I would be a brute if I were not. My misguided friends are being killed. I am a Christian and loyal to the government that keeps a roof over my head. When I cannot be loyal, I will ask you to put me in Fort Lafayette. Is that satisfactory?" More than satisfied, Stanton, according to the story, replied: "Dr. Hall, have you any pews to rent in your church? If you have, you can count on me as a parishioner as long as I live in Washington." Stanton rented Jefferson Davis's vacant pew, prompting Hall to recall Stanton as a "true and great friend of Epiphany," whose worship there solidified Epiphany's pro-Union loyalty. Hall would be among four clergy who presided over Lincoln's White House funeral.[12]

On Easter Sunday the day after Lincoln's death, Hall preached on the spiritual lessons of the assassination for the nation: "We are not the Christian people I wish and pray we may be; we are in many things too careless and profane; we have too often forgotten God, and neglected too many of the duties that we owe Him; but there is yet a deep consciousness under all these visible faults of character, which will suffice to carry us through these dangers."[13]

Of Lincoln, Hall carefully noted: "I would that he had been a church member in all the proprieties of our appointed modes of thought. But I wish yet the same of very many of you . . . he has always declared himself to be a believer in the Christian religion. He has, beyond question, believed himself to be an appointed apostle of the rights of man, as he conceived them. And then, with his heart full of the grand principle of reconciliation and peace, I can leave him to the mercy of Him Who is the Resurrection and the Life, and to Whom we too shall appeal for mercy, rather than justice."[14]

Of Lincoln's assassins, Hall implored: "May He give repentance to the wretched criminals who have stained their hands wantonly and stupidly with innocent blood, before they are called upon to meet the just punishment of their atrocities."[15]

Hall apparently abandoned his aversion to politics later in life while pastoring churches in New York, where he befriended famed preacher Henry Ward Beecher. A New York obituary recalled Hall had "stood for all that was good in the Democratic Party," believing there "were times when religion owed a duty to politics and frequently took an active part in campaigns." Hall's obituary in a Washington newspaper in 1895, recalling the "stormy period" of his years at Church of the Epiphany, described his writing and speaking as "lucid and direct," and his sermons "conversational." The placing of a plate marking Jefferson Davis's pew had ignited a "storm of indignation" and questions about his loyalty, it noted, but War Secretary Stanton "always stood ready to vouch for his rector's loyalty."[16]

PYNE AT ST. JOHN'S EPISCOPAL CHURCH

No less pro-Union was Rev. Dr. Smith Pyne of prestigious St. John's Episcopal Church, where he had served since 1845. Pyne prayed at the Peace Conference on February 7, when he was age fifty-eight. He was born in Ireland and grew up in South Carolina, although he studied at seminary and was ordained in New York City. Pyne had baptized and buried former First Lady Dolley Madison in the 1840s, and he had presided over the White House funeral of President Zachary Taylor in 1850.[17] In 1852, during the presidential campaign of General Winfield Scott, Pyne defended Scott's contested devotion to the church, based on their twenty-six-year "intimate acquaintance." Scott attended St. John's Church for eight years during that friendship, evincing that the general was "much attached to the Protestant Episcopal Church," and that "nothing but the most imperious necessity ever prevents his attendance upon the worship of that church" on Sunday. Pyne insisted the whole congregation could testify to Scott's "decorous and devout attention to the public services," which Pyne wanted known not because he participated in "any politics" but as a "mere act of justice."[18] After the election, Pyne officiated the wedding of US Attorney General John Crittenden, who would be prominent as a US senator in the 1861 peace negotiations. Attending celebrants included General Scott and the man who had just electorally defeated him, president-elect Franklin Pierce, with much of official Washington. Crittenden's fellow Kentuckian, incoming US Treasury secretary James Guthrie, was a prominent future leader at the Peace Conference, as were many others present that day.[19]

In 1859 Pyne testified in the infamous murder trial of his occasional parishioner, New York Democratic congressman Daniel Sickles, who had shot his wife's lover in Lafayette Park just steps away from Pyne's church. Pyne had spotted Sickles the day before the killing, looking "very peculiar." Sickles of course would also figure prominently in the events of early 1861 and beyond.[20]

St. John's Episcopal opened for worship in 1816, just two years after the White House and other government buildings were burned by the British. Every president since James Madison had attended there at least once. James Monroe, as an Episcopalian, was there routinely. John Quincy Adams was not Episcopalian but still frequently attended. President Andrew Jackson, a Presbyterian, started attending St. John's after his public feud with his pastor at Second Presbyterian Church over the virtue of the war secretary's wife in the infamous Eaton Affair. That pastor had sided with much of official Washington in shunning Mrs. Eaton because of her alleged loose morals as a Washington tavern keeper's daughter before her marriage. Presidents Martin Van Buren and William Henry Harrison were regular worshippers at St. John's, the latter having planned to join the church before his untimely death. His successor, John Tyler, worshipped regularly there and purchased a pew whose purpose was to remain permanently as a presidential seat. Zachary Taylor, another short-lived president, was a regular there, as was Millard Fillmore. Presidents James Polk, Franklin Pierce, and James Buchanan were Presbyterians who sometimes attended services at St. John's.[21]

At least one Episcopal rector in the federal city was skeptical of the Union and refused, after Lincoln's inauguration, to pray for the new president, quitting Washington for churches in Richmond, Virginia. But Reverend Pyne was stalwartly Unionist before and during the war, prompting one St. John's parishioner to complain to the local Episcopal bishop about Pyne's "violent political sermons" that were "so insulting" that some church members were leaving. Pyne also opened his pulpit to US Army chaplains during the war. Pyne's grandson would later recall, not entirely accurately, that his grandfather had "practically stood alone, among the clergy of that city, in his strong support for the Union during the Civil War," "in spite of the fact that his people were from South Carolina—an Irishman not 'against the government.'" On Sunday, February 24, 1861, during the Peace Conference and shortly after his arrival in Washington, Lincoln was taken to worship at St. John's by his future secretary of state William Seward. They sat in Seward's pew, although Pyne did not realize Lincoln was in the congregation until shaking hands at the conclusion.[22] In May he presided over the White House funeral of Lincoln's beloved close subordinate Colonel Elmer Ellsworth, who was shot removing a Confederate flag from a Virginia tavern within telescope view of the White House. Both Lincoln and his wife wept during the ceremony, as Pyne implored, according to a Washington newspaper, that "peace might be restored to our once happy country, but not at the expense of the great principles of justice and equality, upon which this great government was founded."[23]

BUTLER OF TRINITY CHURCH

The third Episcopal clergy who appeared at the Peace Conference was Clement Butler of Trinity Church. Trinity stood about thirteen blocks from Willard's and was founded in 1828, counting among its members great statesmen like Henry Clay and Daniel Webster. Trinity's twin gothic spires, built in 1851, arose amid largely empty lots, silhouetted against the unfinished Capitol dome and surrounding construction debris. At age fifty, Butler had recently returned for his second appointment to Trinity's pastorate. He prayed with the peace delegates on either February 8 or 23. (C. H. Chittenden's minutes of the Peace Conference do not distinguish between the two prominent Washington, DC, clergy named "Butler" who likely appeared.) He had previously been chaplain to the US Senate and had eulogized Henry Clay and John Calhoun. Butler also had served a Cincinnati church attended by Salmon Chase. In 1852 Chase had attended a White House dinner with President Fillmore that included Butler, then Senate chaplain and Trinity's rector. Also in attendance was later peace delegate Reverdy Johnson. After the dinner Chase brought Butler home for more conversation. In 1855 he preached in Cincinnati on the "highway to redemption," which his parishioner Chase thought "good."[24]

Butler also preached the funeral sermon for President Zachary Taylor in 1850. Taylor's death had propelled Fillmore to the presidency. In his sermon, Butler explained that "we are taught by the career and character of our departed President, that those qualities which win wide and permanent admiration and regard are moral qualities." He hoped this "sad dispensation has been marked by incidents and feelings which should inspire us with new hopes for the union and peace of our beloved land." Butler also noted that the "quiet transfer of the vast power of the Executive without murmur, remonstrance, or excitement, is evidence that we love our Constitution and our laws." With sentiments that would perhaps inform his Peace Conference prayer, Butler hoped "however local interests may temporarily alienate our affections, we love one another . . . [and] the nation has been made to feel that it indeed is one," as "one broad and undivided Republic." He implored: "God grant it may be so; for civilization, liberty, prosperity, peace, religion, and the hopes of coming millions hang trembling on the issue." Exploiting the spiritual opportunity of a grieving nation, Butler was also pleadingly evangelistic, warning:

> Let us then prepare for that life beyond the present, which God, in his mercy, has provided for the penitent and believing and obedient. If we are in Christ, we may be ready for the hour of death and the day of judgment—Are you yet young? Is your "half a tale" that is just begun? Oh, ennoble all its incidents, and give to its progress a healthful and happy character, by connecting with it now, and weaving into it, as the

pervading element of its power and beauty, the name of your Savior! Are you more advanced in life? Has the story of your existence become complicated and tedious with petty incidents and common-place events; and do you, with listless indifference, turn page after page of the life-tale on which frivolity, unrest, and inanity are written? Be assured it will be so even to the end, if there be not introduced upon it a name of power at the name of your Savior. Then the narrative which crept shall soar! Then the scene of your being, the object of your life, the end towards which you tend, will all become glorified and changed. Is old age upon you? Is the story of your life almost ended? Are the last words of it falling on the ear of your friends and of the world? Have the characters which figured in its earlier or later chapters, dropped off one by one the playmates of your childhood, the parents of your youth, the children of your maturity, the actors with you in the stirring scenes of middle life have they departed, and left you to totter off the stage desolate and alone? Ah! What is there then left for you, but to close up the story of your mortal life with the experience of a Savior's love?[25]

BUTLER OF ST. PAUL'S LUTHERAN CHURCH

The other Reverend Butler who prayed at the Peace Conference was Rev. John George Butler of St. Paul's Lutheran Church. After the war, he would become chaplain to the US House of Representatives and to the US Senate. St. Paul's was founded in 1842. Known as the English-speaking Lutheran church, it was located at Eleventh and H Streets, about five blocks from Willard's. John Butler was only thirty-five years old, from Western Maryland, with an illustrious ministerial career ahead of him. It started with attendance at Lutheran Theological Seminary in Gettysburg, Pennsylvania, whose stately brick building with an observation widow's nest atop was occupied and fully exploited by both Northern and Southern forces during the great battle. The seminary served as a hospital for the war's final patients even over four months later when Lincoln delivered his address at the nearby cemetery.

Butler came to the federal capital and his pastorate at St. Paul's in 1843. The relatively new church was in "deplorable condition," heavily mortgaged and with a tiny congregation. The church revived under his leadership. In the days preceding the war, Butler "declared himself squarely for the government and against secession," as one biography recounts. Some of his congregation quit in protest while others "rallied" to him, with the church ultimately growing. During the war he was chaplain to a Pennsylvania regiment while continuing his pastorate at St. Paul's. He also worked as a chaplain to military hospitals, ministering to both Northern and Southern wounded. His church was filled to "overflowing" by war's end. At that point, Butler helped found two new Lutheran congregations in Washington, including Memorial Lutheran and what became Thomas Circle Lutheran Church, "in memorial for God's goodness in delivering the nation from slavery and from war." He eventually pastored Memorial Church and helped erect the large statue of Martin Luther clutching the Bible that prominently stands outside Thomas Circle Church overlooking the traffic circle. Butler also taught at the seminary at Howard University for black students.[26]

More than fifty-five years a pastor in Washington, Butler was known for "sanctified common sense" and commitment to social reform, which included not only devotion to the Union and opposition to slavery but also founding a Lutheran church for blacks.[27]

When celebrating St. Paul's twentieth anniversary after the war, Butler asked: "Has God used us to further the cause of truth and righteousness in this capital of the nation?" And he wondered, darkly, "how many during all these years have rejected Jesus and hardened themselves in unbelief and worldliness?" On a more hopeful note, he wondered what his congregation could not accomplish for the "Master" if they would accept their divinely appointed responsibility "amid the corrupting influences of this great, growing metropolis." He recalled that St. Paul's had nearly died thanks to the "indifference of some, the opposition and slander of others . . . but the gates of hell have not prevailed." More than a few had "assumed the fearful responsibility in turning away from this pulpit, by reason of its loyalty to truth, to freedom, to the great principles of this Holy Word, the only infallible rule of faith and practice." The gospel applies to "every relation of life," he affirmed, citing the "domestic, social, civil and ecclesiastical." Butler said "men have regarded me as their enemy because I have told them the truth." Yet through "trying years" he stood "firmly," fighting "battles of freedom—the freedom wherewith Christ makes free."

"We stand here near the nation's heart, and the influence of the pulpit of this city is felt everywhere throughout the land and the world," Butler concluded. "The hope of the government is in the Gospel; the Gospel that enlightens and liberates and restrains and sanctifies and saves." With his opposition to slavery in mind, he declared, "The sentiments of the nation, so long dwarfed and distorted by legalized bondage, cannot be purified save by the diffusion of the whole Gospel."[28]

EDWARDS OF FOUNDRY METHODIST EPISCOPAL CHURCH

Four days after Butler's prayer at the Peace Conference, Rev. William Edwards of Foundry Methodist Episcopal Church opened the Peace Conference with his invocation on February 13. Foundry Church stood just one block north from Willard's, and one block east from the massively columned US Treasury Department still under construction and emerging next to the White House. It was the closest sanctuary to the Peace Conference after Church of the Epiphany, with which it shared a block on G Street. It was first founded on that site in 1815, only a year after Washington's burning. The property was donated by a devout English Methodist lay preacher and successful businessman whose foundry in the city produced cannons for the US military. Possibly his donation came in thanks for the providential sparing of his foundry from the invading British. The church was likely named after both the founding donor's business and John Wesley's London headquarters church, the Foundry. Although it had been refurbished in the previous decade, even gaining a marble pulpit of which old-style Methodists disapproved, in 1861 it was still a plain brick sanctuary, not yet the ornate temple it became even as the Civil War still raged. During the 1864–1865 rebuilding, the congregation worshipped at Reverend Hall's Church of the Epiphany, while Sunday school convened at Reverend Gurley's New York Avenue Presbyterian Church. Foundry belonged to the denomination of Northern Methodism, Southern Methodists having created their own denomination in a schism over slavery in 1844.[29]

Edwards was ordained in 1859, and only became Foundry's pastor in 1860. He would leave in 1862, having presided over a membership drop from 268 to 203, although he was described as a good preacher and was highly educated, knowing five languages. It was in 1863 that famed Methodist Bishop Matthew Simpson electrified Foundry with his preaching, attracting on one Sunday President Lincoln, Treasury Secretary Chase, Secretary of State William Seward, War Secretary Stanton, and Iowa US Senator James Harlan, who like Chase had been a peace delegate. Over the decades Foundry Church had supported African colonization of freed slaves without supporting abolitionism. During his pastorate and afterward, Reverend Edwards was involved with pledges of support for the Union. In 1863 Lincoln's secretary thanked him for the "expression of piety and patriotism" by local Methodists. In 1864 Edwards was among several clergy who persuaded local Methodists toward formal support of the federal government in war and peace, rejection of any new disloyal clergy, and opposition to slavery.[30]

STOCKTON OF GEORGETOWN

Another Methodist who prayed at the Peace Conference was the Reverend Thomas H. Stockton, who pastored a church in the Georgetown area of Washington, DC, and became chaplain of the US House of Representatives in March 1861, just after the Peace Conference closed. He had already served several times in that capacity in the 1830s. He also had pastored Philadelphia, Cincinnati, and Baltimore churches, and he was an editor of a church magazine. Stockton had started his career as an itinerant preacher on Maryland's Eastern Shore. He had helped found the Methodist Protestant denomination, which split off from the Methodist Episcopal Church in 1830 in protest over the authority of bishops, among other disputes. Most notably, Stockton delivered the "eloquent and thrilling invocation" at the dedication ceremony for Gettysburg Cemetery in 1863, where Lincoln delivered his famed address. That prayer reveals Stockton's thoughts on the Union and slavery.[31]

The Prayer

Oh God! Our Father, for the sake of Thy Son, Our Saviour, inspire us with Thy spirit and sanctify us to the right fulfillment of the duties of this occasion. We come to dedicate this new historic centre as a National Cemetery.

Oh, had it not been for God! for lo! our enemies came unresisted, multitudinous, mighty, flushed with victory, and sure of success. . . . They prepared to cast the chain of slavery around the form of Freedom, and to bind life and death together forever.

One more victory, and all was theirs; but behind these hills was heard the feebler march of a smaller but still pursuing host; onward they hurried, day and night, for their country and God; footsore, wayworn, hungry, thirsty, faint—but not in heart—they came to dare all, bear all, and to do all that is possible to heroes.

At first they met the blast on the plain, and bent before it like the trees; but then led by Thy hand to these hills, they took their stand upon these rocks and remained as firm and immovable as they. In vain they assaulted; all arts, all violence, all desperation

failed to dislodge them. Baffled, bruised, and broken, their enemies retired and disappeared.

But Oh, the slain, in the freshness and fullness of their young
and manly life; with such sweet memories of father and mother,
brother and sister, wife and children, maiden and friend; from the
coasts beneath the eastern star, from the shores of the northern
lakes and rivers; from the homes of the midway and the border,
they came here to die for us and for mankind.

Bless the bereaved, whether absent or present. Bless our sick
and wounded soldiers and sailors. Bless all our rulers and people;
Bless our army and navy. Bless the efforts to suppress the rebellion, and bless all the associations of this day, and the place and
the scene forever.

Reverend Stockton concluded with the Lord's Prayer, during which
he was "spontaneously joined by almost the entire multitude, whose
feelings seemed most deeply solemnized during the offering up of the
devout and the sublime prayer that had preceded it."[32]

Stockton's intense Unionism and patriotism were demonstrated further
in one of several hymns he wrote, called "In The Name of Jehovah Our
Banner We Raise," described as a "national hymn." It unapologetically celebrated the American flag for "its stars and its stripes," as an "ensign of truth"
and "standard of right," as well as the "herald of liberty, union, and right."
It points to "one sky and one land," both "harmonious and free," from the
"north to the south, from the east to the west, with no treason to part it, no
war to molest." And it hopes the "down-trodden nations in triumph may
rise, with their feet on their chains, and their brows to the skies."[33]

Offering his prayer at the Peace Conference on February 21, Stockton
must have cut quite a figure. A colleague later poetically recalled Stockton
as "tall slender, yet majestic; graceful in every motion, with a dignity and
gravity that awed us into solemn silence, as his large blue eyes rolled in
their orbits seeming to visit with a glance each and every auditor. Hark!

That voice speaking so solemnly, so beautifully, such correctness of elocution, that each word has its relative volume of sound; with its strange and unheard sweetness, thrilling your every nerve with like the low murmur of the wind in pine tree tops."[34]

A Baltimore native, Stockton was raised Methodist but turned more devoutly to God after his beloved mother's death, joining famed St. George's Methodist Episcopal Church in Philadelphia, one of Methodism's earliest congregations. After working in printing and studying medicine, he preached his first sermon in 1829 in the countryside outside Philadelphia. His circuit riding sometimes took him on two-hundred-mile trips, when he often preached thrice on the Sabbath, sometimes to "immense" congregations. He also wrote devotional books and poetry in addition to his hymnody.

"Our departed brother burned with divine love and with lustrous genius and grace," Stockton's eulogist declared, comparing him to John the Baptist for opposing "sectarian bigotry and ecclesiastical monopoly," the "one great Christ the one great Bible as sufficient for the fellowship and of all the churches and for the salvation of the world." The eulogist insisted Stockton was an orator "without a rival in the American pulpit," moving "congregations as the wind moves the trees." Henry Clay himself, as a "prince of orators," had called Stockton the "most eloquent man in America." Indeed, "his smile was eloquent; his tears were eloquent; his very infirmity of body was eloquent." Even in his final days, he professed that "All I can say just now is, that, if I die, I wish to die as a Christian: nothing more, nothing less—a Christian, an humble disciple of our Lord and Savior Jesus Christ; to be acknowledged by him, I trust, through grace. . . ."[35]

SMITH OF FOURTH PRESBYTERIAN CHURCH

Stockton was one of two Methodists who prayed at the Peace Conference, and there were at least three Episcopalians. But Presbyterians were the most common, with at least four appearing at Willard Hall in February 1861. Rev. John C. Smith of Fourth Presbyterian Church, known as the "church builder," had planted numerous other Presbyterian congregations in Washington, DC, over the decades. Fourth Presbyterian dated to 1828, with Smith becoming pastor in 1839. Realizing a new sanctuary was needed, he preached on Nehemiah 2:18: "And they said, 'Let us rise up and build.'" This resulted in the city's then largest church building, measuring sixty-one feet by eighty feet. It was at Ninth and I Streets, about half a mile from Willard's.[36]

President Tyler and his cabinet were present in 1841 for the new Fourth Presbyterian Church's dedication, with "the seats . . . all filled, and the aisles and the pulpit-platform crowded," as Smith later boasted, also noting he had already raised the needed funds, so it was "paid for and made meet for their Master's use, to offer unto Him this their free gift." Himself "tall and spare and frail," Smith called the church's then remote location a "land of gullies and marshes," which later transitioned into a bustling neighborhood. In 1845 President Polk and the First Lady would entertain Reverend Smith at the White House, along with the Sunday school of his Fourth Presbyterian Church. In 1855, Smith would recall that his church had been founded in a very different Washington, the "number of churches, population, and resources of the city" having "increased more than threefold" in twenty-eight years. The streets were not even graded, much less paved, and "houses very few and widely scattered and the people in the neighborhood in very moderate circumstances." He boasted that the building of their church had "promoted the interests of landholders in this section of the city more than anything that had previously been done" in what was almost a "wilderness." He admitted even in 1855, the street was still "the receptacle of every kind of rubbish that any one may choose to throw in." Yet he confidently exclaimed that "the building of church edifices is the most direct means of improvement a city can have, and in this respect we have done not a little."[37]

It was said that Smith was "born [and] living among the colored people," always "deeply interested in their welfare." Several years before his arrival at Fourth Presbyterian, the congregation had defeated an effort to shut down its controversial school for black children in deference to "public opinion." Smith continued that policy and was, although a Southerner, an "intense Union man," taking no "council from flesh and blood." He immediately offered himself to the US Army at the start of the Civil War, dramatically declaring to his congregation, "I am now ready to be offered."

Smith offered his church as a military hospital, for which it was used for eight months. Although defiant about his Unionism, he professed to avoid "mooted questions of politics" in his sermons in favor of the Word of God, he explained. The son of a Scots-Irish immigrant, and raised in Baltimore, he studied some at Princeton. He was first licensed to preach in 1828, served a church in Portsmouth, Virginia, and later a church in Georgetown within Washington, DC. "My ministerial life began with the life of this church, to which I have so cheerfully devoted my energies," he would tell his congregation at Fourth Presbyterian in 1855.[38]

That year Smith recited his sixteen years of accomplishments to his church; he estimated he had paid nineteen or twenty thousand visits to church members, the sick, the dying, and the bereaved, "most of them on foot, in this city of magnificent distances," as "no Presbyterian minister in Washington owns either carriage or horse." He also noted he had rarely missed a funeral or taken more than a few days off, always preaching thrice weekly, "unless some brother is providentially with me," preaching up to seven times weekly during revival season for weeks. Smith also noted he had never "preached the same sermon, or from the same preparation, twice to the same people or in the same church," always "joyfully given to this church, to this city, and to the Presbytery of the District of Columbia, that which I can give never again. Freely have I given, and I rejoice that the Master has permitted me to spend and be spent in His service in this Metropolis. All His gifts of mind and heart have I consecrated to God, and offered upon this altar and for your service."[39]

Smith boasted that the Sunday school had a library of more than 1,100 volumes and had 210 children, male and female, with 32 teachers.

On a fund-raising trip for the church he had "met with the disaster" on a Virginia railroad in 1854, "which disabled me for a season," including a "violent concussion of the brain." He recalled that in sixteen years he had received 678 church members, including 400 infant and 64 adult baptisms, while excommunicating 40, with a current membership of 352. He enthused, "Now, let us walk about Zion, and go round about her, that we may tell it to the generation following; for this God is our God for ever and ever: He will be our guide even unto death."[40]

In 1876 Smith was likely in his late seventies (he was vague about his age). He was still actively preaching at Fourth Presbyterian until hit by a Washington horse-drawn streetcar. With diminishing powers, he died two years later.[41]

SUNDERLAND OF FIRST PRESBYTERIAN CHURCH

Rev. Byron Sunderland had been pastor of First Presbyterian Church since 1853 and would remain there forty-five years. He was US Senate chaplain starting in 1861 and was like Reverend Smith a revered clergy figure in Washington. Unsurprisingly, he prayed twice at the Peace Conference, on February 16 and 22, at a relatively youthful age forty-one. His church dated to 1795, though some of its members had peeled off in 1803 to join the new F Street Presbyterian Church that would build what became Willard Hall. The Presbyterian Church's old sanctuary had arisen on Capitol Hill out of donations from James Madison and James Monroe. The newer church, which could seat 1,000, was built more central to downtown, about one mile from Willard's. It endured numerous controversies across the years. In 1866 some church members quit when Frederick Douglass lectured at the church about "The Assassination and its Lessons" as a fund-raiser for the National Home Association of colored orphans, with then Chief Justice Salmon Chase present in a racially mixed audience.[42] "It was the only church open to him in the city and the event cost us dearly, but it was the prestige for free speech for the colored race in this country."[43]

Like many anti-slavery personages, Reverend Sunderland was active in the American Colonization Society. After the war he was also president of what became Howard University, a black college in Washington. He was from Vermont and attended Union Seminary in New York. In 1857 he started preaching against slavery from the pulpit of First Presbyterian. In the postwar years he was pastor to President Grover Cleveland, whom he first opposed, but whose White House marriage he conducted.[44]

At the start of the Civil War Sunderland preached a stirring call to spiritual arms at a worship service in the US Capitol. "The soldier of Christ must expect to endure hardness, must follow his Captain, must obey His orders, must smite down temptation on every hand, and reach the object of the campaign at every cost," he proclaimed. "Discipline is the life of the hero. Through this, and only this, he marches to victory. The life to which God calls us is a time-long conflict, from which there is no discharge and no retreat, and from which we may thank God there is none. The true soldier wants none, else he would be willing to turn back from the conquest and the final rewards of triumph." He made clear his commitment to the Union: "Next to the service of our God is the service we owe our country. The one implies the other. Christianity fosters patriotism." Sunderland added: "Spiritual religion and free government are both ordained of God. He that is right with his Maker is most likely to be true to the interests of his country in her hour of danger; and therefore, there is a political, yea even a militant, as well as a religious sense, in which the declaration is true, 'whosoever shall endure unto the end, the same shall be saved.'"[45]

Sunderland unequivocally denounced Secessionists:

For a long time a certain subtle poison of dissatisfaction and disloyalty to the General Government has been diffusing itself among a portion of the people of our country. The cloud of insubordination has been rising and spreading itself on our political horizon, and the muttering of the thunder of dissolution has been heard until at length a settled plan and purpose to break up this great political structure has been undertaken, and its progress has been fearfully rapid. Forbearance and conciliation have been wrested and perverted to stimulate and encourage this proceeding.

And Sunderland offered fulsome support to President Lincoln and General Winfield Scott:

We cordially approve of the earnest efforts now being made by the President, aided as he is by our war-worn General, the venerable Chieftain of the American people, to preserve the Government and to maintain the Constitution and the laws; and we feel that he has "an oath solemnly recorded in Heaven" to use his best endeavors to this end. We discountenance all efforts from every quarter to interfere with this object. We disapprove of all appeals made to him from whatever motive, to embarrass or cripple him in his work. This is emphatically his work; and therefore to entreat him to desist from it, is to undertake to seduce or to solicit him to perjury. The principle and spirit of my text applies to him and his work, as well as to you and to me and to our work. Our only salvation lies in "enduring to the end."[46]

Sunderland commended the "religion of the Cross" as the "only solace which can assuage our sorrows" and a "refuge and support which alone is adequate to life's solemn undertakings."[47] In 1862 he would meet with President Lincoln, later recounting that after Lincoln's "joke and fun," the president had "for one half hour poured forth the deepest volume of Christian philosophy I had ever heard."[48] Sunderland had worried that the president might renege on issuing the Emancipation Proclamation. But after listening to Lincoln by the dim light of a single gas fixture, he thought he sounded like "one of the old prophets," and Sunderland "went home comforted and uplifted, and I believed in Abraham Lincoln from that day."[49] On April 30, 1863, on a day of national prayer and thanksgiving, Sunderland "preached a sermon of pronounced anti-slavery and anti-secession character," according to a New York newspaper.[50]

GURLEY OF NEW YORK AVENUE PRESBYTERIAN CHURCH

The most frequent and prominent clergy who prayed at the Peace Conference was Reverend Gurley of New York Avenue Presbyterian Church, who delivered invocations before the delegates at least four times, on February 5, 11, 18, and 27. He both opened and closed the Peace Conference. He was age forty-four, from upstate New York, and had pastored churches in Indiana and Ohio. He arrived in Washington in 1854, quickly gaining a reputation and becoming US Senate chaplain in 1859. He had attended Princeton Theological Seminary and was a loyal student of Old School Presbyterian theologians Charles Hodge and Archibald Alexander, who espoused Calvinist orthodoxy and were skeptical of modern revivalism and most church political activism.[51] After the April 12, 1861, firing on Fort Sumter, Gurley preached a typical sermon on God's sovereignty at New York Avenue Presbyterian with Lincoln in the audience. "God in His merciful providence had afforded another opportunity for counsel, for pause, for appeal to Him for assistance before letting loose upon the land the direst scourge which He permits to visit a people—civil war." The pastor's simple, insistent style appealed to the new president. "I like Gurley," President Lincoln once said. "He don't preach politics. I get enough of that through the week, and when I go to church, I like to hear the gospel."[52]

A journalist observed in 1862 the growing popularity of the New York Avenue church: "Last Sunday [November 30] I saw the President and his wife at church at Dr. Gurley's (Presbyterian), where they habitually attend. The building was crowded, as usual, with dignitaries of various grades, besides sinners of lesser note and rank. Conspicuous among them all, as the crowd pour out of the aisles, was the tall form of the Father of the Faithful, who is instantly recognized by his likeness to the variety of his published likenesses."[53]

Not everyone was an automatic fan of Gurley's, especially sophisticates who didn't share Lincoln's taste for middlebrow Protestantism. In 1865, the Marquis Adolphe de Chambrun, an expatriate French aristocrat, groused: "We had to submit to an hour's discourse by Dr. Gurley. He has the sort of eloquence belonging to this denomination; that is, no high-sounding phrases but a stock of dry commonplaces marshaled in good order."[54] President Buchanan had also been Gurley's parishioner, although perhaps more from a policy of simply attending the "nearest" Presbyterian church.[55]

In a tribute to Gurley's quickly established reputation in Washington, DC, he was first nominated to become chaplain of the US House of Representatives in 1857, after having been in town for only three years. The nominating congressman made clear he was advancing Gurley's name "without the knowledge or consent of the gentleman," describing him as a member of the Old School Presbyterian denomination and distinguished for his social propriety and position, "in politics, as in religion he is a Christian."

During the rollicking debate, one congressman nominated a female Presbyterian as chaplain, admitting he previously was accused of "being an infidel" when last nominating her, and prompting laughter in the House of Representatives. One member responded: "In view of the injunction of St. Paul for woman to 'keep silence in the churches,' I think it would be decidedly out of order." Another member nominated a "Hardshell Ironside Baptist," explaining he was a "very pious man, and though not of eminent ability, he has enough talent to pray for such a crowd as this," prompting more laughter. In the end Gurley came in third place, with 22 votes, losing to a Congregationalist clergy with 106 votes out of 204 cast. But Gurley would become US Senate chaplain two years later.[56]

Gurley preached a stern Calvinism not uncommon to the era. This appealed especially to Lincoln, who came from a Calvinistic Baptist background, as well as to other leaders in Washington who looked for national purpose in a guiding Providence. Gurley preached at the funeral for Lincoln's son in 1862: "All those events which in any wise affect our condition and happiness are in His hands, and at His disposal. Disease and health are His messengers; they go forth at His bidding and their fearful work is limited or extended according to the good pleasure of His will."[57]

Gurley would preach at Lincoln's White House funeral:

> Though our beloved President is slain, our beloved country is saved. And so we sing of mercy as well as of judgment. Tears of gratitude mingle with those of sorrow. While there is darkness, there is also the dawning of a brighter, happier day upon our stricken and weary land. God be praised that our fallen Chief lived long enough to see the day dawn and the daystar of joy and peace arise upon the nation. He saw it, and he was glad. Alas! alas! He only saw the dawn. When the sun has risen, full-orbed and glorious, and a happy reunited people are rejoicing in its light—alas! alas! it will shine upon his grave. But that grave will be a precious and a consecrated spot. The friends of Liberty and of the Union will repair to it in years and ages to come, to pronounce the memory of its occupant blessed, and, gathering from his very ashes, and from the rehearsal of his deeds and virtues, fresh incentives to patriotism, they will there renew their vows of fidelity to their country and their God.[58]

SAMSON OF FIRST BAPTIST CHURCH

The only Baptist clergy to pray at the Peace Conference was forty-one-year-old Rev. George W. Samson, pastor of First Baptist Church. He had been president since 1859 of Columbian College in Washington, DC, an originally Baptist school that later became George Washington University. First Baptist Church dated to 1802, and its sanctuary was on Thirteenth Street, very close to Willard's. Samson became pastor in 1860, serving without pay for several years to help the church revive after a merger. Challenges for the church were compounded by severe hurricane damage in 1862, followed by its temporary seizure for a military hospital, which compelled the congregation to meet for a time at nearby New York Avenue Presbyterian Church. Federal troops were also quartered at Columbian College, and Samson likely was suited to such adversity across his varied career. He was from Massachusetts, of old Puritan stock, studying at Brown University and Newton Theological Seminary. He later taught and pastored several Baptist congregations, but he was maybe best known for his numerous writings against alcohol consumption, including an 1885 work called *Divine Law As To Wines*, commissioned by both Northern and Southern Baptist Conventions. "The conviction that Jesus did not use intoxicating wine grows with every new development in tracing His life and teaching," Samson insisted.[59]

Starting in 1846 Samson had befriended legendary Texas US Senator Sam Houston, who called Samson a "young man, but one of the most able divines, that I have anywhere heard . . . [he] gave us a rich feast on the spiritual and practical duties of the followers of the Lord Jesus Christ, I have never heard anything superior—extempore, or written. That he is a pious man, I have no doubt, it is my determination, while we are detained here, to attend his church, as often, as he preaches."[60]

Samson was anti-slavery but politically cautious. In September 1861 on a national day of fasting and prayer, a speaker at Samson's church denounced slavery as an "abomination in the sight of God," prompting Samson's pastoral rebuke. Likely Samson agreed with President Lincoln that it was too early in the war for such sharp denunciations from a prominent church, when border slave states and moderate Northern opinion were crucial, not to mention sensitivities in historically Southern Washington, DC.[61]

BULLOCK OF BALTIMORE

The only clergy who prayed at the Peace Conference who had pronounced pro-Southern and subsequent Confederate sympathies seems to have been forty-eight-year-old Rev. Joseph J. Bullock, a native Kentuckian and Baltimore pastor of southern Presbyterianism. In 1864 he was arrested by military authorities and charged with "harboring a rebel colonel at his house," who was a relative and fellow native of Kentucky.[62] In 1865 he was leading Baltimore Presbyterian clergy in trying to assist southern Presbyterian ministers living in "destitute conditions."[63] As a young man he had pastored a Presbyterian church in Frankfort, Kentucky, where he was recalled as "distinguished and attractive" with a "towering frame." His parishioners included prominent families such as relatives of Senator Crittenden and Governor Morehead. Morehead was later a peace delegate, which might explain Bullock's invitation to the Peace Conference.[64] He had also as a young man faced down a Kentucky mob set to attack the Ohio abolitionist editor James Birney, while making clear his disagreement with him. He shared that experience with Salmon Chase, who had similarly defended Birney in Cincinnati.[65] He studied theology at Princeton and had headed a women's academy in Kentucky before the Peace Conference. In 1878 Bullock became chaplain of the US Senate and later became the moderator of Southern Presbyterianism.[66]

Bullock's relatively quiet pro-Southern sentiments in Baltimore contrasted with many of the other clergy who prayed at the Peace Conference. Most were steadfastly pro-Union, becoming more outspoken as the national crisis progressed. A Louisiana Presbyterian minister was disgusted by much of what he heard from fellow clergy, including several who were at the conference, during his Washington visit, his tart observations appearing in a Presbyterian newspaper:

> The religious condition of Washington has sadly deteriorated since the commencement of the war. The political preachers have become more political in their prayers and sermons. You could once hear the gospel in its purity, but he who attends the Church of Dr. Sunderland, or Mr. Noble (a chaplain in the Navy,) or Mr. Brown, who now fills the place of the Rev. Dr. Bocock, will hear tirades upon the wickedness of the South, and harangues upon the glory and power of the pious North.

An Elder in Dr. G.——'s Church said to me—"religion is dead in the Churches; our prayer meetings have been converted into abolition enclaves, and the best class of attendants have ceased to come."

Mr. Brown has disgusted his congregation, and the Government was compelled to give him a chaplaincy to save him from suffering. Dr. Gurley, up to this time, has continued to give his people the unadulterated gospel, unmixed with the hypocrisy and humanitarianism of Northern fanatics. A lady remarked to me, "It was awful to hear the prayers of blood and imprecation which were sometimes hurled, in the name of God, at the South!" To "crush," "confound" and "destroy" were no unusual epithets.

Nevertheless, there are a few good and noble spirits who cry day and night for peace. They are sick of the awful scenes of the wounded and dying which Washington City has so often witnessed. Dr. Sampson, a Baptist minister, on the day of our "fasts," called the attention of the Union Prayer meeting to it, and desired that God would bless the day to our everlasting good. It met with the approbation of some, but Dr. John C. Smith remarked if this was to be converted into a "secesh" meeting he would come no more, and his majesty has since kept at home to curse the South and invoke blessings on the head of President Lincoln. Although I was once a teacher in his Sabbath School, and a member of his congregation, yet I was afraid to attend his church, lest he should recognize and report me to the provost marshal and have me imprisoned. We do trust the prayers of the few righteous will be heard, and that he who is Head over all things to the Church will grant them and us the speedy blessings of peace. Christ does not delight in bloodshed and the horrors of war, therefore they and we may humbly draw nigh and earnestly pray that this dreadful sacrifice of human life be stayed.[67]

SCHISM IN THE CHURCH

Divisions had been brewing for years along sectional lines in most of the great Protestant denominations. In 1837, after a takeover by orthodox

Calvinist Old School Presbyterians, the Presbyterian General Assembly expelled more revivalistic and ecumenical New School Presbyterians, who tended to be more Northern and sometimes abolitionist. New Schoolers had about 1,200 congregations and about 100,000 members, or just under half of the total.[68]

Old Schoolers looked to Princeton Seminary, while New Schoolers created Union Seminary in New York. Southern Presbyterians had mostly sided with Old Schoolers, with famed Northern preacher Lyman Beecher crediting South Carolina's US Senator and arch Southern partisan John C. Calhoun for being "at the bottom of it . . . writing to ministers, and telling them to do this and do that. . . . It was a cruel thing . . . and 'twas slavery that did it."[69]

After Methodists and Baptists divided along strictly sectional lines in the 1840s, Presbyterians in the Old School and New School denominations struggled to keep their communions intact. In 1845 Old School Presbyterians carefully affirmed the church as a "spiritual body, whose jurisdiction extends only to the religious faith, and moral conduct of her members," not able to "legislate where Christ has not legislated."[70]

Southern theologian James Henley Thornwell insisted in 1851 that "we deplore a schism in the body of Christ . . . [and] among the confederated states of this Union," warning that "continued agitation of slavery must sooner or later shiver this government into atoms." He warned that if slavery was consistent with the Bible, "their responsibility is tremendous, who in obedience to blind impulses and visionary theories, pull down the fairest fabric of government the world has ever seen, rend the body of Christ in sunder, and dethrone the Savior in His own Kingdom."[71]

In 1850 the New School Presbyterians reaffirmed an earlier 1818 Presbyterian stance condemning slavery as a "gross violation of the most precious and sacred rights of human nature," and that slave holding should be, with some exceptions, a "matter of church discipline." In 1857 the New Schoolers overwhelmingly denounced the defense of slavery by some Southern Presbyterians. This prompted twenty-one

Southern and border state presbyteries, with 15,000 communicants, to create the United Synod of the Presbyterian Church in the United States of America.[72] In 1861, dominated by Northerners, the New Schoolers assertively declared: "There is no blood or treasure too precious to be devoted to the defense and perpetuity of the government in all its constituted authority."[73]

In 1861 Northern Old School theologian Charles Hodge admitted that "we alone retain, this day, the proportions of a national church." But in May 1861, the Old Schoolers' general assembly in Philadelphia affirmed support for the federal government, although broadly defined. Southerners predictably withdrew and created the Presbyterian Church in the Confederate States of America in Augusta, Georgia, that December.[74] There, theologian Thornwell explained that "political problems" connected with slavery "transcend our sphere" and were not entrusted by God to the church.[75] This new Old School denomination of the South affirmed its loyalty to the Confederacy and defended slavery's moral legitimacy. In 1864 the Southern Old Schoolers merged with the Southern New Schoolers in what became the Presbyterian Church in the United States.[76]

The Methodist Episcopal Church, representing the country's largest religious movement, had divided at its 1844 general conference, which voted 110 to 68 to urge a Georgia bishop to "desist from the exercise of his office" so long as he had a "connection" to slavery. This resolution was unacceptable to Southern Methodists, and the general conference organized a relatively orderly sectional division of the denomination. But many saw the fracturing as ominous for the nation. A Virginia Methodist warned that church schism could lead to "civil disunion . . . the North against the South . . . civil war and far-reaching desolation." But a Southern Methodist publication suggested schism would warn the North of the "limits" of "southern forbearance" toward the "pseudo-religious frenzy called abolitionism," checking further threats to "political union."[77]

Famed Methodist evangelist Peter Cartwright was anti-slavery but not abolitionist, and once had run unsuccessfully against Lincoln for

Congress as a Democrat. In 1856 he lamented that "this dreadful rupture of the Methodist Church spread terror over almost every branch of the Church of Christ . . . it shook the pillars of our American government to the center . . . as the fearful step toward the downfall of our happy republic . . . [and] the horrors of civil war."[78]

Hoping to avert schism, the 1844 General Convention of Baptists, representing America's second largest religious group, disclaimed any stance on slavery or anti-slavery, affirming free expression of views. But Baptists from mostly the Deep South objected even to this pronouncement and convened in Augusta, Georgia, in 1845 to create the Southern Baptist Convention. The national ramifications were evident, especially after the Methodist division. Washington, DC, Baptists had warned earlier in 1845 that Baptist schism would "have an unhappy bearing not only on the cause of Christ but upon our national union."[79]

In 1850 Southern diehard Senator John Calhoun remarked on the US Senate floor that "the ties that held each denomination together formed a strong cord to hold the whole Union together, but powerful as they were, they have not been able to resist the explosive effect of slavery agitation," noting only the Episcopal Church of the "four great denominations" yet "remains unbroken and entire."[80]

Yet these great denominational divisions seem not to have directly touched the 1861 Peace Conference, at least in terms of clergy who attended and prayed. None of the more than one dozen ministers, except Reverend Bullock, were from the separated Southern branches of fractured denominations. None of the clergy except Bullock were partial to secession or slavery, even though several were decidedly Southern in origins. Yet all the clergy, and the Peace Conference itself, were ultimately responding to a religious disagreement over the morality and spiritual implications of slavery.

A year before, in June 1860, a Washington newspaper reported the sermons from the previous Sunday of several clergy who would appear at the Peace Conference. Foundry Methodist's Reverend Edwards preached on Christ's words in John's gospel, "I am the vine, ye are the branches"

(15:5 KJV), emphasizing the organic unity of the body of Christ, with God often slicing off the vines that bear poor fruit. "If God sees something in me which divides my heart or affections by His providence He will take that something away and prune me," Edwards explained. Meanwhile, Reverend Stockton preached at the US Capitol on Second Corinthians: "For he hath made him to be sin for us, who knew no sin" (5:21 KJV), in which the Methodist preacher addressed the suffering of the innocent for the sins of the guilty. And Reverend Butler at Trinity Episcopal preached on Christ's admonition from Mark's gospel, "Come, take up the cross, and follow me" (10:21 KJV), in which he explained the steep costs of discipleship. All three sermons would be relevant in the city's and the nation's troubled days ahead.[81]

FIVE
THE COMPROMISE

The eyes of every true patriot in the nation are turned toward this body.

—James Guthrie of Kentucky

We hold property, yes, our property in slaves, as rightful and as honorable as any property to be found in
the broad expanse between ocean and ocean.

—James Seddon of Virginia

Absent authorized reporting from the convention, rumors about its proceedings and underlying agenda swirled around the country. A Richmond
newspaper's anonymous correspondent breathlessly reported: "It is now
believed that the Peace Congress owes its origin to Messrs. Seward,
Douglas and Crittenden, who have coalesced to form a Union party." A
Staunton, Virginia, newspaper skeptically responded on February 13 that
such speculation was calculated for "prejudicing the public mind against
the action of the Peace Conference, by creating the impression that

Seward was instrumental in the inauguration of this great movement to which the patriotic, union-loving men of every section of our distracted country are earnestly looking with so much of anxiety and hope."[1]

More abstractly, an Ohio newspaper, citing "rumors," reported on February 21 that the "debate in the Peace Conference was of an exciting character among the Northern and Southern extremists," with "another effort made to admit reporters."[2]

A more level account from a Nashville newspaper reported that the Peace Conference was to reaffirm the "principles of the Missouri Compromise north of 36 degrees and 30 minutes, and popular sovereignty south of it," but acknowledging the recommendation was not unanimous, and predicting it would precipitate "warm debate" among the commissioners. The convention "may not fully accomplish its object," it granted, which should be to "settle this mischievous question [of slavery], and to banish it forever from American politics, to release the American mind from the curse of its agitation, and once more inaugurate a feeling of universal confraternity, and thus bring back our erring friends in the South into the old cherished Union of the fathers of the Republic."[3]

Many were looking with "hope to an agreement on the part of the conference," a Cincinnati newspaper reported, but "many difficulties" remained. The Resolutions Committee itself was "far from being harmonious," as "evinced by their having spent over a week" in deliberation and emerging with only a "trifling majority," even from a committee comprised of "more conservative men" than in their respective state delegations who were disposed to defer for the sake of "harmony." Their report would "certainly be overhauled in debate," especially by Republican delegates. It would be "unlikely to favor a scheme which yields so much that is vital of the slavery inhibition principle," such as making slavery "subject to judicial cognizance in the federal courts" in the territories where it was allowed, and surrendering the "whole doctrine of prohibition of slavery by the people of a territory into the hands of the Supreme Court."[4]

Noting the limitations of analysis when the "proceedings of this convention are supposed to be kept in secret," a Vermont newspaper suggested, "it seems hardly probable that a majority of the states represented in this conference will agree to Mr. Guthrie's report." The articles were "ambiguous, unsatisfactory, and if adopted, will settle nothing," although "they are very carefully drawn and their language is skillfully adapted to cover their real intent," being "nothing more nor less than the Crittenden Compromise toned down to render it more palatable to northern compromisers." And the South would exploit the language to protect slavery "in any territory hereafter to be annexed on our southern border," with the North resisting that "interpretation." The newspaper predicted "neither this nor any other plan of compromise that the convention may be called upon to consider will be of any value as a final settlement of pending territorial questions." It suggested submitting the "whole matter to a convention of all the states to consider and adjust, after the present temporary excitement shall have passed away."[5]

A New York newspaper reported that a "majority of Pennsylvanians, and some from all the northern states, it is now thought, will accept the majority report, which, with all the border state compromisers, will secure its adoption by a close vote," with a canvass that morning showing "only about half-a-dozen majority in its favor." Slave state delegates lamented that adoption by such a vote would be of no avail and "not be accepted as settlement, as it will not be an expression of the wishes of the free states."[6]

"It is rumored that the Peace Convention is likely to adjourn without agreeing upon any plan for the pacification of the country," a Washington newspaper mournfully related on February 18. "It is said that it contains on the one hand Disunionists from the South, who seek to defeat any adjustment by extreme demands, and on the other hand semi-Abolitionists from the North, who are opposed to any concession, and that these united outnumber the conservative of both sections." Neither faction has any business there, it insisted, warning, the people "are not prepared to sustain a set of men who prefer their party to their country."[7]

The Conference
Debates Proposals

Amid such speculation, hopes, and worries, the Peace Conference reconvened for its tenth day at noon on Saturday, February 16, 1861, ready finally to substantively debate actual proposals for saving the Union and averting civil war. Rev. Dr. Byron Sunderland of First Presbyterian Church opened with prayer.

Despite that prayer, the session lasted less than three hours but was packed with debate about the core issues fracturing the country. Kentucky's Charles Wickliffe proposed that no delegate be permitted to speak longer than thirty minutes, explaining that time was short and Congress, which was needed to ratify any proposal, was shortly to adjourn. Another delegate suggested ten minutes instead, pointing out that "opinions are formed" and "will not be changed by debate."

But Virginia's Seddon objected, saying he needed more time for his own proposal, and Ohio's Chase supported him, pointing out that no delegate had yet abused his time to speak. Wickliffe postponed his proposal.[8]

Connecticut's Roger Sherman Baldwin then motioned for his minority report to become the substitute motion; it urged a national constitutional convention, echoing a request from the Kentucky legislature. Coming from such an outspoken slavery opponent, this call likely confirmed suspicions from Southern critics like a Memphis newspaper, which warned that the "Black-Republican party are now lustily clamoring for a national convention," having "humbugged us into waiting for Congress to meet," then "hoodwinked the people into delay by supporting the project of a 'peace' conference," a "swindle" that was "carried out, and now promises to 'fizzle out.'" Not withholding contempt, it further derided the Peace Congress as "worse than the Jacobin club that ruled the mobs of Paris when France quaked with terror."[9]

Doubtless Baldwin was undeterred by such derision. In an "elaborate" speech, according to a Washington newspaper, he urged a national convention, as all other remedies would fail in Congress.[10] And he asserted that the Resolution Committee's majority report was "contrary to the spirit of the Constitution," which did not recognize any group like the Peace Conference to originate amendments. "Any attempt to coerce Congress, or to influence its action in a manner not provided by the Constitution, is a disregard of the rights of the people."[11]

Baldwin asked rhetorically: "Are we the representatives of the people of the United States? Are we acting for them, and as their authorized agents, in this endeavor to press amendments upon the attention of Congress?" Kentucky's appeal for a constitutional convention asked for the president to lay the proposal before Congress, which was the "correct, the legal, the patriotic course."[12]

This appeal from Kentucky noted that the "people of some of the states feel themselves deeply aggrieved by the policy and measures which have been adopted by some of the people of the other States," and "an amendment of the Constitution of the United States is deemed indispensably necessary to secure them against similar grievances in the future."[13]

Baldwin then shifted to arguing that the Peace Conference was not representative. "Why should we assemble here and express our wishes to Congress in reference to the Constitution without permitting California, Oregon, or many other States not here represented, to unite in our deliberations?" he asked. "I cannot assent to such an unfair proceeding toward other states."

Baldwin suggested the Resolutions Committee was a "revolutionary proceeding." He also pointed out that some Peace Conference delegates were elected by state legislatures, others appointed by governors, some delegates may act on their own judgment, while others have instructions from their states, leaving the delegates as a whole "not standing upon equal ground."[14]

The Virginia resolutions calling for the Peace Conference warned that without a quick settlement there was "danger of the disruption of the Union," Baldwin recalled. But even if so, the Constitution "knows no such danger" and is "self-sustaining," not subject to amendment except by "deliberate action of the people themselves," whose rights Baldwin would "not disregard."

Baldwin, on a rhetorical roll, also disputed that any state could secede from the Union, as there was no "such thing as *legal* secession, for there is no power anywhere to take the people out of the protecting care of the Government, or to relieve them from their obligations to it."

The Peace Conference had no more authority to propose constitutional amendments than did the "so-called Southern Confederacy," Baldwin added in another jibe that must have provoked frowns from Southern peace commissioners like Seddon and perhaps even Tyler, although the latter was sufficiently self-composed to hide it. For good measure, Baldwin also quoted from George Washington's Farewell Address:

> You should properly estimate the immense value of your national union to your collective and individual happiness; that you should cherish a cordial, habitual, and immovable attachment to it; accustoming yourselves to think and speak of it as the Palladium of your political safety and prosperity; watching for its preservation with jealous anxiety; discountenancing whatever may suggest even a suspicion that it can in any event be abandoned; and indignantly frowning upon the first dawning of every attempt to alienate any portion of our country from the rest, or to enfeeble the sacred ties which now link together the various parts.[15]

"It appears to me, that in adopting the line of policy proposed by the majority of the committee, we are doing the very thing which Washington warned us not to do," Baldwin exclaimed. Again citing Washington's counsel:

> If, in the opinion of the people, the distribution or modification of the constitutional powers be in any particular wrong, let it be corrected by an amendment in the way which the Constitution designates. But let there be no change by usurpation; for though this in one instance may

122

be the instrument of good, it is the customary weapon by which free governments are destroyed.[16]

"Entertaining these opinions, and with these convictions, I should be untrue to my sense of duty to the Government and the State I represent, and to the people of the United States, if I should consent to disregard the Constitution and my obligations to it," Baldwin insisted. "My report leaves everything to the people, where I think every such question should be left." He pledged to "bow" to the people's decision, "whatever it may be."[17]

Saying he had studied the Constitution his whole life, Kentucky's James Guthrie, who chaired the Resolutions Committee, was the first respondent to Baldwin. He delivered what a Washington newspaper called an "able speech" that urged "speedy action" if the conference wanted to restore peace among the states.[18] He acknowledged the Constitution's "strength was intended to be placed in the affections of the people, and I had hoped it would endure forever." But he regretted that "one portion of the people has lost confidence in the government, and now seven states have left it."[19]

In a circuitous argument repeated later by other delegates, Guthrie effectively granted the right of secession by saying the American War of Independence had "established the right of revolution, and that right gave to the world this splendid government," a precedent that "will stand for all time" and "will always be acted upon when the people have lost confidence in the government."[20]

"I *hate* that word secession, because it is a cheat!" Guthrie admitted. "Call things by their right names!" He said the departing Southern states had "framed another government" for which the Constitution offered no warrant, but it was like the "right of self-defense, which every man may exercise." He reminded Baldwin that Congress was constitutionally the recipient of petitions from the people. And he noted that twenty states were present at the Peace Conference because Congress, even after in "shameful" session for two months, had lacked the "sagacity to give the necessary guarantees, the proper assurances to the slaveholding states," while the government was "falling to pieces." Even the "proudest governments" were often compelled to give guarantees to their people, yet Congress had failed, he lamented.[21]

The Peace Conference was the assembly of the people's representatives who had every right to petition Congress, to repair the "foundations of government" and "save the country," Guthrie insisted. Whoever refused to respond to the crisis now would be called to "fear account," he warned. "When the building is on fire, it is no time to inquire who set it on fire. The North say the South did it, and the South say the North did it."[22]

All present loved the Union and Constitution, Guthrie declared, and all hoped to "lay the foundation" for bringing back the seceded states by "reason and not the sword." But what Baldwin was proposing would take "too long," given the pressing national crisis of the moment.[23]

Unsurprisingly, Guthrie as a Kentuckian also took umbrage and challenged Baldwin over his citation of Kentucky's call for a national convention. "I don't want the gentleman to come between me and the people of Kentucky," he fumed. "He has no right to speak for the people of that State—her representatives here have that right and will exercise it." He recalled that Kentucky's resolution specifically accepted Virginia's invite to the Peace Conference. Guthrie predicted Kentucky would in fact accept his Resolution Committee's proposals.[24]

Very likely Guthrie was aware that many Republicans and abolitionists were now favoring a national convention. It could be both a delaying measure and an arena where presumably the North's population advantage could have maximum sway. The nation's most famous abolitionist, Horace Greeley, editorialized somewhat sarcastically in his *Liberator* newspaper that the "Constitution does not seem to find favor with the Old Gentlemen's Conference at Washington," where they "evidently suppose that such a Convention may possibly make alterations in favor of freedom, and not in favor of slavery hence their reluctance. We must say we think they are more than half right."[25]

Maybe with such infamous support in mind, Guthrie denounced Baldwin's proposal as a "new excuse for inaction" and representing "those who are willing to stand by and see this Government drift toward destruction—to see this country involved in civil war." Guthrie wanted no part of it. The choices were clear.[26]

"The eyes of every true patriot in the nation are turned toward this body," Guthrie pronounced. "The people are awaiting our action, with anxious and painful solicitude." He said it was well known that unless the Peace Conference could "quiet the apprehensions" of the slaveholding states, a "disruption of the Government is inevitable." And if Baldwin's proposal to "go home and do nothing" were adopted, then effectively they were all accepting the "responsibility of breaking up the Government."[27]

Fifty-six-year-old Congressman Samuel Curtis of Iowa was born in New York, anti-slavery, and both a lawyer and engineer. He was one of the first Republicans elected to Congress, a West Point graduate, and a Mexican War veteran who would soon serve as a successful Union general in the impending war. He rose to challenge Guthrie. A tall man with commanding military presence and "deep-set, black, penetrating, yet, kind, eyes," Curtis often carried a "stern expression," but was "animated and winning in conversation, his countenance lighting up with remarkable brilliancy and attractiveness when interested." He was recalled later for his unblemished personal character.[28] During the war in Mexico he had obligingly attended Catholic churches, but he was discomfited by some aspects of Mexican Catholicism and preferred the "Puritanical customs" at home.[29]

A Washington newspaper somewhat sarcastically reported that Curtis delivered a "disquisition upon political affairs generally, and could be interpreted to mean everything or nothing, whatever the case might be."[30] In fact, Curtis was rather pointed in challenging his Kentucky colleague about the Resolutions Committee proposals: "I would ask Mr. Guthrie if the adoption of his propositions, previous to their action, would have prevented the States which have already seceded from going out."[31]

Guthrie replied that his Resolutions Committee proposals would have saved all but possibly South Carolina from seceding.

Curtis quickly rejected Guthrie's answer. "We know, and the gentleman knows, that there has been for a long time a purpose, a great conspiracy in this country, to begin and carry out a revolution," Curtis alleged, noting that Congress had hardly been inactive and in fact had pondered "forty or fifty different propositions" on the current national crisis. He made clear his rejection of Guthrie's proposals because they would render "all territory we may hereafter acquire slave territory."[32]

Maryland's Reverdy Johnson of the Resolutions Committee heartily denied the allegation, but Curtis stood his ground, explaining that Northern non-slave territory was already divided up, so future territory would be bound to slavery. He suggested admitting territory already pegged for slavery to satiate the South. And Curtis denounced the seceded states and President Buchanan; if Buchanan "had acted as Jackson did, there would have been an end of it."[33]

If states can willfully quit the Union, then "this government, in my opinion, is not worth the trouble of preserving," Curtis suggested. He continued:

> The Government is one of love and affection, it is true, but it is also one of strength, and power. Where was there ever a more indulgent people than ours? Our forts have been taken, our flag has been fired upon, our property seized, and as yet nothing has been done. But they will not be indulgent forever. Beware, gentlemen, how you force them further. Gentlemen talk about the inefficiency of Congress; I wish there was some efficiency in the Executive. If there was, or had been, our present troubles would have been avoided.[34]

SUNDAY'S REFLECTION

The Peace Conference did not convene on Sunday, despite its short Saturday session, and despite the quickly expiring amount of time left available for compromise. Instead, delegates likely attended church, especially the closest places of worship such as Reverend Hall's Church of the Epiphany, Reverend Edwards's Foundry Methodist, and Reverend Gurley's New York Avenue Presbyterian. It is likely that many also walked Pennsylvania Avenue, admired the city's great buildings, strolled by the White House, or admired the statue of General Andrew Jackson in Lafayette Square, whom most of the delegates were quite old enough to remember well, and with whom some had even served. Almost certainly nearly all the delegates conferred in Willard's lobby and in its respected restaurant, or caucused more privately with kindred spirits in their rooms upstairs. The mood now must have been more serious, as the previous conviviality among colleagues grew into heated debate among strong-minded, articulate men with often vastly differing understandings about the future and meaning of American democracy.

At 11:00 A.M. on Monday, February 19, the Peace Conference reconvened, earlier than the previous noon start time. Delegates had refused anything earlier than 11:00 A.M. Rev. Phineas Gurley opened with prayer. The delegates turned immediately to internal administrative issues, with Vermont's L. E. Chittenden pleading for the convention to appoint a stenographer. The diligent self-appointed note taker of the proceedings did not then mention his labors. He specified that he didn't propose any contemporaneous publication of their remarks, which some feared would upset the "calmness" of their deliberations, and that the record would be only for posterity, after their adjournment.

"I could not justify myself to my conscience, or to those who have a right to hold me responsible for my acts here, if I failed to do all that lays in my power to have the true history of this convention laid before the country," Chittenden implored. Eleven states, mostly slave states, but also Pennsylvania, Rhode Island, and Connecticut, voted no. Only eight states voted yes, all of them Northern. Ohio was divided. Chittenden would have to rely on his own notes.[35]

Fifty-year-old Amos Tuck of New Hampshire took the floor. He was a former US congressman and a founder of the Republican Party who helped orchestrate Lincoln's presidential nomination in 1860. Tuck was also a devout Baptist, successful businessman, politico, and anti-slavery diehard who had quit the Democratic Party over the issue. He shared a formal appeal to the American people, declaring no interest in interfering with slavery where it was already existing. He affirmed the right of states to appeal violations of their rights, and commended a national convention, for which he credited the legislatures of Kentucky and Illinois. Several delegates objected to Tuck's seemingly aimless disquisition on the Constitution, but President Tyler judiciously affirmed Tuck's right to enter his speech into the record.[36]

North Carolina's fifty-seven-year-old David Reid was a Democrat and former governor, US senator, and US congressman. He put forth a motion to specify that the Resolutions Committee's proposed constitutional amendment would protect slavery in both "present" and also "future" territory, about which the language was confusingly vague. Eight states supported him, all of them slave owning except New Jersey. Twelve states opposed, all of them free.[37]

Maryland's Reverdy Johnson proposed adding the specification that slavery was protected only in "present" territory. It was "odious" to him to signal that the US "proposes to acquire new territory in any way." He aimed his comments at his "southern friends" there in the audience of Willard Hall. "You have sought to extend this provision to territory which shall be hereafter acquired," and "you have had a decisive vote and have been beaten in this conference," during a "fight [that] has been a fair one." Johnson urged them to accept the majority will of the Peace Conference, also knowing Congress would likewise never accept otherwise. He implored them to settle for protections of slavery in current territory, "fairly—recognizing and acknowledging the rights of all, and remain brethren forever with the free states!" Provoking rare applause, Johnson declared, "From my very heart, I say yes." He faulted the national crisis "which has brought this country into its present lamentable condition" on the issue of slavery's expansion. If this had been "disposed of or settled in some way before," he claimed, "many states would have been kept in the Union that have now gone out." He continued:

We have now a territory extensive enough to sustain two hundred millions of people—embracing almost every climate, fruitful in almost
every species of production—rich in all the elements of national
wealth, and governed by a Constitution that has raised us to an elevation of grandeur that the world has never before witnessed. That we
should separate to the destruction of such a government, on account
of territory we have not got, and territory that we do not want, is not, I
believe, the patriotic sense of the South.[38]

Johnson recalled that Virginia had summoned the Peace Conference
because the "country was going to ruin," and the South was "aroused . . .
to a frenzy—not madness, but the frenzy which falls on every patriotic
mind when it witnesses a country going to destruction." The remedy was
to "satisfy the people of the slave States that their rights were secure." As
the Peace Conference endeavored to comply, he appealed for Southern
cooperation. "I speak for the South and to the South," he emphasized.
"I know that we can still labor to keep this Government together. If we
follow the plain dictates of our judgment, any other course would be
impossible."[39]

"The cords that bind you together are a hundred times as strong
as those which ever bound any party," Johnson concluded emotively.
"Unless we do something, and something very quickly, before the
incoming President is inaugurated, in all human probability he will
have only the States north of Mason and Dixon to govern—that is, if
he is to govern them in peace." Johnson carefully denied any right of
secession but admitted a "right of self-defense" and "right of revolution,"
that was "recognized by the Constitution itself." When Virginia's James
Seddon retorted that Johnson was in fact describing a constitutional
"right of secession," Johnson riposted, "Heaven save me from a Virginia
politician!"[40]

Johnson then pivoted to his "friends of the North," asking: "Do you
want us to go out? You are a great people, a great country—a powerful
people, a rich country. No threat or intimidation shall ever come from

me to such a people. I ask you in all sadness whether, in the light of all our glory, of all our happiness and prosperity, whether you will, by withholding a thing that it will not harm you to grant, suffer us, compel us to depart?"

Johnson insisted that the Resolutions Committee's proposed amendments were asking little of the North and only of the South. He pointed out that the Supreme Court's Dred Scott decision had already asserted a right for slavery to spread north of the Missouri Compromise line of latitude 36°30′, which the proposals were now ceding. He only asked "you to give us . . . the territory south of that line; and even as to that, we give you the right to destroy slavery there whenever a State organized out of it chooses to do so."[41]

"We are, in fact, yielding to you," Johnson exclaimed. "We abandon our rights North. Will you not let us retain what is already ours, South?" He said on their decision "hangs the question, whether we shall be preserved a united people, or be broken to atoms." And absent a settlement now, "war will come." He prayed that the Peace Conference's decisions "may at least spare this agony to ourselves, our families, and our posterity."[42]

Virginia's Seddon responded defiantly to Johnson: "I appeal not to forbearance—I ask not for pity." He felt "proud to represent the grand old commonwealth of Virginia here, and prouder still that I only come here to demand right and justice in her behalf." Virginia had come forward in a "great national crisis," distressed as "this glorious temple of our government has been torn away." Very "proud of her memories of the past," she offered "calmly and plainly" what guarantees were needed to safeguard her rights. Seddon added that Virginia did not stand alone but was "supported by all her border sisters" in demanding protections for slavery in any new territory. Indeed, "She and her sister States plant themselves upon it."[43]

Seddon cited Dred Scott's affirmation that slave owners were "entitled to participate in *all* the territory of the United States," which Virginia and her sisters were now willing to cede. But all that was offered

130

in exchange was "getting a little piece of the worthless territory south of the proposed line!" Additionally, Virginia sought "security against the principles of the North, and her great and now dominant party," ending the upheaval that had "convulsed the country and jeopardized our institutions."[44]

Tartly addressing the Northerners, Seddon asked: "Would it not be wise and well as statesmen and as patriots, that you should do what you can for adjustment? do what you can to bring back your sisters of the South who have departed?" Which was the "part of wisdom to settle?" He pointed at the "great and mighty party" arisen in the North that was "determined to exclude the institution of slavery, not only from all future, but from all *present* territory." Their "heated zealots" had resolved that the "natural and patriarchal institution of the South should be surrounded by a cordon of free States, and in the end be extinguished altogether." Virginia was "wise" to resist this scheme to "preserve her dignity and power."[45]

Virginia demanded to be "equal in dignity—equal in right," otherwise the people would be "dishonored," "unworthy" among nations, Seddon adamantly insisted. "We hold property, yes, our property in slaves, as rightful and as honorable as any property to be found in the broad expanse between ocean and ocean," he readily admitted. "We feel that in the existence, the perpetuity, the protection of the African race, we have a mission to perform, and not a mission only, but a right and a duty."[46]

Seddon continued with his rigorous defense of the humanity of slavery, explaining that "these colored barbarians have been withdrawn from a country of native barbarism, and under the benignant influence of a Christian rule, of a Christian civilization, have been elevated, yes, *elevated* to a standing and position which they could never have otherwise secured." The "colored race" fared far better on Southern plantations than did free blacks in the Caribbean or those former slaves transferred to Africa's western coast, evincing that "we have redeemed and kept well our high and our holy trust."[47]

This issue was for the Southern consciences, not the North's, Seddon asserted. "We appeal to you to leave it where it is, to leave the colored people where they are." They were a "people about which you know nothing," and knowing that "we have done that race no wrong." In the South for "scores of years we have been laboring earnestly in our mission," having "contributed far more to the greatness of the North than to our own." Yet the South had been "assailed, attacked, vilified and defamed, by the people of the North, from the cradle to the grave, and you have educated your children to believe us monsters of brutality, lust and iniquity." From the start "abolition societies" had spread their "poison and venom all over the land."[48]

Tracing the original spread of the anti-slavery contagion, Seddon faulted "British, Anglo-Saxon instigation," whose purpose was to "disrupt this republic," claiming slavery as an "evil and a sin." It "manifested in religious societies—first in the largest churches in New England, in the Presbyterian or Congregational churches, next the Methodist, then the Baptist, and finally, the venom spread so widely, its influence separated other churches." This incited members and others "by the vilest motives, to steal our slaves, to destroy our property," with no "effort of the law nor an exertion of public opinion to put them down." He cited the "invasion" of Virginia by John Brown's "robbers and murderers" in 1859, who after meeting the "just reward of their crime," gained "expressions of sympathy" and were hailed as "victims of oppression, as martyrs to a holy and righteous cause."[49]

Moving beyond abolitionism, Seddon assailed the North more broadly for "acquisitive disposition," its "greed of land—the greed of office and power," and its desire to control the national government. This, he said, had led to the "great Republican party; in other words, your great sectional party, which has at length come to majority and power." He accused the party of opposing "admission of slave states in the future," having in mind the "final extinction of slavery," and the "rule of one portion of the country over another." With the "whole united government" now turned against the South, it was now "taking the subject into our own hands." Northerners "would deserve to be spurned by the maids and matrons among you, if you refused to protect yourselves against the dangers" that now surround the South. Seddon professed to speak for the "border States, by all the citizens of the South, by every householder of my State in a greater or less degree."[50]

Finally drawing to a close with his stem-winding defense of Southern slavery, Seddon thought Virginia was in fact demanding too little by accepting the Crittenden Compromise. He alleged that the Union and the Constitution, "as they now stand, are unsafe for the people of the South, unsafe without other guarantees which will give them actual power instead of mere paper rights." He asked the Northern peace commissioners how they expected to retain Virginia and the border states for the Union, when confronted by such an "immense party," absent "added guarantees."[51]

Responding to Seddon's fiery oration was the equally adamant forty-three-year-old former Massachusetts governor George Boutwell. Boutwell was a former Democrat and temperance activist who had become anti-slavery due to convictions that started years earlier, through conversation with a slave woman whose child was sold south. In 1853 he explained his opposition to the "slave power that governs this country," wanting "under the federal Constitution to nationalize and fortify liberty, to localize and discourage slavery." He noted that the "doctrine of equality . . . is the fundamental doctrine of democracy," sustained "by the fiat of the Almighty, and recognized and established in His revealed word. The commandments, 'Thou shalt love thy neighbor as thyself,' and 'Do unto others as you would have them do unto you,' are the foundations of democracy." He extolled the "sacred principle, that, by nature and the will of God, every man is born a freeman, and enters into society with equal rights with every other man."[52]

BOUTWELL WEIGHS IN

On a Sunday shortly after arriving in Washington, DC, for the Peace Conference, Boutwell approached Seddon for friendly conversation. Later he recalled Seddon telling him:

It is of no use for us to attempt to deceive each other. You have one form of civilization, and we have another. You think yours is the best for you, and we think that ours is the best for us. But our culture is exhausting, and we must have new lands. One part of your people say that Congress shall exclude slavery from the territories, and another set of men say that it will be excluded by natural laws. Under either theory, somebody must go, and if we can't go with our slaves, we must go without them and our country will be given up to the negroes.[53]

In his time and place, Seddon's view was not "unreasonable," Boutwell thought, with "no conclusive solution of the problem presented." But Seddon "did not seem to consider that he was warring against nature as well as against the Union in his attempt to extend the area of slavery," and "could only have postponed the crisis for a period." Seddon was most "anxious" to secure an "assurance that in no event should there be war" while at the conference—at least from the Republicans. The "greatest error was the failure of the Northern delegates to assert that in no event should the Union be dissolved except through the success of the South in arms," he determined, for which reason he directly warned of it in his speech. Boutwell was disgusted when New Jersey's Stockton "went so far as to assert that in case of war the North would raise a regiment to aid the South as often as one was raised to assail it." Likewise he remembered conversing with Salmon Chase "as we walked one evening on Pennsylvania Avenue, toward Georgetown," when Chase said: "The thing to be done is to let the South go."[54]

After the preponderance of speeches for the compromise package, the Massachusetts delegation met with New York's Republican delegates and chose Boutwell to speak, as he remembered. He "resolved to say that no scheme would be accepted by us which did not contain an abandonment of the doctrine of secession, an acknowledgment of the legality of Mr. Lincoln's election, and a declaration that it was the duty of the whole body of citizens to render obedience to the government." Yet he "very well knew that these terms would be rejected with scorn" by most delegates.[55]

According to a New York newspaper, Boutwell delivered a "long and eloquent speech" that was "against all compromise" and was said to be the "most elaborate and able speech yet delivered." It gained "much attention" and steered the debate for much of the day, even urging the border states to "conciliating and agreeing with the North for their own safety."[56]

"It is attempted here to put the North on trial," Boutwell observed. "I have listened with grave attention to the gentleman from Virginia today, but I have heard no specification of these charges." Every man in his state would give his life for the Union, he pledged. And Massachusetts has "made war upon slavery wherever she had the right to do it; but much as she abhors the institution, she would sacrifice everything rather than assail it where she has not the right to assail it."[57]

Boutwell reminded his fellow peace commissioners that America's new president had been elected in a "legal and constitutional way," but he surmised that his inauguration was now being made contingent on additional guarantees to the South. In the interests of the Union, the South could not "demand of us at the North anything that we will not grant, unless it involves a sacrifice of our principles," which we "shall not sacrifice—these you must not ask us to abandon," he insisted. And added, more provocatively, that "if the Constitution and the Union cannot be preserved and effectually maintained without these new guarantees for slavery, then the Union is not worth preserving."[58]

Warning against prohibitions on acquiring new territory, Boutwell said there may be a time when Canada may wish to unite with the United States, and the Union should not forswear "acquiring new territory in an honorable way." He warned that seceding Southern states were already eyeing Mexico and her neighbors for annexation, blocking the North's "highway to the Pacific coast."[59]

Boutwell was skeptical that the Resolution Committee's proposals would save the Union and may in fact prove "mischievous," hence the "North, the free States, will not adopt them—will not consent to these new endorsements of an institution which they do not like, which they believe to be injurious to the best interests of the republic." And even if the North could adopt them, the South "would not be satisfied; she would not fail to find pretexts for a course of action upon which I think she has already determined."[60]

More ominously, Boutwell warned the North would "never consent to the separation of the states," and if the South persisted, "we shall march our armies to the Gulf of Mexico, or you will march yours to the Great Lakes," as there can be "no peaceful separation." Union and peace required the South to abide by its "constitutional obligations, and remain in the Union until their rights are in fact invaded," then "all will be well." But if the South precipitates civil war and breaks up the government, then supporters of the government "must and will defend it at every sacrifice—if necessary, to the sacrifice of their lives."[61]

Boutwell later recalled about his hour-long speech, "When I began to speak, I advanced slowly up the aisle until I could look into the faces of the Virginia delegation, who occupied the settee next to the president's desk," while the Massachusetts delegation sat far from the front. William Rives of Virginia seemed particularly pained by Boutwell's militance. "They were not indignant, but grieved rather," Boutwell recounted. "For many days the remark was repeated or referred to with the hope, apparently, of inducing me to retract or qualify it. I allowed it to stand as a truth which they might well accept."[62]

Kentucky's James Guthrie responded to Boutwell with a defense of the South's prerogatives, insisting that there was not the "slightest objection anywhere to the inauguration of Mr. Lincoln," that disagreements should be decided "at the ballot box," and if the question is decided against the South, *we know how to take care of ourselves.*" He reminded Boutwell that the North had contemplated secession during the War of 1812 because of its impact on the Northern economy. Now, he said, it's the South whose "property is depreciating, going down every day," feeling "this want of security very deeply, this want of faith in the Government under which we live," and growing "in agitation." If the North's property values were struck down, he asked, would it not call for "guarantees" and desire "its security restored?"[63]

"There is nothing in the territorial question that we may not settle by a fair compromise," Guthrie declared. And the Peace Conference could make that compromise there and then, without delay. "We shall then go home and tell our people that we can still live on together, in security," Guthrie hoped, "before the inauguration of Mr. Lincoln." After all, "we come to consult together, to give and receive justice."[64]

Guthrie pleaded that the North not "impose upon us the necessity of fleeing our country!" He warned them that war would bankrupt "one-half your merchants, one-half your mechanics," and that "not one man, North or South, but must suffer if the sad conclusion comes." He predicted that "our products will depreciate," and "next year not one-half the fields now whitened by the rich growth of cotton will be cultivated if this unhappy contest goes on." Already the "people of the South are restless and impatient," he warned, and "already in the way of revolution," unlikely to "remain quiet when the fortunes of one-half of them are struck down." He imploringly asked, could "the North remain quiet under like provocations?"[65]

When asked if the Peace Conference would have similarly convened after the election to the presidency of Stephen Douglas or John Breckinridge instead of Lincoln, Guthrie quickly admitted no. All the "discordant elements combined" into the new Republican Party that had "brought the abolitionists into power," producing "this sense of insecurity in the South," which wanted to "guard against" their "combined power."[66]

Former Connecticut governor Chauncey Cleveland, age sixty-two, was a Democrat who turned Republican. He served at the 1860 Republican Convention and in 1861 as a presidential elector for Lincoln. Cleveland challenged the growing acrimony in the Peace Conference debates. "Let us not widen our dissensions; let us do nothing to postpone or destroy the only hope we have for the settlement of our troubles," he urged. "Let us be gentle and pleasant. Let us love one another. Let us not try to find out who is the smartest or the keenest. Let us vote soon, and without any feeling or any quarreling." He wondered why the Compromise of 1850 was not "permitted to stand," bringing the nation to the current precipice. "Nothing but the ambition that has sent so many angels down to hell could have ever brought it up again," he surmised. "In the name of all that is good and holy let us settle these differences here," he pleaded, offering his support for the proposed amendments. He asked why there should be discussion about territory that the United States does not yet have, as the country has "just the same title to it that the devil had to the territory he offered our Savior on a certain remarkable occasion."[67]

Shortly after Cleveland's reference to Satan's tempting offer of all earthly kingdoms to Jesus Christ, the Peace Conference approved Johnson's motion to amend the majority report by limiting slavery to all "present" territory under latitude 36°30′. No doubt exhausted, commissioners then quickly adjourned that Monday, refusing a suggestion they reconvene that evening. Instead, they would meet the next morning, Tuesday, February 19, at 11:00 A.M.[68]

A Cincinnati newspaper account, republished in Nashville, chirpily reported that the Peace Conference had concluded a "harmonious session," having rejected all proposed amendments to the majority report, except for Johnson's, with only Maryland among the slaveholding states voting for it. The newspaper opined that before Friday delegates would "without doubt, agree upon a plan of settlement to be acted on by Congress, which will prove acceptable to the border states." But a Louisville newspaper more grimly surmised that after compromises friendly to the South had failed in Congress, "fears are now seriously entertained that the South will be as unfortunate in the Peace Conference as she has been before Congress and its committees." The reporter speculated that Republicans and other die-hard Unionists were now pushing for a national convention as yet "another project to induce delay, and if possible forever prevent the remaining southern states from going into the Southern Confederacy." It published a "letter from Washington" mocking Tennesseans awaiting "evidences of Republican devotion to their constitutional rights," noting that all who had "hope of obtaining guarantees through the Peace Conference or through Congress, have been woefully deceived." It wondered "how Virginia ever fell into the blunder of supposing that a satisfactory settlement could be made in the order proposed by her."[69]

John Tyler occasionally stepped down from the rostrum and temporarily transferred his presidential duties to others. The elderly president may not have been in the best health. But he was actively working to sway delegates toward compromise, often working behind the scenes. A New York newspaper described Monday's session as "very spirited," but still insisted that the "most amicable feelings were displayed on all sides." It reported that Tyler "asked some of the anti-compromisers to-day, in a private conversation, if they would yield the Virginia proposition, the Crittenden Compromise, or anything against the spirit of the Chicago Platform." Tyler also asked advocates of a national convention if some other more direct compromise were not acceptable. But he "received a negative answer," to which he replied that "if they maintained that position through this week, without action in the right direction for a settlement, there would no longer be any hope of adjustment, and they must prepare to recognize the consequences, or involve the country in civil war."[70]

Reputedly Tyler had not yet abandoned hope in the Peace Conference he had been instrumental in creating, but he had to have been discouraged and increasingly aware of narrowing opportunities for conciliation. Similarly, the same newspaper reported that James Guthrie approached Northern Republicans like Boutwell and Crowninshield to assure them he was not wedded to "any particular measure," and "as an alternative, asking what they would give, and intimating that they would agree to anything which presented a basis of adjustment." Their reply was to offer a national convention, which they thought was "rapidly gaining in favor, and express the belief that now no other can pass."[71]

TERRITORIAL QUESTIONS

On the following day, February 19, a Washington newspaper reported that "some or more delegates to the Peace Conference say that they will agree upon a plan of adjustment which will be satisfactory even to the Virginia Commissioners." This optimism was perhaps excessive, but the report accurately predicted the "territorial question" would feature prominently in that day's proceedings, with the debate "directed to the object of securing unanimity on that point," which was again an optimistic projection.[72]

Citing the fast-moving calendar, Kentucky's Wickliffe again proposed a thirty-minute time limit on speeches, with one motion suggesting ten minutes. Their labors might be "useless" unless they agreed to resolutions before Congress adjourned.

"Massachusetts will never consent to this," quickly replied Boutwell from that state, to which Wickliffe sarcastically retorted, "If we cannot get Massachusetts to help us, we will help ourselves. We got along without her in the war of 1812; we can get on without her again. The disease exists in the nation now. It is of no use, or rather it is too late to talk about the cause, we had much better try to cure the disease."[73]

Several Northern delegates, one professing to speak for "commercial interests," protested that sufficient Northern voices had not yet been heard before the advent of such a time limitation on speech. One delegate proposed evening sessions. Another proposed an end to all debate by 3:00 P.M. that day, since "our minds are all made up." But sixty-three-year-old former Massachusetts congressman Charles Allen protested that "nothing but harm can come from these limitations upon the liberty of speech." The grand nephew of Revolutionary era patriot Samuel Adams, Allen observed that the "questions before us are the most important that could possibly arise," and the Constitution itself was "examined in Convention for more than three months." He pointed out the Peace Conference was "practically making a new Constitution," and predicted that further discussion would "bring us nearer together." And he complained that Wickliffe seemed "disposed to apply a plaster to the foot, to cure a disease in the head." Allen also warned that a forced vote, gaining a majority but not a consensus, would have little weight with Congress and popular opinion.[74]

Salmon Chase affirmed Wickliffe's proposed thirty-minute time limit, but was against stricter time limits, pointing out that speakers could always ask for extended time. Kentuckian Charles Morehead reiterated the imperative to "act speedily," emphasizing, "I came here to act for the Union—the whole Union. I recognize no sides—no party."[75]

Supporting Morehead was New Jersey's Robert Stockton, a fellow Resolutions Committee member. His family and service encompassed the whole history of the Union. His grandfather had signed the Declaration of Independence, his father had been a US senator from New Jersey, and Stockton himself was a longtime naval officer who had served in the War of 1812. He had also been the first US naval officer to capture a slave ship during the US Navy's decades-long struggle against the slave trade. Stockton, who was Catholic, declined President Tyler's invitation to become his navy secretary. In 1844 he captained the new USS *Princeton*, during a demonstration of its latest artillery technology on a Potomac River cruise. Much of official Washington was on board, including President Tyler. A defective cannon called the "Peacemaker" exploded, killing two cabinet members and several others, including a New York congressman. The congressman's daughter, Julia Gardiner, fainted into the arms of the president, who would soon after marry her. During the Mexican War, Stockton's naval command helped seize California from the Mexicans. Stockton then served in California as military governor. After the war, he became a US senator from New Jersey, serving as a Democrat.

So unsurprisingly, Stockton spoke at length and passionately at the Peace Conference about the urgency of their mission, although with odd timing, interrupting a debate about whether to limit the length of speeches. He asked: "Upon what, let me ask gentlemen, does the salvation of the Union depend at this moment? What is it alone that prevents civil war now?" His answer, of course, was that only "this convention—this august convention!" was forestalling an "awful danger!" and the "throes of an earthquake which threatens to bring down ruin on the whole magnificent fabric of our Government!" Surely with personal remembrance of his own grandfather as a Founding Father, he warned that "this edifice which our fathers constructed" could "crumble to pieces" unless they, "by trusting in God, who guided our ancestors through the stormy vicissitudes of the Revolution, should this day resolve that the Union shall be preserved!" Citing his own military service, Stockton recalled his "love" for the people of every state, who had served "under my command and I have been under theirs." He declared: "I know them, and I know that this Union can never be dissolved without a struggle," when we "shall begin to shed each other's blood." To this prospect he shouted, "No, gentlemen, no!"[76]

The national crisis was essentially about slavery in the territories, Stockton noted, and as such, "better that the territories were buried in the deep sea beyond the plummet's reach, than that they should be the cause of such a deplorable result" as civil war. He reported that although the territory "south of 36° 30´ had been ten years open to Southern colonization, only twenty-four slaves had been introduced into it." So the real question, he surmised, was "whether pride of opinion shall succumb to the necessities of the crisis." Stockton observed that Lincoln, as "The Premier of the incoming administration, has declared that parties and platforms are subordinate to, and must disappear in the presence of the great question of the Union," which "gives me hope." If the new administration did act upon this commitment, then the Peace Conference could in a mere six hours, "in conjunction with a committee of his political friends, adjust such terms of settlement as will save the Union."[77]

An oracle had informed a hero of ancient Rome that the sacrifice of his own life would save his country, Stockton recalled. But on this day, no one was called "upon to give up life, property, or honor, but to concede justice and equal rights to our Southern brethren," needing only "courage to yield extreme opinions." He warned Republicans that without conciliation, they would "govern a little more than half of" the country, "and with that you have to provide for war." He warned against "stigmatizing" the seceding states as treasonous, when they encompassed "territory equal to half of Europe," making it a "revolution." The federal government could not subjugate his own New Jersey alone, much less fifteen slave states, he warned. And even if it could, what next? He recalled that when Oliver Cromwell's Puritans had subjected all the British Isles, when Cromwell dismissed Parliament, the "Republican party of that day" left the "whole country, tired of war, crouched under the iron heel of the Puritan soldier." And now America must ponder whether to commence its own civil war "to maintain the Chicago Platform" of the Republican Party. Surely it would not, as that platform must "disappear."[78]

Stockton argued the "mad action of South Carolina does not truly represent the South." Such Disunionists existed in both the South as well as the North, requiring "patriotic men to checkmate" them in both sections. He inveighed against the "enormous bribe with which the Republican leaders would seduce the North into fratricidal war." That would include the "expenditure of uncounted millions, the distribution of epaulets and military commissions for an army of half a million of men, the immense patronage involved in the letting of army contracts, the inflation of prices and the rise of property which would follow the excessive issue of paper money, made necessary by the lavish expenditure." If the question were about the tariff, he suggested, the North "would hesitate and look at the awful consequences." So could the Peace Conference "fix it in a minute, if you will be calm and act like brothers."

If only the "hostile attitude which the North assumed at Chicago [would] give place to the recognition of the rights of the South," Stockton predicted, it would produce an "outburst of loyalty to the Union throughout the entire South, like that which welcomed to old England its constitutional sovereign after a long and bloody civil war, forced upon the English people by the Puritans. It is the spirit of the same fanatic intolerance which has caused our present troubles." He sternly told his fellow peace commissioners, "You shall not go home; you shall never see your wives and families again, until you have settled these matters, and saved your good old country, if I can help it." And he implored in his soaring conclusion: "Spread aloft the banner of stripes and stars, let the whole country rally beneath its glorious folds, with no other slogan on their lips but the unanimous cry, The Union, it must be Preserved!" [79]

Responding to Stockton's artful peroration was sixty-eight-year-old former New York congressman Francis Granger. Granger was an old Whig who was postmaster general under President William Henry Harrison, resigning shortly after Tyler's accession to office to return to Congress. He had supported President Fillmore and the Compromise of 1850, against anti-slavery Whigs like William Seward. He informed the Peace Conference that the New York delegation was divided. He posited that even though New York had given Republicans a fifty-thousand-vote majority in the 1860 election, "if the noble propositions of the majority of your committee . . . could be submitted to them, the people of New York would adopt them by even a larger majority." The people everywhere knew that "the politicians who have brought the country to the verge of ruin can be trusted no longer," he declared. "The time has come when they must act for themselves. Be assured, gentlemen, they will do so."[80]

Granger recalled having opposed "this Republican party from the outset—to avert, if possible, the adoption of its pernicious principles by the people of New York." Of Lincoln, he said, "I believe in him although I opposed his election . . . would trust his Kentucky blood to the end, if all else failed . . . [and] I think he is honest." Granger expected him to heed not "hotheaded zealots" but "cool, dispassionate, and conservative men; not men who are driven to the verge of insanity upon this question of slavery." The "northern mind," unlike the Southern, was "not started by slight scratches, but strike the rowel deep, and there is a purpose in it that nothing can conquer or restrain. The people of the North will carry that purpose into execution, with a power as fierce as that of the maddest chivalry of South Carolina. The rowel was struck deep and the consequences were not considered."[81]

Some Northerners, Granger admitted, were "rash enough to say, 'Let these Southern slaveholders go. The [negro] will rise upon them and cut their throats!' The action of such men, I admit, gives some color and justification to your charges and prejudices against the whole Northern people." He originally thought only four Southern states would secede, and now Virginia stood ready to leave. And as the country faced the possibility of war he foresaw the "awful legacy of widows' tears—of the blighted hopes of orphans—with a catalogue of suffering, misery, and woe, too long to be enumerated and too painful to be contemplated." Such a war inevitably would be "long and terrible," with both sides rising "in their majesty at both ends of the line," devoting themselves "with terrible energy, to the work of death."[82]

Granger warned Republicans not to think they won New York on the basis of opposing slavery, as voters for Lincoln had a "great variety of motives." Some wanted the Homestead Act and others changed in the tariff. He promised that most New Yorkers, if offered the Resolutions Committee's "fair and noble propositions," would "accept them with a unanimity that will gratefully surprise the nation."[83]

"Mr. Lincoln is coming," Granger noted. "And all along the route the people are doing him honor. But that triumphal march is insignificant compared with the anxiety felt throughout the country that this convention should agree upon some plan that will save the government and the Union."[84]

After Granger's appeal, North Carolina's Thomas Ruffin rose. About seventy-five years old, with a mop of white hair covering his crinkled head, he was a former state Supreme Court chief justice who once ruled for a master's "absolute" power of his slave. He was himself a plantation owner. Despite his "advanced years and enfeebled health," Ruffin told his applauding fellow peace commissioners he had come to "maintain and preserve this glorious government! I came here for Union and peace!" Doubtless impressed by Granger's dramatic words and elderly appearance, Ruffin explained: "My health is such that if I could avoid it, I would not mingle in this discussion . . . would not say one word, if I did not know perfectly well that life or death to my part of the country was involved in the action of this Conference." He appealed for them to "discard politics and party—let us be brethren and friends." There was a "new and strong party . . . coming into power, which our people believe entertain views and designs hostile to our institutions." Absent decisive actions with "constitutional guarantees" to restore confidence, Ruffin declared, "we are ruined, and we must see this noble government go down." He observed that his own state and Tennessee were now "border states" between two nations and would form the "theater of war," with their "slave property . . . in even greater peril."[85]

"Gentlemen, we of North Carolina are not hostile to you; we are your friends," Ruffin insisted to his Northern colleagues. "Brothers in a common cause—citizens of a common country . . . loyal to our country and to our Constitution," but losing "both of them, unless you will aid us now." As an "old man" with a "very full" heart regarding the country's "unhappy and distracted condition," he noted his birth even "before the present Constitution was adopted," and prayed "God grant that I do not outlive it." He implored the convention to endorse the proposals before it and submit them immediately to state conventions without waiting on slower state legislatures.[86]

Fifty-year-old New York jurist and temperance activist William Noyes spoke next, after Ruffin's appeal on behalf of North Carolina. He had burnished his famed courtroom oration skills to speak for New York, not of "a time gone by . . . but young, breathing, living New York, as she exists today . . . full of enterprise, patriotism, energy—her living self, with her four millions of people, among whom there is scarcely to be found a heart not beating with loyalty to the Constitution and the Government."[87]

Getting confrontational, with all his prosecutor's zeal, Samuel Curtis intoned, "gentlemen of this Convention, beware of false prophets." Pointing at his Democrat colleague Granger, he exclaimed: "This day, the Scripture is fulfilled among you," adding, "A prophet is not without honor save in his own country, and in his own house!" He warned New York would not yield to "intimidation," not even from New Jersey, prompting audible protests from Stockton. Returning the debate to the motion before them, he protested limitations on speeches, especially "after one section has had an opportunity of expressing its views." Although Virginia had no right to call the convention, and "no possible good could come from her doing so," still New York and others came. Now, peace commissioners were asked to alter "our fundamental law" at the same time being told "we must not discuss" the proposals but simply ratify them. "I submit to the Conference, is it kind, is it generous, is it proper to stop here? Is it best to do so?"[88]

Noyes's speech was interrupted by the reading of a telegram from Missouri, announcing that its state convention's delegates would be strongly pro-Union, prompting "much applause" from the delegates, and to which Noyes responded: "This news is indeed cheering. It is an additional evidence of the depth to which love for our country has struck into the hearts of its people—another inducement to make us agree—another reason why we should not be led off upon false issues." But he concluded by calling Virginia's mechanism for amending the Constitution through the Peace Conference "unconstitutional," asking why there should be such "indecent haste."[89]

Responding to his New York colleague and "false prophet," Noyes insisted their state had not voted Republican based on "collateral issues" but upon the Chicago platform. They thought it embodied the "true principles upon which the government should be conducted," and believing the "destinies of this nation should no longer be left in the hands of men who would use them only to promote the interests of one section of the Union." Noyes proclaimed, contrary to Curtis's claims, "the great heart" of New York was "still loyal and Republican." Threats of dissolution from the South would only strengthen that majority.[90]

Sixty-seven-year-old William Rives then rose, not willing to remain silent amid the "reproach" from Noyes that Virginia had behaved unconstitutionally. He took the time during debate on that Wednesday, February 19, 1861, in Willard Hall to explain his state's "motives and purposes." A Virginia planter and patrician, Rives was another living link to the Founders. He had studied law under an aging Thomas Jefferson, who was a neighbor. He had known James Madison, whose biography he wrote, as well as James Monroe and other Virginia luminaries. A longtime Whig and pro-Union moderate, he had served in the US Congress, succeeded John Tyler in the US Senate, and was US minister to France under President Zachary Taylor. Like Tyler, he would soon serve in the newly formed Confederate Congress.

Rives had sought solace in religion after his infant son died, joining the Episcopal Church. He was a large landowner and slaveholder, having inherited some of both from his father, who had 8,000 acres and 283 slaves. When his boyhood friend, the grandson of Thomas Jefferson, proposed in 1831 that the Virginia legislature gradually abolish slavery, Rives accused him of "striking at our lives and our property," and warned that the proposal could bankrupt Virginia. Rives served as an officer of the American Colonization Society, believing that deportation of slaves to Africa would expel "this consuming cancer of our permanent prosperity." Living abroad in Europe Rives had pondered the "melancholy anomaly of domestic slavery in our free institutions." In an 1837 US Senate debate, Rives admitted slavery was "in the eye of religion, philanthropy and reason an evil," telling pro-slavery senator John C. Calhoun, "You shock the generous sentiments of human nature . . . you outrage the spirit of the age." Rives would later claim that Southern slavery would fade if the North would not interfere "in the free and spontaneous action of the state sovereignties, under the humane influence of a humane and enlightened public opinion . . . the moral and Christian sentiments of the people of the South."

He once claimed he was a slave owner "from considerations of humanity than of interest." Although he liberated a few of his slaves, Rives sold 114 slaves in 1860, only a year before the Peace Conference. One of the purchasers was future fellow Peace Delegate James Seddon.[91]

In defense of Virginia's honor, Rives rhetorically asked of his fellow peace delegates: "Can she not call together a convention of this kind and suggest measures to be considered by it for the purpose of saving an imperiled country?" He explained that Virginia "knew well" that the Peace Conference would be merely an "advisory conference." He chidingly asked Noyes if he knew the history behind the Constitution, reminding him that Virginia "did the same thing previous to the adoption of that Constitution, which she is doing now."[92]

Speaking in the tones and cadence of an old Virginia statesman who had long moved in rarified social and political strata, Rives pronounced:

"There are occasions, sir, in the history of nations, when men should rise far above the rules of special pleading. This is one of them." He recalled that in the country's early days, "there were gentlemen then, who took the same ground that gentlemen do now, who sought by the use of dilatory pleas, by interposing objections, temporary in their nature, to prevent and delay action upon the great national questions then under consideration." Now Virginia, "in a time of great peril, when the whole country is convulsed, when the existence and perpetuity of the Government is in danger," has again invited her "sister states" to "see whether they cannot devise some method to avoid the danger and save the country."[93]

Always looking stately beneath his white hair and in dark suits, Rives wondered: "What purpose can gentlemen have in interposing these dilatory pleas, objections merely for delay, when we all know that Congress is now waiting for—actually inviting the action of this Conference?" He stressed that the crisis was "infinitely more important now than it was then," at the time of the Constitution, when there was "no disintegration of the states," compared to the seven who had recently seceded. "Virginia loves the Union," Rives exhorted. "She cherishes all its glorious memories . . . proud of its history and of her own connection with it." But she has "no apprehension as to her future destiny," surviving either in the Union or out of it, and standing in "her own strength and power if necessary." Virginia's delegates were not there at the Peace Conference in a "spirit of supplication" or "intimidation." Rather, they called the delegates "here as brothers, as friends, as patriots," whose future suffering Virginia would share "equally."[94]

Virginia was "now the neutral ground between two embattled legions, between two angry, excited, and hostile portions of the Union." To expect her to ignore the "excitement" and "apprehensions which pervade the country; to expect that they should not begin to look after the safety of their interests and their institutions, were to expect something superhuman." Virginia wanted to "save the country, to allay these apprehensions, to restore a broken confidence." Turning to his "Republican friends," Rives asked if they would "not take warning" and ignore the example of "pretended prophets of old, who cried, 'Peace! Peace! when there was no peace.'" Today's "political prophets" were claiming no danger, he fretted.[95]

Rives pointed out that the "loyal South," after the secession of seven fellow slave states, was "reduced to an utterly helpless minority" of seven or eight states to "stand in your national councils against a united North!" The remaining South could not retain its rights by "mere sufferance, and we will not." If the other Southern states had remained in the Union, "we might have secured our rights in a fair contest." Rives recalled his own observation of other revolutions, especially as ambassador in France, "where interest was arrayed against interest, friend against friend, brother against brother. I have seen the pavements of Paris covered, and her gutters running with fraternal blood! God forbid that I should see this horrid picture repeated in my own country; and yet it will be, sir, if we listen to the counsels urged here!"[96]

For thirty years he had opposed any "constitutional right of secession," Rives recalled, but now theories had been replaced by facts. "I condemn the secession of States," he proclaimed. "I am not here to justify it. I detest it. But the great fact is still before us." Since "force will never bring them together," there must be negotiation, for which Virginia would present "herself as a mediator to bring back those who have left us." Addressing himself to "Republican gentlemen," he made clear his "wish to inaugurate your power and your administration over the whole Union," with a nation "worth governing." He asked how the new administration would function in a divided country convulsed by civil war. "You cannot carry on your Government without money," he said. "Where is the capitalist who will advance you money under existing circumstances?"[97]

"You may spend millions of treasure, you may shed oceans of blood, but you cannot conquer any five or seven States of this Union," which was an "utter absurdity," Rives pronounced. "I respect the power which our army and our navy give to our nation, but our army and navy are impotent in such a crisis as this." He melodramatically recalled from his years in France the scenes of revolution as "regiment after regiment throw down their arms and rush into the arms of the people, of their fellow-citizens, and thus oppose, by military strength, the government under which their organization was formed. Will you repeat such occurrences here? Will you 'destroy the imperishable renown of this nation'? No! I answer for you all—you will not. Now, we, representatives of the South and of Virginia, ask of this Convention, the only body under heaven that can do it, to interpose and save us from a repetition of the scenes of blood which some of us have witnessed."[98]

Rives emphasized that the "patriotic" Resolutions Committee had labored for two weeks "earnestly and zealously," with a final result that while "not satisfactory to Virginia in all respects, will yet receive her sanction, and the sanction of the border states." Virginia was "yielding much" to "give peace to the country." Now "just in sight of land," he demanded, "when we are just entering a safe harbor, shall we turn about and circumnavigate the ocean to find an unknown shore?" Rives admonition was resolute: "No, sir! no! Let us enter the harbor of safety now opened before us."[99]

Indignantly, Rives noted his Massachusetts colleague had stated "he abhorred slavery," which "grated harshly on my ears." In contrast, he claimed, "we of the South, we of Virginia, may not and do not like many of the institutions of Massachusetts, but we cannot and we will not say that we abhor them," chastising the Northerner for his bad manners. And Rives reminded him that "it was New England that fastened this institution upon us" by its long advocacy of the slave trade. He wondered: "Shall she reproach us for its existence now?" New England's present attitude was "very unfair," Rives regretted, since "she is herself responsible for the existence of slavery" and "is now our fiercest opponent." This was unlike New Jersey and Pennsylvania, Rives pointed out with political acuity, "who have not this responsibility, have always stood by the South, and I believe they always will."[100]

Rives explained that Southerners better understood this subject, knowing it was "not a question of slavery at all . . . but of race."

Southerners knew from long experience that the "best position for the African race to occupy is one of unmitigated legal subjection," he insisted. "We have the negroes with us; you have not. We must deal with them as our experience and wisdom dictate; with that you have nothing to do." How would Massachusetts handle this race if roles were reversed, he asked. Rives insisted that the "present position of the negroes of the United States is the best one they could occupy, both for the superior and inferior race."[101]

His history instruction complete, Rives exclaimed to his Northern colleagues, but especially to Massachusetts: "It will cost you nothing to yield what we ask. Say, and let it be said in the Constitution, that you will not interfere with slavery in the District, or in the States, or in the Territories. Permit the free transit of our slaves from one State to another, and in the language of the patriarch, 'let there be peace between you and me.'"[102]

Ohio's Thomas Ewing did not disagree with Rives. He proclaimed he had always "discouraged" talk about slavery by Northerners, as "we have faults enough ourselves; let us consider and try to correct them, before we interest ourselves so much in those of our neighbors." He would oppose any extension of slavery into the North, for which there was no threat whatsoever, as everybody knew. "As one northern man, I do not want the negroes distributed throughout the North," he confessed. "We have got enough of them now. I have watched the operation of this emigration of slaves to the North. Ten negroes will commit more petty thefts than one thousand white men. We cannot permit them to come into Ohio. Wherever they have been permitted to come, it has almost cost us a rebellion. Before we begin to preach abolition I think we had better see what is to be done with the negroes."[103]

Had Virginia freed her slaves thirty years earlier, as debated, "her power would have increased tenfold," as "free labor would have come in to take the place of slave labor, and the banks of the Potomac and the James would have blossomed as the rose," Ewing imagined. But Northerners had effectively discouraged the South from independently freeing its own slaves by taking the "abolition into its own hands, and from the day she did so, we hear no more of abolition in Virginia." Coercing the South would never work, he knew, but "these northern men will not listen to reason," preferring to "keep on making eloquent speeches—their pulpits thunder against the sin of slaveholding," with "all grades of speech and thought are made use of, and the sickening sentimentalism of some of them is disgusting" and "full of falsehood." Quoting Scripture, Ewing himself preached, "It would be far better for each man to look for the beam in his own eyes before he troubles himself about the mote in his neighbor's."[104]

Ewing also chided England for its abolitionism, citing "misery" in India, where he noted "two hundred thousand of her subjects were starved to death in one province of Hindustan." And then there was Ireland! There two million died from famine, and "God knows how many more would have perished but for the relief sent from this country," he said. Ewing boasted he had never favored "any of these denunciations of southern slaveholders and slavery." Instead, he urged acknowledging "mutual faults," admitting the North turned anti-slavery only after it became no longer profitable, and should now permit the South to "deal with it as she chooses."[105]

The white and black races could never unite, Ewing opined, nor could they "occupy the same country upon an equality." He asserted that free laborers would never work with blacks. The only solution was to "divide the common territory—divide it fairly, honestly." The North had territory enough, enough for 150 million for another 150 years, and need not worry about what happens in New Mexico, he said, pleading: "If gentlemen are found here who wish to make trouble, who cannot see the peril we are in, and how easily we can avoid the danger which threatens us, I shall be much pained, but not half so much as I shall be, to see this Union broken up and the government destroyed."[106]

Maine's US Senator Lot Morrill rose in response to Ewing's "superfluous" commentary about the North and its "sentimentalism." He had been described derisively by a North Carolina newspaper "as a signer to a paper contributing money for running of fugitive slaves."[107] Morrill

asked Ewing and others: "Do you propose to make war upon the sentiments, the principles of the North? If you do, we may as well drop the
discussion here." He pledged, "The people of the North will never sacrifice their principles." It was "entirely useless for you to urge war upon
the sentiments or opinions of the North." Too much talk was focused
on the North, he complained, when the "true question here is, 'What
will Virginia do? How does Virginia stand?'" Virginia held the "keys
of peace or war," he announced, able either to block the government's
"attempts to assert its legal authority" or "dictate the terms upon which
the Union is to be preserved." Morrill complained that Virginia was
abetting secession, arming her people, and gathering funds for resistance
to the government.[108]

Unsurprisingly, Virginia's firebrand, Seddon, responded. He
affirmed clearly that Virginia would go a "little farther than that" and
would "not permit coercion," while still seeking the "very last means of
restoring peace to the Union" with hope to "preserve the peace and to
save this country from war."[109]

Not relenting one bit, Morrill retorted that he did "not misunder-
stand the position of Virginia" at all, that she in fact was "armed to the
teeth" and had adopted an "attitude of menace," giving "aid and comfort to those who trample upon the laws and defy the authority of this
government." He posed to Seddon a "plain question" in need of a "frank
answer." If the Peace Conference accepted the Resolutions Committee's
amendments, would Virginia then "sustain the government and maintain its integrity, while the people are considering and acting on the new
proposals of amendment to the Constitution? If she will not do this, if
this proposition does not meet the heart of Virginia, there is no use," he
declared.[110]

Unhesitatingly, Seddon promised Morrill that Virginia "solemnly
pledged to resist coercion . . . to the very last extremity," with resolve that
was "unchanged and unchangeable," considering that "this a government
of love and not of force." And he shot back at Morrill his own question:
"Is it the purpose or is it the policy of the incoming administration to

attempt to execute the laws of the United States in the seceded States by an armed force?"

Morrill replied he could not and would not "answer his inquiry from any personal knowledge of my own." Instead, he was confirming that Virginia would not promise to accept the majority report but would "resist the enforcement of the laws in the seceded states," making her "mediation" unacceptable.

Stockton of New Jersey demanded to know why Morrill was pressing "such charges" against Virginia, when so "unfounded; we don't wish to hear them." This was followed by "considerable confusion in the conference, which was promptly suppressed" by President Tyler. Morrill insisted that the "gentlemen need not be disturbed or excited. I have accomplished my object."[111]

Vermont's L. E. Chittenden later recalled a nearly violent altercation between Stockton and Morrill, with Stockton shouting, "Silence sir!" while rushing, as a "gigantic form," toward Morrill with "violent and angry gesticulations." Reputedly Stockton exclaimed: "We will not permit our Southern friends to be charged with bad faith, and with violating an agreement! No black Republican shall—" Then twenty or thirty Republicans "surrounded" Morrill like a "living wall," with one of them telling Stockton, "Back to your seat, you bully!" Tyler decisively intervened, shouting, "Order! Shame upon the delegate who would dishonor this conference by violence!" Although nobody was "proud" of the episode, Chittenden thought its "influence was excellent," showing the unflappability of the slightly built Maine senator.[112]

THE PLEA OF VIRGINIA

As to Seddon's question about Lincoln's plans, Morrill surmised that if "he and his administration do not use every means which the Constitution has given them to assert the authority of the Government in all the States—to preserve the Union, and the Union in all its integrity, the people will be disappointed. I have felt and now feel the importance of the action of Virginia, and I have done what I could to learn here what we may expect from her."[113]

Virginia's George Summers then rose to speak, professing "my heart is full!" Disavowing any "coolness and deliberation," he emotively pledged his love to the Union, saying "there is not an incident in its history that is not precious to me," and "I do not wish to survive its dissolution." But he could "not shut my eyes to events which are daily transpiring among a people who are excited and anxious, who are apprehensive that their rights are in danger—who are solicitous for—who will do as much to preserve their rights as any people," and who must be "calmed and quieted." The Peace Conference "must act," or "I almost fear to contemplate the prospect that will open before us." Noting they had already been in session fifteen days, he said "if we are to save this country we must act speedily."[114]

Summers insisted Virginia had presented no ultimatum but only "invites a conference—she asks the States to confer together," expecting "reasonable concessions, reasonable guarantees, and with these she will be satisfied." Challenging his Maine colleague, he said they were there for one "single Purpose:—that purpose is to save the Union. Virginia claims no greater rights than any other State. She would not take them if they were offered." He announced he would support his fellow Virginian's proposals, which he conflated with Crittenden resolutions. He thought the states could adopt them "without any material sacrifice, and that they will adopt them if they have the opportunity."[115]

Otherwise, Summers wondered, "Shall we dissolve this body, and go home? Shall we risk all the fearful consequences which must follow? No, sir! No! We came here for *peace*. Virginia came here for *peace*. We will not be impracticable. You, representatives of the free states, will not be impracticable. Therefore, I tell you that it is my firm belief that the people of Virginia WILL accept the proposals of amendment to the Constitution as reported by the majority of the committee."[116]

Summers said Virginians were "for the Union, provided their rights

can be secured; provided, they can have proper and honorable guarantees. It is useless to discuss now whether they are right or wrong. Such
is the condition of affairs now, and it is too late to enter into the causes
which produced it. We must deal with things as they are." He appealed
to his New England colleagues especially for "every consideration which
can move a friend, which can influence a patriot, which can govern the
action of a statesman . . . to consider our dangers, and not to refuse us
the little boon we ask, when the consequences of that refusal must be so
awful." He implored, "Can you not afford to make a little sacrifice, when
we make one so great? Can you not yield to us what is a mere matter of
opinion with you, but what is so vital with us? Will you not put us in a
position where we can stand with our people, and let us and you stand
together in the Union? I have no delicacy here. The importance of our
action with me, transcends all other considerations. I do not hesitate to
appeal to New England for help in this crisis."[117]

But even if New England "refuses to come to our aid, it will not
alter my course or change my conviction," Summers promised. "I will
never give up the Union! Clouds may hang over it, storms and tempest
may assail it, the waves of dissolution may dash against it, but so far as
my feeble hand can support it, that support shall be given to it while I
live!" He promised to do as George Washington had promised during
the Revolution to "gather the last handful of faithful men, carry them
to the mountains of Western Virginia, and there set up the flag of the
Union." It "shall be defended there against all assailants until the friends
of freedom and liberty from all parts of the civilized world shall rally
around it, and again establish it in triumph and glory over every portion
of a restored and united country."[118]

Summers suggested, if necessary, a new confederation centered on
the Ohio River Valley, if the "representatives of the two extremes will not
give us the benefit of their counsel and assistance, the Central States, and
the great Northwest, must take the matter into their own hands. North
Carolina, Virginia, Kentucky, Tennessee, with Pennsylvania, New Jersey,
and other States near them, must unite with Ohio and the Northwest to

save the country. They have the power to do it—they must do it," but only as a "last alternative," and "one to which I hope and pray we may never be driven."[119]

His oratorical finale appealing to hope for the future, Summers warned that the "consequences of farther disagreement are too great, the crisis is too important to permit mere sectional differences, mere pride of opinion, party shackles or party platforms to control the action of any gentleman here. The Republic shall not be divided. The nation shall not be destroyed. The patriotism of the people will yet save the country against all its enemies."[120]

Responding to Summers, Seddon, and Rives, a Republican newspaper in Washington, DC, complained that "position in which Virginia has been placed by the expressed opinions of her legislature, and of a majority of her representatives in the Peace Congress, is a cause of great and increasing humiliation to the citizens of that patriotic state." The newspaper discerned that according to "her men in authority, Virginia is here negotiating for terms of accord, but declaring at the same time that, whatever terms of accord may be agreed upon, she will take sides against the government, if any attempt is made to enforce the laws in the (so called) seceded states." Virginia had "armed herself to protect rebellion, and pledged herself to protect rebellion, and yet comes here on a pretended errand of conciliation. She is, in one breath, asking for terms for herself, and, in another breath, declaring that no terms will dissuade her from her purpose to resist the government, if the government attempts practically to assert its authority." The paper also cited Virginia's "extremist demands upon the slavery question," and credited Maine's Senator Morrill for having "unmasked" Virginia's real agenda.[121]

An Ohio newspaper reported a widely repeated assertion that a majority of state delegations were on course to voting for the Resolution Committee's proposals; Virginia, North Carolina, and Missouri were among the slave states voting no, and Kentucky, Maryland, and

Tennessee were to vote affirmatively. On the key Virginia delegation, Tyler, Seddon, and John Brockenbrough would urge their state's convention to reject the proposals, while Virginia's Rives and Summers would urge approval.[122] A Cincinnati newspaper reported that the Virginia commissioners "think the object of the Peace Conference unattainable, and will attempt, to-morrow, to force a vote. Failing this they will probably move an adjournment." According to a New York newspaper, "Mr. Tyler expresses a fear that nothing will be accomplished, and the belief that unless something is done by the convention, Virginia, North Carolina, and Maryland will secede as soon as possible after the 4th of March. He hopes something will yet be done, but is much depressed at the prospects of the country."[123]

Trying to sound hopeful, an Indiana Democratic newspaper looked to the Peace Conference "as a last resort; if they fail in agreeing on some peaceable adjustment, and Mr. Lincoln persists in his purpose of coercing; seceding States into the Union, then, indeed, it is only left for the future historian to record the downfall and utter ruin of the noblest government, the light of heaven ever shore upon." But it also more forlornly reported that "faint hopes are entertained at Washington for any basis of adjustment will be reached by the Peace Conference," whose members "have telegraphed to their friends to the above effect."[124]

"Already several members of the Peace Conference have left," claimed a skeptical Vermont newspaper. "It is not likely to serve any other purpose than to gain time, which is of itself an important object," for "if the border states can be induced to wait for the inauguration of Mr. Lincoln and the development of the policy of his administration, as they now seem likely to do, we think they would find they have no valid cause of complaint, and that their interests will be better promoted by remaining in the Union than by joining the Southern Confederacy under the lead of Jeff Davis."[125]

A Cincinnati newspaper was even more acerbic: "There is going to be no Union saved nor reconstructed on the foundation of treason, rebellion and stealing, whatever the convention of ancients at Washington may advise, nothing of that sort will ever be done." The Peace Conference if nothing else, would compel waverers to decide: "The time is at hand when all the folly, subterfuge and falsehood of concession, coercion and new guarantees will be swept away, and the border states will have to meet the naked question of Union or disunion."[126]

A Wheeling, Virginia, newspaper warned, "If the recommendations of this Conference should so fail, they will do much more harm than good, for this fact will tend to intensify the feeling in the Border slave States, and give a foothold for secession to say that any hope of reconciliation is at an end." The paper offered a conspiratorial view on the organizers' real purpose:

> We have heretofore expressed the opinion that the intensifying, at a critical juncture, of the secession feeling in Virginia, with a view to precipitate the action of the convention, was the secret motive of the originators of the peace conference. We have not yet seen anything in its action to the contrary; and, in further confirmation, it will be observed that, as yet, the Convention at Richmond is doing nothing, but awaiting the action of the Conference.[127]

The peace commissioners adjourned, no doubt exhausted by the soaring oratory, the confrontations, the implied threats, the emotional pleas for conciliation, and the repeated citations of civil war as the inevitable and blood soaked penalty of their failure. They rejected a motion to meet earlier than the usual 11:00 A.M. the next morning, even though they had much still to do, to debate, ponder, and anguish over. Most if not all delegates were hoping for compromise yet, but had very little time yet to achieve it. Secession conventions were meeting in states like Arkansas, Missouri, and above all Virginia. And a train carrying the president-elect was slowly but inexorably meandering through the Midwest, into the Northeast. Lincoln was giving speeches that avoided specifics, exuding good cheer, shunning firm commitments, and listening carefully, very carefully, for all hints of the opinions of the throngs who came to see the spectacle of their new rustic chief executive from the prairie of Illinois. The Peace Conference, all of official Washington, and both the North and South anxiously awaited his arrival in the federal capital, which General Scott was desperate to secure.

SIX
SECURING THE CAPITOL

I have said that any man who attempted by force or unparliamentary disorder to obstruct or interfere with the lawful
count of the electoral vote for President and Vice President
of the United States should be lashed to the muzzle of a
twelve-pounder and fired out of a window of the Capitol.

—Lieutenant General Winfield Scott

Abraham Lincoln was formally announced as president of the United
States on February 13, 1861, in a joint session of Congress. The Electoral
College vote was read aloud by outgoing Vice President John Breckinridge,
a pro-Southern Kentuckian who had been one of Lincoln's three opponents in the 1860 election. All 131 members of the Peace Conference had
been authorized by special vote of the US House of Representatives to
attend the historic session. Of course, it was this election of the first openly
anti-slavery president that had ignited the national crisis that prompted
the creation of the Peace Conference. Many peace commissioners shared

162

carriages together for the 1.3-mile ride down Pennsylvania Avenue from Willard's Hotel to the expanding US Capitol, whose sprawling edifice sat amid stone blocks and lumber, with timber construction cranes perched overhead, preparing to mount the new giant dome.

US Army commander Lieutenant General Winfield Scott had, with others, heard many reports of plots to block the electoral vote count. From his new headquarters at Winder Building by the White House he diligently reinforced the federal city with what forces he could to deter any disruption to constitutional process. The forces totaled about 480 men of the army, supplementing 240 marines already based in the city. In January he told a congressional committee that he had received "80 to 90" letters, half of them anonymous, alleging plots aimed at Washington. Targets included the electoral vote count, but also the inauguration. He testified, "Some sort of conspiracy obviously exists, either for mischief or creating a false alarm."[1]

The presence and exertions of the aged general and war hero were reassuring to Unionist Washingtonians, and perhaps to many others who simply hoped for order. He personally inspected much of the city in his carriage, and when he arrived at army headquarters he was greeted by passersby who removed their hats and shouted, "God bless you, General!"[2]

Others were less grateful, and many Southerners saw his securing the capital by armed force as intimidation, during the Peace Conference no less. This was a special betrayal, since Scott was a Virginian. A month before the electoral vote count, a Virginia congressman attacked Scott in a speech to the House of Representatives:

> There was a time in her history when Virginia . . . when asked for her jewels, could point to her sons . . . Jefferson, Henry, Madison, Monroe, and the immortal Washington. . . . She too, in this age, has been proud of another son, whom, she gave to the nation as the commander-in-chief of its armies. That son I, together with her representatives in the leg-islature, in her name, have honored with a sword for his brilliant

163

achievements in arms. Little did I think . . . that that sword was so soon to be drawn against her who gave him birth. Here, sir, in sight of her own blue hills . . . is this ungrateful son planning his campaign, and planting his batteries for her subjugation. . . . She discards him from her bosom.[3]

On February 8, somewhat "impulsively," after that day's session of the Peace Conference, Vermont's Lucius Chittenden headed the few blocks over from Willard's to General Scott's office, to "learn whether any preparations had been made to secure the undisturbed counting of the electoral vote." After sending in his card, Scott summoned him in while prone upon a sofa, then raising "his gigantic frame to a sitting posture." The "infirmity in the movements of his body . . . was forgotten the moment he spoke, for there was no suspicion of weakness in his mind," Chittenden observed.[4]

"A Chittenden of Vermont!" Scott had bellowed in greeting, with a "voice which rang like an order through a clear-toned trumpet," proving his vigor. "Why, that was a good name when Ethan Allen took Ticonderoga! I know the Vermonters—I have commanded them in battle. Well, Vermont must be as true today as she has always been. What can the commander of the army do for Vermont?"

After hearing Chittenden's concern about the electoral vote, Scott told him he had "suppressed that infamy" and that he had the "assurance" of the Vice President Breckinridge, whose word was "reliable." Breckinridge would announce the election of the president and vice president, and "no appeal to force will be attempted." Scott surmised a "few drunken rowdies may risk and lose their lives" but no "revolution" would occur.[5]

No stranger to martial rhetoric and flamboyance, Scott further assured Chittenden:

I have said that any man who attempted by force or unparliamentary disorder to obstruct or interfere with the lawful count of the electoral vote for President and Vice President of the United States should be lashed to the muzzle of a twelve-pounder and fired out of a window of the Capitol. I would manure the hills of Arlington with fragments of his body, were he a senator or chief magistrate of my native state! It is my duty to suppress insurrection—my duty.[6]

Five days later, Chittenden was among the attending peace commissioners at the US Capitol to see for himself if Scott's promise of calm during the electoral vote count was validated. He carefully recalled that his "certificate of membership enabled me to pass the guard without difficulty, and by the courtesy of a doorkeeper I secured a seat in the gallery, where my view of the hall was unobstructed." By noon, he remembered, the galleries were "comfortably filled, and all the seats and standing-room in the hall were occupied, except the seats reserved" for senators and representatives.[7] No gentlemen were admitted to the ladies' galleries, not even their escorts, as one Washington newspaper described the strictness.[8]

In the US Capitol that day only visitors with passes signed by the US House Speaker or vice president were given entrance to the electoral vote count in the House chamber. Passes from senators and representatives did not count, nor could they usher in their friends. "Consequently the amount of profanity launched forth against the guards would have completely annihilated them if words could kill," Chittenden said. "The result was that, although solid humanity outside could have been measured by the acre, the inside of the building was less crowded than usual, and there was no difficulty in passing from room to room in all parts of the Capitol."[9] A Washington newspaper confirmed there was "considerable amount of swearing" from certain "amiable individuals" angry about their lack of access.[10]

As a zealous New England Republican, Chittenden was very aware that Southerners were a "vast majority" and Northerners "very few" among the audience thronging the gallery of the still relatively new, expansive and windowless House chamber, whose light poured down from skylights spanning the ceiling. "To one who knew nothing of the hot treason which was seething beneath the quiet exterior of the spectators, the exercises would have appeared to be tame and uninteresting," he suspiciously observed. From within the chamber, except guards at the doors checking passes, there were no soldiers visible.[11]

Sitting next to Chittenden in the gallery was a friend who lived in Washington and recognized the Vermonter:

> Aware that he had organized a selected body of loyal men into a regiment of which he was colonel, more than a month previously, I expressed my surprise at his presence in citizen's dress, and said, "I supposed you would be on duty to-day with your regiment." He smilingly replied, "We are minute men, you know; that is, we enter a room as private citizens, and come out of it a minute afterwards, a regiment, armed with loaded repeating-rifles. Such a thing might happen here to-day, if the necessity arose. My men are within easy call, and their rifles are not far away. Some men get excited on election day, and require control. However, I think this is to be a very quiet election."[12]

Chittenden noticed two adjoining committee rooms on the chamber's north side closed to all persons; he supposed the rooms were to serve as the arsenal for these "minute men" if needed.

The crowd quieted as the House of Representatives came to order and formally summoned colleagues in the US Senate to join them for the official count of the Electoral College's votes. This vote count from the presidential electors of each state was nearly always a relatively unexceptional technicality. Everyone already knew the result. But this particular result would split the country, and many wondered how exactly, or even whether, it would actually happen according to law and procedure.

Chittenden saw a "gathering of Southern members on the floor below me, which a young member from Virginia (whose name is omitted, because he is now, I have no doubt, an earnest friend of the Union) was addressing with much gesticulation," urging that then was "the best time to give them some music, before the Senate came in." By music he apparently meant disruptive protests, but was unpersuasive. Members of the US Senate were then announced and processed forward, led by Vice President Breckinridge, taking their seats in front as Representatives respectfully stood in silence. Breckinridge took the chair usually reserved for the Speaker of the House, while one senator and two representatives, as vote counters, sat nearby at the house clerk's desk, amid "absolute silence."

In a clearly audible but conversational tone, Breckinridge announced, "It is my duty to open the certificates of election in the presence of the two Houses, and I now proceed to the performance of that duty." He was easily heard, without any projection, because the new chamber was carefully crafted for acoustics, the previous chamber having been infamously inhospitable to the hearing of speeches. It had been, ironically, Jefferson Davis, soon to be the Confederacy's new president, who oversaw this accomplishment, first as US war secretary, then as US senator. He had been determined that the fast-growing nation should have a great and timeless temple for its lawmakers.[13]

"There is an unmeasured, latent energy in the personal presence of a strong man," Chittenden admiringly said of Breckinridge, despite their deep political differences. "If he could be remembered only for his services on that day, Vice-President Breckinridge would fill a high place in the gallery of American statesmen, and merit the permanent gratitude of the American people."[14] Now age forty-nine, Breckinridge had become America's youngest ever vice president four years earlier. Clean shaven and imposing, from a famous Kentucky political dynasty, he would soon face federal treason charges for accepting commission as a general in the new Confederate army, even while still a newly appointed US senator from Kentucky, replacing John Crittenden. In 1864 Breckinridge was part of a Confederate army that unsuccessfully attacked the federal capital, and late in the war he became Confederate war secretary, replacing James Seddon.

But on February 13, 1861, Breckinridge punctiliously followed his script. "He knew that the day was one of peril to the republic—that he was presiding over what appeared to be a joint meeting of two deliberative bodies, but which, beneath the surface, was a cauldron of inflammable materials, heated almost to the point of explosion," Chittenden recounted melodramatically but accurately. "But he had determined that the result of the count should be declared, and his purpose was manifested in every word and gesture." The Vermonter abolitionist Republican was effusive about the pro-slavery Democrat and soon to be Confederate that day: "Jupiter never ruled a council on Olympus with a firmer hand. It was gloved, but there was iron beneath the glove."[15]

One House member rose in an attempt to disrupt the proceedings, drawing a firm rebuke from Breckinridge: "Except questions of order, no motion can be entertained." But the congressman insisted on a point of order to protest the heavy security presence: "Was the count of the electoral vote to proceed under menace? Should members be required to perform a constitutional duty before the janizaries of Scott were withdrawn from the hall?" The vice president rejected the objection: "The point of order is not sustained."[16]

Breckinridge began opening envelopes from the various states, starting with Maine, which voted Lincoln, provoking slight but suppressed applause. US Senator Stephen Douglas successfully proposed dispensing with reading aloud from various state certificates, so the electoral votes ended more quickly. Chittenden recalled the only other interruption to the somber proceeding was an audible "expression of mingled contempt, respect, ridicule, and veneration" when South Carolina's vote was declared. And then, "In a silence absolutely profound, the Vice-President arose from his seat, and, standing erect, possibly the most dignified and imposing person in that presence, declared: 'That Abraham Lincoln, of Illinois, having received a majority of the whole number of electoral votes, is duly elected President of the United States for the four years beginning on the fourth day of March, 1861; and Hannibal Hamlin, of Maine, having received a majority of the whole number of electoral votes, is duly elected Vice-President of the United States for the same term.'" The vote was 180 for Lincoln, 72 for Breckinridge, 39 for John

Bell, and 12 for Stephen Douglas, although Douglas had been second in the popular vote.[17]

It was done. But then Chittenden observed that "a dozen angry, disappointed men were on their feet before the door had closed upon the last senator, clamoring for recognition by the speaker," and for "a few minutes the tumult was so great that it was impossible to restore order," with the "concentrated venom of the secessionists was ejected upon the General of the Army," Winfield Scott. "There were jeers for the 'rail-splitter,' sharp and fierce shouts for 'cheers for Jeff. Davis,' and 'cheers for South Carolina.'" But mostly "hard names and curses for 'old Scott' broke out everywhere on the floor and in the gallery of the crowded hall," as the previously quiet "spectators seemed in a moment turned to madmen." They shouted, "'Superannuated old dotard!' 'Traitor to the state of his birth!' 'Coward!' 'Free-state pimp!'" among "any number of similar epithets . . . showered upon him." The now unruly mob demanded the "old traitor" remove his "minions," his "janizaries," his "hirelings," his "bluecoated slaves," from the Capitol. Chittenden "glanced around" to notice "my military friend, and the quiet gentlemen I had noticed near by, had vanished—where and for what purpose I knew only too well," and for a "few moments I thought they would officiate in a revolution."[18]

Fortunately, Chittenden found that the "power of the human lung is limited, and howling quickly exhausts it." As the House Speaker pounded the chamber back to order, the "danger inside had passed." Chittenden left the Capitol by the north, Senate chamber side, and "entering the first carriage I found, I ordered the colored driver to take me to my hotel." There the carriage driver maneuvered "without difficulty" through the crowd, which was "orderly and undemonstrative," thanks to two batteries of artillery across the street from the Capitol. The troops were "quiet themselves, but none the less causes of the quiet around them." Beyond view of the intimidating guns placed by General Scott, Pennsylvania Avenue heading northwest toward Willard's Hotel was "choked with a howling, angry mob," around which Chittenden's carriage, and presumably other peace commissioners returning from the Capitol, "escaped" to the rear entrance of Willard's Hotel on F Street, avoiding the main entrance on the chaotic avenue.[19]

With Chittenden and other delegates safely in their hotel rooms, the "mob had possession of the avenue far into the night," as "reputable people kept in-doors, and left the patriots who were so injured by the election of Mr. Lincoln to consume bad whiskey and cheer for Jeff Davis undisturbed." Crittenden was relieved there was "much street-fighting, many arrests by the police, but no revolution." He credited the "joint influence" of General Scott and Vice President Breckinridge, between whom "perfect understanding existed" about upholding their duties. To them the "country was indebted for the peaceful count of the electoral vote, the proclamation of the election of Mr. Lincoln, and the suppression of an attempted revolution on that day," Chittenden was certain. "These two men, both Southern-born, on the 13th of February conducted the republic safely through one of the most imminent perils that ever threatened its existence."[20]

Afterward an Arkansas congressman indignantly "suggested that Lieutenant General Scott be also informed that there is no use for mercenaries around the Capitol, as the electoral votes have been counted."[21]

The son of Senator William Seward privately reported: "General Scott had his troops all under arms, out of sight, but ready, with guns loaded and horses harnessed; so they could take the field at a few minutes' notice. But there was no enemy."[22] Seward himself would later claim that he had personally hired one hundred local ruffians to stand by in the House galleries in case needed.[23]

Less dramatically, a Washington newspaper given to understatement reported that "police and other officials" at the Capitol had taken what "looked like precautionary measures against any possible interruption, from whatever quarter" during the Electoral College vote, with Capitol police "stationed in the passages around the Hall to keep back the crowd." The US House of Representatives' galleries were more "crowded than on any previous occasion this winter," but "thus far everything has passed off quietly." There had been a "crowd of rather hard-looking boys about the lobbies of the House Hall, and considerable hard swearing among them, but no further demonstration," with General Scott "keeping military forces stationed here in active readiness today, if perchance their services should have been needed."[24]

The "imposing ceremony of counting the electoral votes passed off in perfect quiet," a New York newspaper asserted, "yet not without the exhibition of the bad passions which animate the Breckinridge wing of the sham Democracy." During the opening prayer by the House chaplain, the Methodist Reverend Stockton, a "chivalrous Virginian" rudely "strode out of the Hall with the air of old Booth in 'Richard III,'" referring to famed actor Junius Booth, father of John Wilkes, "stamping his feet with such emphasis as to attract the attention of the crowded galleries." In the House cloakroom he greeted colleagues "with a loud, horse laugh, accompanied by words equally loud and disrespectful to the House and to the solemn occasion." The newspaper lamented that if "conduct like this is consistent with the character of a gentleman, and the dignity of a legislator, in Virginia, at the present day, the fact only furnishes another sad illustration of the decay of civilization in that ancient commonwealth." Also to be regretted was the procession of senators, who appeared like "animals in Noah's Ark," paired off two by two, typically with sectional political allies instead of showing bipartisan unity. Not noticing the acrimony reported by others, the newspaper reported the House galleries were "filled with an audience of unusual respectability," almost "filled exclusively with well-dressed gentlemen, to the exclusion of rowdies and ruffians, and this fact will account for the good order which prevailed." Yet the New York newspaper admitted that "in addition to other fears" about the Electoral College vote, the "blowing up of the Capitol was regarded as an event not impossible," so every night "thorough examination of the cellars and vaults of the building was made by the Capitol police, to be sure that no explosive materials had been clandestinely deposited there."[25]

A Pennsylvania newspaper sarcastically reported, with exaggeration, that "for the first time in the history of this country has it become necessary to overawe the members of the National Congress with a military force of 2000 men, in order to make them do their duty, and to act as a body guard to the Black Republican members of the Senate and House." It claimed the capital of the United States now "presents the appearance of a European capital filled with glittering swords and bayonets, and the upholders of all despotic governments, the soldiers." It called the claims that a "Gunpowder Plot was on foot, to prevent the counting of the votes on Wednesday last . . . only a pretext to enable the leaders of the Black Republican Party to perfect their plans" in what was an "outrage upon civilization."[26]

In contrast, a Vermont newspaper hailed the "resolute and soldierly arrangements of Gen. Scott to put down by force of arms any attempt on the Capitol by revolutionary mobs and traitorous concocters of insurrection." There could be no doubt of an "intention to break up Congress and to prevent not only the inauguration of Mr. Lincoln, but also the formal counting and announcement of the electoral vote in his favor and at the same time to start the Southern Confederacy as the government of the nation." If the plot was abandoned, "it is from a conviction in the minds of the plotters that the attempt would fail, and with the failure would come the destruction of all their nefarious and traitorous schemes."[27]

LINCOLN'S WHISTLE-STOP TOUR

The focus of all this controversy, president-elect Lincoln had been traveling by train for much of six days at the point of the electoral vote count. He had left his native Springfield, Illinois, early on the morning of February 8, not reaching Washington until the 23rd. In the late afternoon on February 14 he received word of the completed Electoral College vote, about which he had worried some, while at a public event at the state Capitol in Columbus, Ohio.

He slowly meandered through the Mideast, stopping at rail stations, greeting crowds, and giving optimistic but vague speeches. At a reception on February 12 in Cincinnati he declared in typical fashion for that period: "I deem it my duty . . . that I should wait until the last moment, for a development of the present national difficulties before I express myself decidedly what course I shall pursue."[28] Later that day he told German immigrants: "It is not my nature, when I see a people borne down by the weight of shackles—the oppression of tyranny—to make their life more bitter by heaping upon them greater burdens; but rather would I do all in my power to raise the yoke, than to do anything that would tend to crush them."[29]

At times Lincoln was humorous. On the previous day, February 11, he remarked in Indianapolis, amid laughter, that Secessionists viewed the Union not as a marriage but a "sort of free love arrangement, to be maintained on what that sect calls passionate attraction." Earlier that day he had deployed biblical imagery when telling another Indianapolis crowd, likening the Union to the indefatigable church, provoking applause, "When the people rise in masses in behalf of the Union and the liberties of their country, truly may it be said, 'The gates of hell shall not prevail against them.'" The next day in Columbus, Ohio, he told a crowd that he had "not maintained silence from any want of real anxiety" but hoped first to "gain a view of the whole field" while "being at liberty to modify and change the course of policy, as future events may make a change necessary." In Cleveland on February 15 he called the national crisis "artificial" and elicited laughter by saying, "Let it alone and it will go down of itself."

In a private letter to Senator William Seward on February 1, while still in Springfield, Lincoln was more specific, describing himself "inflexible" on extending slavery into the territories, opposing any "compromise which assists or permits the extension of the institution on soil owned by the nation," and to "any trick by which the nation is to acquire territory, and then allow some local authority to spread slavery over it," which was "obnoxious." Such compromises strove to "put us again on the high-road to a slave empire." He declared, "I am against it." As to "fugitive slaves, District of Columbia, slave trade among the slave states, and whatever springs of necessity from the fact that the institution is amongst us, I care but little, so that what is done be comely, and not altogether outrageous." Nor did he "care much about New Mexico, if further extension were hedged against."[30]

Lincoln's largely public silence about the Peace Conference was persuading Southern delegates that Republican delaying tactics were timed around Lincoln's arrival in Washington and his inauguration. "The convention cannot move a wheel until Lincoln gets here," privately wrote Missouri's fifty-two-year-old Peace Delegate Alexander Doniphan, a slave-owning Unionist and Mexican War hero who had legally defended Joseph Smith's Mormons on February 22. Late in life he turned to Christian faith after the death of his sons, joining the Christian Church in Liberty, Missouri, only one year before the Peace Conference. "But for my unchanging and undoubting faith, I should be the most miserable of men, but I have a most implicit confidence of again meeting my loved and lost ones in a brighter world," he wrote only months before coming to Washington. Doniphan faulted Abolitionism for precipitating national division. "Harmony and union," he said, required removing slavery from the "arena of politics," otherwise not even "Spalding's glue or anything else in the world" can plaster the nation back together.[31]

Of course, Doniphan did not trust Lincoln and assumed he was beholden to different Republican politicos: "If he is under Seward's guidance we will compromise in a day—if he is under the Chase and Greeley faction, then we may go home and tell Gabriel to blow for the nation will be dissolved in a few days or months at most, [Virginia] leading and all the rest following as they get ready."[32]

Doniphan, an old Whig, complained that "the Pubs," or Republicans, had "thirteen states to our seven and of course they can baffle us to all eternity—they are determined to know Lincoln's wishes in regard to the adjustment—whether we are to have any or none & what guarantees they will give." He claimed there were "at least fifty open and avowed office seekers in our Convention who have availed themselves of the opportunity of visiting Washington at the expense of their respective states & haveing [sic] at the same time some decent pretext for being here, so as not to seem to be mere cormorants & birds of prey." These Republican office seekers "only want to know Abraham's wishes in order to perform them," Doniphan surmised.[33]

"It is very humiliating for an American to know that the present & future destiny of his country is wholly in the hands of one man," Doniphan opined about the president-elect, and "that such a man as Lincoln—a man of no intelligence—no enlargement of views—as ridicously [sic] vain and fantastic as a country boy with his first red Morocco hat—easily flattered into a belief that he is King Canute & can say to the waves of revolution, 'Thus far shalt thou come and no farther.'"

As the "most adroit flatterer and manager," Doniphan fretted, Lincoln was "for the time being the arbiter of the destinies of this mighty nation—if rash may at any time ruin all beyond redemption. The Convention cannot move a wheel until Lincoln gets here."

Doniphan at least rejoiced that at the Peace Conference he and his allies had "beaten the ultras on every test vote since Lincoln's Buffalo and Albany speeches."

> But we are constantly looking for him to ruin everything by his ridiculously childish displays of eloquence and presidential taste and literary attainment. If his future administration should compare in statesmanship, diplomatic skill and military strategic [sic] with the speeches that have adorned and embellished his triumphant march to the Capital the slave states may well quake in their boots—for Austerlitz and Waterloo will be heard of no more after the victories of Black Republicanism are recorded.[34]

In Buffalo on February 16, Lincoln had once again avoided articulating clear policy, instead saying that since "these difficulties are without precedent, and have never been acted upon by any individual situated as I am, it is most proper I should wait and see the developments, and get all the light possible, so that when I do speak authoritatively, I may be as near right as possible." He added, "When I shall speak authoritatively, I hope to say nothing inconsistent with the Constitution, the Union, the rights of all the States, of each State, and of each section of the country, and not to disappoint the reasonable expectations of those who have confided to me their votes."[35]

On February 18 Lincoln addressed the New York legislature in Albany, once again demurring on his specific plans, explaining: "I do not propose to enter into an explanation of any particular line of policy, as to our present difficulties, to be adopted by the incoming administration." He preferred "that I should see everything, that I should hear everything, that I should have every light that can be brought within my reach, in order that, when I do so speak, I shall have enjoyed every opportunity to take correct and true ground; and for this reason I do not propose to speak at this time of the policy of the Government." He offered instead, "In the meantime, if we have patience, if we restrain ourselves, if we allow ourselves not to run off in a passion, I still have confidence that the Almighty, the Maker of the universe, will, through the instrumentality of this great and intelligent people, bring us through this as He has through all the other difficulties of our country."[36]

Back at the Peace Conference, Doniphan thought Lincoln's seeming equivocation infuriating and unbecoming. "Jesting aside Old Abe is simply an ignorant country buffoon who makes about as good stump speeches as Jim Craig, and will not be more fitted intellectually as President, but perhaps as disinterested," the Missourian harrumphed. In contrast, Doniphan praised the eloquence of peace commissioners like William Rives of Virginia and New Jersey's Frederick Frelinghuysen, the latter of whom had delivered "by far the most eloquent and able speech that has been made," having been "chaste, logical, learned, highly ornate & abounded in the most lofty appeals to our patriotism."

Yet overall Doniphan believed the Peace Conference speeches were

The Peace Conference, held in the Concert Hall
attached to Willard's Hotel in Washington DC

Abraham Lincoln in Willard's Hotel in Washington
on the eve of his inauguration, March 1861

Ladies' parlor at Willard's Hotel in 1861

*Gentlemen's parlor, reading, and sitting room at Willard's Hotel,
Washington, during the inauguration week in 1861*

Reverdy Johnson

Mrs. Stephen A. Douglas

*Early photographic view of Washington DC
from the Capitol, looking northwest*

*Historic American Buildings survey copy of old photograph,
east front of Capitol dome under construction*

*Brown's Indian Queen Hotel, Washington City, north side of Pennsylvania
Avenue about midway between the Capitol and the White House*

John Jordan Crittenden

James Buchanan, bust portrait

James A. Seddon,
Secretary of War

Varina Davis

Harriet Lane Johnston

Believed to be: Julia Gardiner
Tyler, wife of President John Tyler

Robert Field Stockton

*Salmon P. Chase, US
Senator from Ohio*

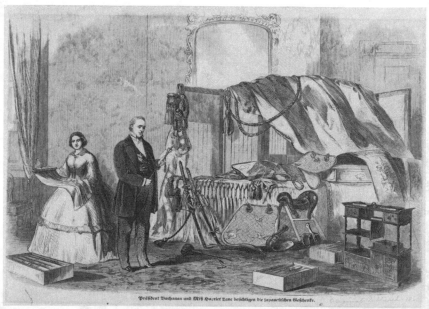

Präsident Buchanan und Miß Harriet Lane besichtigen die japanesischen Geschenke.

President James Buchanan and Harriet Lane inspecting gifts from Japan

Thomas Ewing

Winfield Scott

Lucius E. Chittenden

Rev. Phineas Gurley

John Tyler

James Guthrie

The F Street Church, the site of the Washington Peace Conference

Willard's Hotel, Washington DC

no more able than what he had heard over the years in Missouri, as "there is not much difference between great men—at last 'Tis distance lends enchantment to the view—the magic fades as we approach to familiarity." He was pleased with himself for having "maintained my reputation here well among all men." And he suggested that if "these Black Republican cormorants had any sense they would avail themselves of the lull in the storm to make an adjustment," since "if ever the red lava spouts forth again from the revolutionary volcano—all the border states are gone forever. I thank God we have staid it in its mad course if it is only for a time to let people think."

Doniphan was glad that his Missouri delegation was unified behind the Crittenden Compromise as an "ultimatum—but still we must demand what the other slave states demand and accept what they accept—we cannot go out of the Union before them nor remain—as a unit—and by one act—and form a new gov't or go with the South—& this last is best as one respectable republic in numbers and power is better than twenty little rickety concerns."[37]

Such private pondering aside, Doniphan told the Peace Conference that he was "a Union man. I go for the whole Union, the entire Union. I go for it North, South, East, and West. I do not intend to bring about a calamity that will destroy the Border Slave States and the whole Union." When Lincoln finally met Doniphan in Washington he told Doniphan, who was six foot four, or about Lincoln's height, that he was the only man he had ever met who measured up to his expectations in appearance. It was a tall compliment, as Doniphan had a soaring reputation for courage and accomplishment. In 1838, as a commander of the Missouri militia during the Mormon War, he had received the surrender of Mormon leader Joseph Smith and refused to obey an order to execute Smith, later defending him at trial, as he had before. During the Mexican War he had led Missourians on an epic march from Fort Leavenworth, Kansas, to Santa Fe, New Mexico, later winning military triumphs in Mexico.[38]

AWAITING LINCOLN'S ARRIVAL

While Lincoln was careful to avoid public comment about the Peace Conference, certainly he was in contact with Republican allies in Washington, foremost of all William Seward. Seward's Lafayette Square home, overlooking the White House and General Andrew Jackson's equestrian statue, was only four blocks from Willard's. Doubtless he conferred with many delegates, scores of whom he personally knew across the decades of his political career. While the Resolutions Committee was still deliberating, Seward had invited Massachusetts's George Boutwell over to confer, prompting Boutwell later to recall that Seward was "different from the conversation and bearing of most of the public men of the time," as he "spoke as though the subject of conversation was the chance of a client and the means of bringing him safely out of his perils." Seward told Boutwell about his recent remarks in the Senate and said, "My speech occupies the mind of the South for the present, then the proceedings of the Peace Congress will attract attention, and by and by we shall have the President's inaugural which will probably have a good influence." According to Boutwell, Seward "did not assume the possibility of war," and shared with Boutwell the copy of a recent Richmond newspaper editorial, which accused Seward of a "scheme for delaying definite action in Virginia and the other states of the South, until the inauguration of Mr. Lincoln, when he would use both whip and spur." Boutwell "inferred that he intended to have me understand that such was his purpose," and he "may have thought that war could be averted by dilatory proceedings."[39]

Seward described to Boutwell the momentous speech he'd given to the Senate a month earlier. On January 12, before packed galleries, he had advocated sweeping compromises to save the Union, including a constitutional amendment to protect slavery where existing, and a constitutional convention to address slavery in the territories. Senator Crittenden had listened tearfully, finally covering his face in a handkerchief, and the Senate replied with unusual applause. Seward's wife privately chastised her husband for advocating that "compromise based on the idea that the preservation of the Union [which] is more important than the liberty of nearly 4,000,000 human beings cannot be right . . . cannot be approved by God or supported by good men." Seward assured her he was trying to "gain time for the new administration to organize and for the frenzy of passion to subside."[40]

A month later on February 7, only three days into the Peace Conference, Massachusetts Peace Delegate John Goodrich wrote his governor: "Good nature and masterly inactivity is the policy till Lincoln is inaugurated."[41] Republican congressman Preston King on February 11 similarly celebrated delay, noting, "it is probable that the Peace Congress . . . will carry us over a good many days and aid to bring the 4th of March innocuous." He explained that "Providence . . . is helping us along here."[42] Recognizing this political reality, fifty-four-year-old Peace Delegate Daniel Barringer, a former Whig North Carolina US congressman, telegraphed home on February 23: "Delay is part of their game."[43]

THE BIRTH OF THE CONFEDERACY

In Tennessee, a statewide plebiscite on February 9 rejected secession by 54 to 46 percent. In Missouri, a statewide vote took place on February 18, electing delegates to a state convention to consider secession, with conditional and unconditional Unionists winning nearly all seats. Their convention began on February 28. A state convention in Maryland on February 18 and 19 declined to take a position on secession. In December 1860, Kentucky's legislature was asked by its governor to authorize a state convention to consider succession but refused.

The Provisional Confederate Congress opened its first meeting in Montgomery, Alabama, on February 4, the same day the Peace Conference opened. It was nearly as cold there as in Washington, the temperature almost plunging below freezing that morning, and reaching forty degrees by noon when the Congress convened, the same time as the Peace Conference in the federal capital. And as in Washington that day, so in Montgomery, the clouds cleared, and the sun eventually emerged. There were other similarities. In the state Senate hall where the Confederate delegates met, a large portrait had been hung specially for the occasion, just as one was brought to Willard Hall in Washington to remind peace commissioners of their national duty. In fact, at the Montgomery meeting, there were two Washington portraits, as if to emphasize their revolutionary heritage.

But there were also differences between these two historic gatherings eight hundred miles apart that chilly Monday. Willard Hall was closed to all but delegates. The Montgomery event was open to all spectators. The town's women, in a display of Southern hospitality, had even equipped the Alabama Senate chamber with tables laden with cold food, replenished every day, and open to all. Female spectators sat in the galleries above. Male visitors sat on the main floor, screened from the delegates. More dramatically different from the Peace Conference, which repeatedly rejected press observers, about twenty reporters sat near the speaker's desk, unlikely to miss much. One prominent delegate suggested their gathering had been foreshadowed by the creation of the Southern Baptist Convention fifteen years before. There were thirty-seven delegates there that day, and ultimately forty-four in the coming days. The youngest that first day was age thirty-five, but a thirty-one-year-old soon joined. The oldest was seventy-one; the average age was forty-seven. Overall, with the food, spectators, presence of women, reporters, fewer elderly delegates, and an overall sense of anticipation about creating a new nation, the atmosphere in Montgomery was likely more electric than the somber event in Washington. The Montgomery event differed in another way; the vast majority of delegates were slave owners.

A Southern Baptist minister opened the Confederate event by praying: "Oh, thou heart-searching God, we trust that Thou sees we are pursuing those rights which are guaranteed to us by the solemn covenants of our fathers, and which were cemented by their blood." The

Peace Conference that day had no similar invocation but voted to invite clergy thereafter.[44]

That same day John Tyler in Washington received a "dispatch" from Montgomery reporting the convention there had adjourned to "await the action and result of this meeting," the Peace Conference. Julia Tyler interpreted that "this shows a desire to conciliate and do what is right up to the last moment."[45] In fact, the Confederate gathering had ended early that day so that a rules committee could organize its procedures. But it soon would move far more quickly than the Peace Conference; within a week, the Confederate delegates had drafted a constitution and elected former US senator Jefferson Davis as president and former US senator Alexander Stephens of Georgia as vice president, both for six-year terms. Davis was a longtime statesman and experienced military officer, and the undisputed selection for the Confederacy's chief executive, nominated and elected in less than an hour on February 8. The new Confederate constitution replicated the US Constitution but specifically protected slavery and prohibited a protective tariff, while more assertively affirming states' rights. Amid much excitement, the halls and galleries of the Alabama state Capitol were "crowded to an unusual extent." Models for possible flags for the new Confederacy were "made by some ladies of South Carolina, with a blue cross on a red field, and seven stars on the cross," which was "greatly admired" along with "another model," from a South Carolina man, with a "cross of fifteen stars on a field of stripes." The day concluded with a 100-gun salute.[46]

Davis and his wife, Varina, had quit Washington in January, enduring what she regarded as a "very unpleasant" trip home plagued by crowds and tensions. But by early February they had comfortably ensconced themselves at their plantation on the Mississippi River south of Vicksburg, Mississippi. There he found himself enmeshed in the "most agreeable of all labors planting shrubs and trees and directing the operations of my field . . . ploughing and cleaning up for another crop." His retreat into farm life was short lived. His state had appointed him a major general of the new Army of the Mississippi. "In this hour of my country's severest trial [I] will accept any place to which my fellow citizens may assign me," he resolved.[47]

On February 9 Davis received word of his election as Confederate president from a hard riding messenger on horseback. He was in the garden on a warm evening helping Varina with their rose bushes. She recalled that he "looked so grieved" that she assumed it was terrible news, telling her, after several minutes of silence, the news "as a man might speak of a sentence of death." He sent word of his acceptance by the same messenger and announced his impending departure to his assembled slaves. The next day was Sunday, but on February 11, several slaves rowed him into the Mississippi River to catch a steamer. He would not return home again for seven years. His train trip from Vicksburg to Montgomery, Alabama, took a circuitous five days. It was a short version of Lincoln's procession by train, as Davis addressed excited crowds in "one continuous ovation" along the way in Mississippi, Georgia, and Alabama, except in Tennessee, which had not yet seceded. When he arrived in Montgomery, he told the welcoming crowd: "Our separation from the old Union is complete. No compromise; no reconstruction can be now entertained."[48]

On February 18, Davis was inaugurated at the white, domed Alabama state Capitol with a large clock perched over Doric columns, declaring 1:00 P.M. A lady who witnessed the scene was quoted in *Harper's Weekly*:

> The President is a pleasant-looking old gentleman, of about fifty years of age; he was escorted to the Capitol by the military, he being in an elegant carriage drawn by six white horses. After he took his seat on the platform in front of the Capitol, and a short prayer had been offered, he read a very neat little speech, not making many promises, but hoping, by God's help, to be able to fulfill all expectations. He took the oath amidst the deepest silence; and when he raised his hand and his eyes to heaven, and said, "So Help Me God!" I think I never saw any scene so solemn and impressive.
>
> He puts much in the mind of General Jackson in appearance and

character, though he is much more of a gentleman in his manners than the old General ever wished to be. He had a reception last night which I attended. I walked about and exchanged greetings with my friends, but would not shake hands with the President, for I thought I would not be recognized today, and so would rather wait for a more private introduction. The Vice-President is a constant visitor at the houses where I stay; he is very slight and delicate looking, has more the appearance of a dead man than a living one, until he begins to speak, when you forget entirely how ugly he is."[49]

About five thousand spectators stood before the Alabama state Capitol on that initially frosty morning. A band played "La Marseillaise," cannons boomed, and a Southern Baptist minister gave the invocation (a proposed Methodist had been disqualified by his Unionist sentiment). "Turn the counsels of our enemies into foolishness," the Baptist implored of the Almighty.[50]

Davis, speaking from the portico to the crowd on the lawn below, carefully read the remarks he had composed the day before on Sunday. He declared: "Our present condition, achieved in a manner unprecedented in the history of nations, illustrates the American idea that governments rest upon the consent of the governed, and that it is the right of the people to alter or abolish governments whenever they become destructive of the ends for which they were established." Stressing that their separation had been "a necessity, not a choice," he explained the purpose of the old Union had been "perverted from the purposes for which it was ordained." So sovereign states through a "peaceful appeal to the ballot-box declared that so far as they were concerned, the government created by that compact should cease to exist." Several times citing God, Davis intoned: "He who knows the hearts of men will judge of the sincerity with which we labored to preserve the Government of our fathers in its spirit."

Acknowledging the possibility of war, Davis warned "we must prepare to meet the emergency and to maintain, by the final arbitrament of the sword, the position which we have assumed among the nations of the earth," stressing that their new independence "must be inflexibly pursued." Keeping the door open to new states joining the Confederacy that also desired to be "freed from the sectional conflicts which have interfered with the pursuit of the general welfare," while not disrupting the overall "homogeneity" of the new nation. He also alerted his people that "care and toil and disappointment are the price of official elevation," and they should expect "errors to forgive, many deficiencies to tolerate, but you shall not find in me either a want of zeal or fidelity to the cause that is to me highest in hope and of most enduring affection."[51]

Davis closed with a virtual prayer: "Reverently let us invoke the God of our fathers to guide and protect us in our efforts to perpetuate the principles which, by his blessing, they were able to vindicate, establish and transmit to their posterity, and with a continuance of His favor, ever gratefully acknowledged, we may hopefully look forward to success, to peace, and to prosperity."[52] When then sworn in, his hand on a Bible, tears welled in his eyes as he twice exclaimed, "So help me God." Among the well-wishers who swarmed him at that evening's celebration were two sisters of Abraham Lincoln's wife, who stressed their relation to fellow Kentuckian and pro-Southern John Breckinridge.[53]

A Nashville newspaper praised Davis's inaugural as "calm, determined, statesmanlike in its tone," proving that the new Confederacy was "determined to meet war" and "conscious of right, never can be subdued." It also compared the "chief magistrates of the two republics," one of whom, from the North, was a "coarse, second-rate hoosier lawyer, without education, with no experience in statesmanship, and of manners and attainments that unfit him for the society of refined gentlemen and ladies, and who has never given the slightest evidence of that energy and force of character which sometimes induces people to overlook defective education and rude manners." The president of the South was a "soldier, a statesman and orator," with "no superior in the late Republic of the United States."[54]

But Mary Chesnut, the wife of a South Carolina member of the

Provisional Confederate Congress, cryptically commented of Davis's inaugural: "Down here they do not like the President's message." She also recorded an overheard joking explanation of General Winfield Scott's zeal for the Union, which included "season[ing] every dish and every glass of wine" with a pro-Union toast: his $17,000 US Army salary. "I can imagine the scorn of old Scott's face," she retorted in her diary.[55]

Varina and the Davis children joined President Davis in Montgomery on March 1. He had of course returned to his usual, intense work routine, describing himself as "crowded and pressed," examining every paper addressed to him, seeing hordes of visitors, and convening lengthy cabinet meetings. He seemed "'overwhelmed' with paper," as one interlocutor recalled. A British journalist described Davis looking "anxious" and having a "very haggard, careworn, and pain-drawn look, though no trace of anything but the utmost confidence and the greatest decision could be detected in conversation."[56]

Before leaving Mississippi, Varina had written outgoing President Buchanan, telling him she would have been happy to stay at their plantation. In January he had told her of his good wishes "wherever your lot may be cast." During a stop in New Orleans, she was too "depressed" to speak to a crowd of well-wishers. "I deprecated his occupying the civil position," she privately admitted of her lack of enthusiasm for her husband's new office. In Montgomery the Davises initially occupied a clapboard house rented by the Confederate Congress a few blocks from the state Capitol, and Varina was now hailed as "First Lady." She still very much missed Washington, DC, and maintained contact with Northern friends there. Aware of the lack of developed state protocol for the new Confederate government, she explained, "We are Presidents in embryo here, shorn of much of our fair proportions."[57] The same British journalist described Varina at this time as "a comely, sprightly woman, verging on matronhood, of good figure and manners, well-dressed, ladylike and clever." Varina's friend, Mary Chesnut, recalled her as "awfully clever-always," but she also thought Varina found "playing Mrs. President of this small Confederacy slow work after leaving . . . Washington."[58]

If Varina Davis was uncomfortable with her new situation in Montgomery, much Northern opinion was even more discomfited by the implications of the new Confederate regime. Many Peace Conference delegates likely read a Washington newspaper's reprint of a Philadelphia newspaper's editorial, warning that the Southern Congress had its eyes on Washington, DC, as its potential capital.

"That there is at this moment a very powerful and dangerous conspiracy going on, with Jefferson Davis at its head, to form a new government for the seceding States, and pull down the National Government at Washington, there need now be no doubt," it warned. "The only question among those engaged is, whether its seat shall be at Montgomery, Alabama or Washington, D. C." The newspaper surmised that "in order to coax Virginia into the conspiracy, and for the sake of the prestige of the national name and authority, the possession of the capital of the United States, if only for one month, would be worth millions to the seceders, and no cost of hundreds of millions to the country in its peace and power and history." After all, "he who holds Paris rules France, and Jefferson Davis maintaining himself in Washington would demand recognition of European powers, and would win over one half or three quarters of the regular army, he would at least attempt the entire seizure and command of the navy, form a powerful military despotism, and create a civil war in every town and village of the country by all possible falsehoods and deceptions."[59]

The Philadelphia newspaper would have been more alarmed had it known that in Montgomery, former Buchanan–era US Treasury secretary Howell Cobb, a longtime Davis friend from Washington social life, had tried to cheer Varina by suggesting that if Virginia seceded, she might be sitting in the White House by Christmas. The Confederate First Lady just smiled in response and said nothing.[60] She likelier would be in better spirits if she were instead in the federal capital, during the Peace Conference, surrounded by so many old friends from her cherished years in that city.

THE VIRGINIA CONVENTION

Meanwhile, many of Varina Davis's friends at the Peace Conference were paying closer attention to the Virginia Convention considering secession, which first convened on February 13. They were less concerned about events in Montgomery; to many, the already seceded states seemed almost hopeless. Virginia Peace Delegate William Rives assured his brother, Alexander, a Virginia state senator and convention delegate, of the "ability, patriotism and good feelings" of some peace commissioners, which pointed toward "reaching good results." Alexander replied hopefully on February 11 that "with so little to settle," it is "scarcely credible that such men as Guthrie, Ewing, Ruffin of N.C. etc. etc. cannot bring about a harmonious result." But a few days later Alexander wrote William, "We are all anxiety here about the result of your labors in the conference." He worried that "many prayers are put up by the disunionists for its failure, but we are not discouraged. The salvation of the country depends on your success." Alexander further warned his brother in Washington on February 20, "Delay is breeding great trouble." He wondered, "I do not see how we can maintain ourselves in this state, unless we soon obtain a specific plan, upon which we can rally the people." And he implored, "in this fearful dilemma, we all beseech you for some adjustment; and its speedy submission by Congress. That alone, I fear, can save us."[61]

Rives was hearing from others in Richmond beside just his increasingly anxious brother. "It is idle and wicked for those of us who have already nullified personal and political associations to make further sacrifices in a hopeless cause," fretted a member of Virginia's House of Delegates. "If the public men at the North hold themselves in their cold repelling position our course is marked and plain. We put [Virginia] out of this Union never to return." He assured Rives his was also the "feeling of all the young vigorous controlling Union men here."[62]

The Virginia Convention in Richmond was widely deemed a momentous affair for the state and nation. Most of its delegates were elected as Unionists in January, with only about 25 out of 152 supporting secession, which had cheered many Unionists nationally before the Peace Conference began. John Tyler was himself an elected delegate, although choosing not to take his seat until the Peace Conference concluded, presumably confident no decisive action would occur in Richmond until proceedings ended in Washington. He had been elected by six to one at a local district convention near the James River, where many of his otherwise old-line Whig neighbors supported him against a prominent Whig. Before the vote, according to a Richmond newspaper, a supporter told the local delegates that "there was no man in the country more ardently attached to the Union or more anxious to preserve it in its integrity, than was ex-President Tyler; yet there was no more thoroughly aroused to a sense of the wrongs which had been inflicted on his section, who would guard more watchfully or more certainly defend the honor and interests of Virginia." A statement from Tyler was read aloud affirming his support for reconciliation and peace plus Virginia's sovereignty. Another supporter urged the convention to set aside "party bias" and elect this "distinguished" person.[63]

The Virginia Convention in Richmond was largely in a holding pattern for the duration of the Peace Conference. This was doubtless encouraged by Tyler, who reputedly advised the convention "to adjourn from day to day, until some final adjustment is made or a definite understanding reached," in Washington.[64] Likely other Virginia peace commissioners were exercising similar influence. "The convention is waiting the action of the peace commissioners at Washington," a Washington newspaper's Richmond correspondent reported. "This is perhaps the most safe and conservative body of Virginians ever assembled, embracing among its members some of the ablest and best men of the commonwealth."[65]

But proceedings in Richmond, despite the reputed conservatism, were often rambunctious. They received national attention, as Virginia was the South's largest state and its ultimate choice would be significant for the Union. A New York newspaper reported on February 26 about a Unionist speech "inimical to the rights of Virginia, the whole South, and the people of Richmond," as it "was decidedly Union in its tendency, and strongly against the action of South Carolina." In reaction, Secessionists "posted bills calling every true Southerner to attend an indignation meeting," while "music was engaged," and fifteen hundred demonstrators assembled outside to hear "strong Southern speeches" by convention delegates. An effort to burn an effigy of the outspoken Unionist delegate was halted by Richmond's mayor. The New York newspaper presumed the "whole decided secession demonstration was gotten up by parties in the negro business and selling interests."[66]

The next day at the convention, one delegate asserted the "duty of Virginia in this trying hour to go with the South as the only method of restoring peace to the country." Another delegate declared that "Virginia is attached to the Union as it was, but that as it is it does not protect her rights; that it becomes her people in Convention to look to every remedy for relief, and to provide, in the event of failure, for the future relations she will occupy, having due regard to her position as one of the Southern States." Still another delegate that day denied the "constitutional right of secession" but admitted there was a "revolutionary remedy for wrongs." He suggested a "Confederacy" with other border states, and while opposing "precipitate action," whenever Virginia quit the Union he would go with her. He reasoned that Virginia would be "insecure in the present Southern Confederacy, but the period for conference with the North has now passed."[67]

A Washington newspaper likely echoed many staunch Unionists in the Peace Conference when it editorialized on February 22 against Virginia's representatives as a "cause of great and increasing humiliation to the citizens of that patriotic state," for having "armed herself to protect rebellion, and pledged herself to protect rebellion, and yet comes here on a pretended errand of conciliation," with "extremist demands upon the slavery question." It praised Maine's Senator Morrill in the Peace Congress for pressing this point in an exchange with Virginia's James Seddon, who admitted "the adoption of the measure proposed in the Peace Congress would not restrain Virginia from resisting the forcible execution of the laws." And it opined that Virginia's people were not responsible for the legislation at Richmond, or for their commissioners to the Peace Congress. Such Disunionists "will be turned out of place, just as soon and as fast as the recurrence of elections places them within the reach of the popular will." Doubtless the newspaper had John Tyler very much in mind.[68]

THE MATTER OF THE FORTS

Besides watching over the Virginia State Convention and presiding over the Peace Conference, Tyler was also trying to fulfill his appointment by Virginia to advocate with President Buchanan against military force with the seceding states, especially regarding the tense siege of Fort Sumter in the harbor of Charleston, South Carolina. Meanwhile, Tyler also encouraged new Confederate president Davis to send commissioners to negotiate with the incoming Lincoln Administration.[69]

Shortly after the Peace Conference began, alarmed by a defiant letter from the secretary of war to South Carolina over Fort Sumter, Tyler and his wife, Julia, had rushed to the White House, both as a courtesy and to offer himself as a mediator. Buchanan authorized Tyler to telegraph a conciliatory message to South Carolina's governor, while Tyler urged Buchanan to withdraw federal forces, which were only seventy-eight men, whose continued presence threatened the Peace Conference's success.

Tyler later recounted:

> I urged the impossibility of sending relief. I saw no chance for a successful defense. I represented to him, in the mildest terms I could, the condition of that noble boy (Major Anderson). I adverted to the state of the garrison; that there were only seventy odd people to man the guns; that after all his vaunting about the strength of the Fort, there were no more than enough soldiers to man six guns, and the ability would fail even to man them after a few days' conflict. Why not, then,

relieve and discharge the garrison? They are ready to perish in defense of their duty—why let them perish?[70]

But Buchanan declined the advice and, at least on Fort Sumter, "remained stubborn to the last," as Tyler's son described.

Immediately afterward Tyler had a telegraph exchange with South Carolina's governor. He relayed this to Buchanan, assuring the president that there was now "no ground to fear any early disturbance," as the "whole subject is referred to the convention at Montgomery," and that South Carolina was committed "to avoid collision and bloodshed," which meant the "inquietude you expressed may be dismissed." On February 13, Julia Tyler wrote her mother in New York that President Buchanan "spent the evening in our parlor evening before last," which she supposed was the "first visit he has paid since being the nation's chief." During the call, Buchanan reiterated a letter he had just sent Tyler "full of gratitude for the relief he had afforded him in probably preventing, through his influence at Charleston, the attack on Fort Sumter." Buchanan's niece and First Lady, Harriet Lane, had also done Julia the honor of a personal visit at the hotel.[71]

Such excitement seems to have grown wearisome for Julia Tyler after her initial exhilaration over returning to Washington. In her Wednesday, February 13 letter, Julia told her mother that if her husband were "detained here indefinitely, I shall run home. I want to be with my children. Probably I shall go on Friday, unless I hear from home in the meantime to my satisfaction." Evidently she delayed her departure, as a Richmond correspondent reported she was at a "hop," or a dance, at Brown's, which was renowned for its raucous weekly hops. On that February 17 evening, on a day of "heavy rains," Mrs. Tyler was "the bright, particular star" of the night.[72]

Julia's husband would indeed be further "detained" in Washington, but not for dancing. The Peace Conference would press on for another two weeks, and Tyler continued to attempt to manage relations between Buchanan and South Carolina. Several days later Buchanan got word

191

of intelligence that South Carolina might attack Fort Sumter. "I do not believe a word of it," Tyler assured Buchanan on February 19, quickly gaining confirmation from South Carolina and explaining to the president that South Carolina would not act without approval from Montgomery. "I think you may rely upon tranquillity at the South," Tyler assured Buchanan on February 24, telling him of the "improbability of any movement until a commissioner shall come on here, and a failure in the mission."[73]

Buchanan's reliance on Tyler for managing the highly sensitive forts issue in the South seems to have continued for the duration of the Peace Congress. A Richmond newspaper's correspondent in Washington reported on February 27 that Sunday morning, the 25th,

> Old Buck was down at Brown's before nine o'clock, it is supposed to see Mr. Tyler. After remaining a few moments, he drove off rapidly in the direction of the Capitol. What be sought in that direction, nobody knows. His anxiety was explained, later in the day, by the report of an attack on Fort Pickens. Through Mr. Tyler's exertions, it is believed the attack will be postponed until Lincoln's policy is announced definitely.

The correspondent continued in a jesting tone, reporting that last night he heard John Tyler had denied he expected a "satisfactory adjustment" from the Peace Congress, but this morning he heard Tyler had "repeated the assertion." Advice from the correspondent: "Believe nothing until your commissioners return home—which they will do tomorrow, the day after, or the next day, in the course of events."[74]

In her February 13 letter to her mother, Julia Tyler wrote from her ample suite at Brown's Hotel on Pennsylvania Avenue. She observed that "here you can realize more than anywhere else the distracted state of the country." She noted that the Resolutions Committee would be reporting in a few days, and then the "end I suppose can be foreseen," but in the "meantime all is suspense, from the President down." Mrs. Tyler expected the New Yorker and Massachusetts men at the Peace

Conference would "no doubt perform all the mischief they can" and possibly "will defeat this patriotic effort at pacification." Either way, she surmised, Virginia "will have sustained her reputation, and in the latter event will retire with dignity from the field to join without loss of time her more Southern sisters; the rest of the slave border states will follow her lead, and very likely she will be able to draw off, which would be glorious, a couple of northern states."[75]

This scenario of national dismemberment likely reflected increasingly pessimistic views of Mrs. Tyler's husband midway through the Peace Congress. She told her mother that "The President," her husband, "has hundreds of letters" complaining about "this state of suspense, which is bringing disaster to trade everywhere," and which she hoped "will soon be removed in one way or another." Explaining she "must conclude" her letter, she rued that amid the press of events both national and familial, "I have so much to say of persons and events, and no time to say it in."[76]

One newspaper, skeptical of the Peace Conference altogether, would report that Julia Tyler was leaving Washington, with her husband shortly to follow, as they realized his exertions for conciliation were for naught. But in fact, the most intense moments of the convention were yet ahead. Tyler himself would take the floor at Willard Hall to meet with president-elect Lincoln, and ultimately to appeal himself before Congress, as the hours and days ran out for preventing further disunion and war.

SEVEN
LINCOLN'S ARRIVAL

Mr. Lincoln, the prayers of many hearts were with you before
you started this journey, they accompanied you all the way here,
and they will follow you as you enter in on this administration.

—William Dodge

On Wednesday, February 20, the Peace Conference convened for its thirteenth day. Prayers were offered by Rev. Dr. George Sampson of First
Baptist Church.

That day a Washington newspaper editorialized that the Peace
Conference would facilitate the "eventual peaceable settlement of the
troubles," despite the unfortunate "presence among them of a few delegations selected palpably to the end of defeating any action," having
been "sent hither in bad faith." Yet the only hope of retaining the border
states in the Union was the Peace Conference's assuring them that their
interests, "so far as slavery is concerned," had not been "practically remit-
ted into the keeping of the radical wing of the Republican Party." The

editorial opined, they saw "clearly that all the Republican members of the convention are not so blinded by anti-slavery partisanship as to render them utterly incapable of reasoning sensibly" and "in the end they will discard extreme party councils" and pursue Unionism, as "the party presenting the highest claim to it will surely be overwhelmingly ascendant."[1]

With such expectations upon the delegates, and with dwindling time left at the convention, debate that morning began almost immediately. Connecticut's sixty-three-year-old retired jurist, legislator, and diplomat Charles McCurdy protested the Resolutions Committee's proposal to constitutionally recognize slavery under common law. The North "will never consent to it," he insisted, speaking as the descendant of old New England patriots whose family home once housed General Lafayette during the Revolution.[2] He was a man of quiet faith, as his obituary noted, "his religious training and tendencies found expression in his familiarity with the Scriptures, and in his never-failing practical efforts for the support of public worship," who was "reticent in regard to his religious experiences and feelings, but his habit of daily prayer and his firm faith in the doctrines of Christ are well known."[3]

McCurdy's obituary would recall that he was at the Peace Conference "one of the first to discover the irreconcilability of the opposing views of the north and south; but after the civil war commenced, and even during its darkest days, he never doubted the final success of the union cause." In Willard Hall, he told his delegate colleagues: "She [the North] understands all the consequences as well as you. No doubt it would be a great point gained for you, to have the Constitution recognize the institution of slavery as part of the common law. For then slavery goes wherever the common law goes."[4]

Ohio's Thomas Ewing responded that the proposal didn't pertain to all US territory but only where already existing "in that little worthless territory we own below the proposed line" of territory south of latitude 36°30′. "Will we agree that it shall remain there just as it is now, so long as the territorial condition continues? That is all. There is no mystery or question of construction about it."[5]

New York's fifty-six-year-old David Field proposed a constitutional amendment against secession, which "would render the majority report much more acceptable to the northern people," while still asserting his own reservations about the majority report or any constitutional amendments. Field, the son of a Congregationalist minister, was a former Free Soil Democrat turned Republican who had chaired the 1860 Cooper Union meeting in New York where Lincoln delivered his famous speech on slavery and the Constitution.[6] He was "one of the first to break" from the Democratic Party over the extension of slavery, which "he fought in conventions, when he stood almost alone."[7] Field warned of the momentous decisions before them: "To found an empire, or to make a constitution for a people, on which so much of their happiness depends, requires the sublimest effort of the human intellect, the greatest impartiality in weighing opposing interests, the utmost calmness in judgment, the highest prudence in decision."[8]

Field also charged: "You have called us here to prevent future discussion of the subject of slavery. It is that you fear—it is that you would avoid—discussion in Congress—in the State Legislatures—in the newspapers—in popular assemblies." He warned that compelling Northern states to pay for unreturned fugitive slaves would toss a "lighted firebrand not only into Congress, but into every state legislature, into every county, city, and village in the land," creating a "consuming fire."[9]

"Stop discussion of the great questions affecting the policy, strength, and prosperity of the Government!" Field exclaimed. "You cannot do it! You ought not to attempt to do it!" Striking a brief conciliatory pose, he professed, "I am still for peace . . . [but] I object to the propositions, sir, because they would put into the Constitution new expressions relating to slavery, which were sedulously kept out of it by the framers of that instrument; left out of it, not accidentally, but because, as Madison said, they did not wish posterity to know from the Constitution that the institution existed . . . because the propositions contain guarantees for slavery which our fathers did not and would not give."[10]

When challenged, Field denied that saving the Union meant

protecting slavery. "I would let slavery slide, and save the Union," he explained. "Greater things than this have been done. This year has seen slavery abolished in all the Russias." He "would sacrifice all I have; lay down my life for the Union . . . but I will not give these guarantees to slavery. If the Union cannot be preserved without them, it cannot long be preserved with them." He pointed out that his Southern colleagues could not promise that seceded states would return, even if guarantees for slavery were constitutionalized. In fact, they were prepared to join them if the compromise failed. "Even if these propositions of amendment are received and submitted to the people, I see nothing but war in the future, unless those States are quickly brought back to their allegiance," he surmised. Citing the absence of states like California and Oregon, he urged a state convention "because I believe it is the best way to avoid civil war."[11]

"We must have either the arbitrament of reason or the arbitrament of the sword," Field warned. "Only last night I dreamed of marching armies and news from the seat of war." Responding to derisive laughter from the Kentucky and Virginia benches, he remarked, "The gentlemen laugh. I thought they, too, had fears of war. I thought their threats and prophecies were sincere. God grant that I may not hereafter have to say, 'I had a dream that was not all a dream.'" He concluded by quoting Longfellow's poem "O Ship of State:"[12]

> *Thou, too, sail on, O Ship of State!*
> *Sail on, O UNION, strong and great!*
> *Humanity with all its fears,*
> *With all the hopes of future years,*
> *Is hanging breathless on thy fate!*
> *We know what Master laid thy keel,*
> *What Workmen wrought thy ribs of steel,*
> *Who made each mast, and sail, and rope,*
> *What anvils rang, what hammers beat,*
> *In what a forge and what a heat*

Were shaped the anchors of thy hope!
Fear not each sudden sound and shock,
'Tis of the wave and not the rock;
'Tis but the flapping of the sail,
And not a rent made by the gale!
In spite of rock and tempest's roar,
In spite of false lights on the shore,
Sail on, nor fear to breast the sea!
Our hearts, our hopes, are all with thee,
Our hearts, our hopes, our prayers, our tears,
Our faith triumphant o'er our fears,
Are all with thee,—are all with thee.[13]

Pennsylvania's Thomas White, apparently unmoved, replied that "all the speeches that have been made, and all the declamation that has been uttered on this floor, have not made a single convert." He explained that Pennsylvania was present because as a "border state" amid "civil, unnatural war," she would be "devastated," with "fields laid waste and trampled down." Citing Virginia's currently meeting convention, he warned against further delays, preferring "speedy action . . . to have some plan laid before the country at once—something fair to all sections—and then, with, the alternatives before them, let the people decide. She wishes to pour oil on the troubled waters." He also reasoned that restoring the Missouri Compromise line, which Dred Scott had inflamed the North by overthrowing, could only be a positive.[14]

New Hampshire's Amos Tuck then spoke, averring, "gentlemen greatly err in assuming that we of the North are acting under some wizard influence, and, out of pure malignity, are plotting the overthrow of slavery," when "there is no plot or general concert in the action of the North on this subject," and "no disposition at the North to interfere with it." Sounding biblical, he pledged, "We will live with you in the Union, under a Constitution that requires us to help you keep the peace. Where you dwell, we will dwell. Your people shall be our people, and where you die, we will die." But he wondered why Southerners would wish to leave, when slavery was protected, and when national governments and the courts had long been partial to their interests.[15]

"You are going out of the Union because you say we propose to immolate you—to turn you over to the mercies of a Government of slaves set free," Tuck deduced. "How unfounded is such a belief!" noting how partiality to the South was dominant even at the Peace Conference. "You turn your backs upon the Government of the Father of his Country, whose portrait is before us, and join your fortunes to a mere southern nationality," he observed, warning about political stability in "southern latitudes" like South America versus the "permanence and power of Russia, France, and England." He rejected "maintaining the Union by force of arms" as "not in accordance with the theory of our Government." Trying to conclude hopefully, he declared, "The end of the Union has not come—it is not coming. The Union will yet outlive us and our posterity."[16]

New Jersey's Frederick Frelinghuysen proclaimed, "it is of little use to make patriotic speeches here," after himself giving a lengthy one about his state's commitment to the Union and the Constitution, including fugitive slave laws. "The South demands guarantees and I feel under obligations to respond to that demand," he said. "I am ready to do it now; and my obligations to do right will not be changed by the 4th of March rolling over my head," citing Lincoln's inauguration. "If civil war is to come, if this land is to be deluged with fraternal blood, when that time comes there will not be a northern State represented here that would not give untold millions to be placed upon that record by the side of New Jersey."[17]

But Frelinghuysen disclaimed against protecting future territory for slavery as "you have no rights in territory which we never owned, and I hope never may." He hoped for a closure to the slavery issue, complaining it had

separated families and neighborhoods; it has broken up and scattered Christian churches; it has severed every benevolent society of the land;

199

it has destroyed parties; it broke up the good old Whig party, and more recently sapped the strength and vigor from the Herculean Democracy. It now threatens the dissolution of the Union. Let us crush the head of the monster forever. Let us do it by restricting and defining its limits in existing territory.[18]

And Frelinghuysen urged Republicans to abandon their stance on slavery, asking, "Is the Chicago platform a law to us?" He suggested too much had changed since the election, and "in fifty days, fifty years of history have transpired. This is enough to release us from the obligation, if any existed." He professed that, "I can go home to the Republicans of New Jersey with a clear conscience and say to them, that by our action here we have not carried slavery one inch farther than it was before." And he added, "Now we have an opportunity, at once and forever, by constitutional enactment, to prohibit slavery from going into three-fourths of the territory, by simply agreeing that as to the other one-fourth, while it remains a territory, the status of slavery shall not be changed."[19]

Extolling the Union as a providential instrument, Frelinghuysen declared, "There is no one here who, as he has witnessed the freedom, the comfort, the prosperity, and the pure religion disseminated among the people, has not hoped this nation was to accomplish great social and moral good for our whole race. Yes, in fond conception we have seen her the Liberator and Equalizer of the world—walking like an angel of light in the dark portions of the earth."[20]

Kentucky's Charles Wickliffe interjected that he would motion to terminate debate the next day to facilitate a vote on February 22, "that we may see whether the same day that gave a Washington to our Fathers, may not give Peace to their posterity." But long speeches resumed, starting with New York's William Dodge, who spoke as a "plain merchant, out of place, I very well know, in such a Conference as this."[21]

Dodge, a founding member of the Young Men's Christian Association and a temperance advocate, came to Washington bearing petitions endorsing the "Border State Resolutions," meeting with seventy

Republican members of the Senate and House of Representatives in a "most satisfactory and delightful interview." He had been "laboring with all the ability, strength, and power with which God has blessed me, to secure the adoption of some plan here, that would settle our difficulties and avert from our beloved country the evils with which she is now threatened."[22]

"My days are anxious and excited—my nights are wakeful and sleepless," Dodge disclosed. "In all the weary watches of last night, I could not close my eyes in slumber," seeing the "certain and inevitable ruin that is threatening the business, commercial interests of this country, and which is sure to fall with crushing force upon those interests, unless we come to some arrangement here." He explained that "had not Divine Providence poured out its blessings upon the great West in an abundant harvest, and at the same time opened a new market for that harvest in foreign lands, bringing it through New York in its transit, our city would now present the silence and the quiet of the Sabbath day."[23]

Dodge asked: "What is it that has thus stopped the wheels of manufactures and arrested the ordinary movements of commerce," producing "this unusual and uncommon stagnation of business?" He blamed "anxiety, distrust, and apprehension," between and over the North and South. And he faulted delegates from New England as the "most obstinate and uncompromising." But their constituents "will not sit quietly by and see their property sacrificed or reduced in value," readily preferring these conciliatory propositions to further turmoil, after which "you will hear no more said about slavery or platforms."[24]

New York's James Smith made what a New York newspaper called a "strong speech against compromise" that "several members" called "one of the best speeches yet made." He declared he had

> nothing to say respecting the morals of slavery. If there is virtue in the institution, you have the credit of it; if there is sin, you must answer for it. And here let me say that you discuss the moral aspect of slavery much more than we do. We hold it to be strictly a state institution. So

long as it is kept there, we have nothing to do with it. It is only when it thrusts itself outside of state limits, and seeks to acquire power and strength by spreading itself over new ground, that we insist upon our objections.[25]

But Smith insisted "no opinion ever took a firmer hold of the Northern mind—ever struck more deeply into it—ever became more pervading, or was ever adopted after maturer consideration" than conversion of free territory into slave territory, to which the North would consent "Never! never!"[26]

"You must not forget that the people of the North believe slavery is both a moral and a political evil," Smith remarked. "They recognize the right of the States to have it, to regulate it as they please, without interference, direct or indirect; but when it is proposed to extend it into territory where it did not before exist, it becomes a political question, in which they are interested, in which they have a right to interfere, and in which they will interfere."[27]

Slavery and free labor couldn't coexist, Smith explained, which was why the North opposed slavery's expansion into new territory. "We want our children to go there, and live on the labor of their own free hands," he said. "They are excluded if slavery goes there before us." So "this contest is between the owners of slaves on the one side, and all the free men of this great nation on the other."[28]

The Fourteenth Day

After Smith's peroration, the Peace Conference adjourned until 10:00 A.M. the next morning, Thursday, February 21. That morning Rev. Dr. Thomas Stockton of the Methodist Protestant Church invoked them, after which debate resumed. An Ohio newspaper reported that day that Virginia, North Carolina, and Missouri stood ready to vote against the majority report, with Maryland, Kentucky, and Tennessee supporting it. Virginia's Tyler, Seddon, and Brockenbrough would urge Virginia's secession convention to reject it, the newspaper predicted, while Rives and Summers of Virginia would advocate the opposite. But Virginia's delegates in Richmond were "somewhat disappointed overall" by the Peace Conference, which "cannot continue more than three or four days longer." Reportedly "Mrs. Tyler left for home this afternoon, and Mr. Tyler expects soon to follow."[29]

That morning, reflecting either frustration or his policy of delay, Ohio's Salmon Chase unsuccessfully offered what a West Virginia newspaper called a "startling proposition" from his state legislature urging the Peace Conference to adjourn, reconvening on April 4. After this Kentucky's Charles Wickliffe motioned for ending debate the next morning. Missouri's Waldo Johnson backed him, explaining, "We Missourians love the Union, but we have fully arrived at the conclusion that the time has come when something must be done to prevent our entire separation."[30]

Chase opposed the Peace Conference holding night sessions since their day sessions were "protracted and very laborious" and night sessions were "dangerous." But Kentucky's Charles Morehead disagreed, having "observed the demeanor of all the gentlemen in the conference, and know that they are as well fitted for business at five o'clock in the afternoon as at ten o'clock in the morning." Thirteen states voted in agreement with Morehead.[31]

Kentucky's James Clay objected to New York's Smith for offering a mixed narrative of his father, the great Henry Clay, whom Smith portrayed as ardent Unionist while also criticizing his Compromise of 1850. Smith credited the elder Clay for believing that compromise is "beneficial to the country," but "experience has shown that he was mistaken." And Smith appealed to the "venerable and able men around me, who bear historic names—who have been themselves long connected with the Union and its Government, to join us in our struggle to save the Constitution."[32]

Connecticut's Chauncey Cleveland was his state's former governor who had become a Republican and was a presidential elector for Lincoln.

He insisted, "We are all friends—friends of the Union and of each other," and "nobody wants to give up the Union, or hurt Mr. Lincoln." "The South . . . thinks the Republicans, since they have got the power, are going to trample upon her rights." What's wrong with reassuring her, he wondered. "If we could go to work at this thing like sensible men, we could settle the whole matter in two hours," instead of "long speeches" persisting until "doomsday."[33]

Missouri's John Coalter asked if Massachusetts "abhors slavery, how long will it be before she will abhor slaveholders?" He asserted the "people of the North know little of the condition of the negro in a state of slavery," but the South knows that the "four millions of blacks in the South are better off in all respects than any similar number of laborers anywhere."[34]

John Goodrich of Massachusetts, the fifty-six-year-old Republican lieutenant governor of his state, offered a lengthy lecture on the Founders' stances toward slavery. This prompted Charles Wickliffe to snap impatiently, "No one from Kentucky or Virginia wishes to alter the ordinance of 1787. For God's sake spare us the argument." The conference adjourned at 4:00 P.M. and reconvened at 7:00 P.M. for its first evening session on that Thursday, February 21.[35]

Lucius Chittenden of Vermont took a break from his copious journaling to take the floor. "Now, it is useless to tell the people of the free States, that such is the present condition of the South, such is the apprehension and distrust prevailing there, that we must give them these guarantees at once, without any longer delay or discussion—that if we do not they will secede," he observed. "This is not the way in which good constitutions are made, for one of the several parties to present its ultimatum, and then insist upon its adoption, under the threat that if it is not adopted they will go no farther." After all, "a Constitution adopted in that way would be good for nothing."[36]

Chittenden noted that the people of the slave states believe slavery is a "desirable," and even a "missionary institution, and that the North, in attempting to overthrow it, interposes between the slaveholder and his Maker, thereby preventing him from performing a duty toward the African race which his ownership imposes upon his conscience." Probably sounding a bit sarcastic, he told Southerners "that is a question between yourselves and your consciences." The North would not interfere in the South but would firmly reject expansion, which would make the North "responsible for the existence, expansion, growth, extension, or anything else relating to slavery." Any compromise must recognize of this Northern view that "sneering at it will do no good; abuse will only make it stronger. You cannot legislate it out of existence. From this time forward, as long as the nation has an existence, you must expect the determined opposition of the North to the extension of slavery into free territory." Chittenden admitted at this point he had no expectation that "much good would come from our deliberations."[37]

Stephen Logan of Illinois, a political associate of Lincoln, warned against the "evil day that brings civil war upon our happy and prosperous country, and to prevent the devastation of that country." Addressing "my brother Republicans," he stressed that the only way for a "united country to rule" was by a "settlement of our troubles," and adopting the committee report. Having won the election, "you can afford to be liberal," he told Republicans. "Liberality is a noble trait in any character, whether it be that of an individual or political party." If the Union is dissolved, "that party will be responsible; responsible, as that party has now the power to prevent it." He implored that they "induce Congress to submit our propositions at once to the people," since "in no other way, in my judgment, can we avoid the disunion that threatens us."[38]

Indiana's Godlove Orth made clear he would never "consent, by word, thought, or deed, to do anything to strengthen the institution of slavery," which he saw as an "evil which all good men should desire to see totally eradicated; and I hope for the day to dawn speedily when, throughout the length and breadth of the land, freedom shall be enjoyed by every human being, without reference to caste, color, or nationality." While "willing to tolerate its existence where it now is, I am unwilling to extend its boundaries a single inch, and will not give it any guarantee, protection, or encouragement, save what it can exact by the strict letter of the fundamental law." He told the South that "you must strike the first blow, cross the Rubicon, commit the foul and damning crime of treason, and bring upon your people ruin, devastation, and destruction, and call down upon your guilty heads the curses of your children and the disapprobation of the civilized world!"[39]

Exasperated by the meandering debate, New York's seventy-one-year-old jurist Greene Bronson likened the "set speeches" to the "circumlocution office in one of Dickens' novels, showing 'how not to do it.'" He dryly suggested: "All this circumlocution might have better been done at home." Disclaiming partisan interests, he claimed if he were a "mere politician, I do not know but I should be in favor of breaking up the Conference, and of doing nothing; but being only a Democrat, I desire to transmit to posterity the blessings of a good Constitution and a good Government."[40]

Bronson thought it "strange to see gentlemen so cool and apathetic under such circumstances," asking, "Is no one alarmed for the safety of the old flag about which so much is said?" He declared, "My only wish is to spend my few remaining days in the United States, and to transmit the blessings of our Government to my children." He commended Republicans who subordinated "their platform to their country. I commend them for it; these are noble sentiments. Men should abandon platforms when they tend to destroy the country." Dismissing British opposition to slavery, he recalled that "she has millions in India worse off than slaves . . . has been the greatest land robber on the earth . . . and has forced the Chinese at the point of the bayonet to eat opium. Do you forget that she ruined the capitol in this city, and blew it up, in 1814? I do not deny her virtues, but I do not care to follow her example." As to slavery's expansion, Bronson thought it a "blessing to the slave if he may be permitted to go with his master into these new territories," away from "old slave States," where "he is compelled to work in gangs under the whip of a driver, with no one to look after his health or comfort." Urging adoption of the resolutions, he declared "in their adoption there is safety; there is great danger in their rejection."[41]

THE FIFTEENTH DAY

The weary delegates adjourned at midnight until 10:00 A.M. the next morning, Friday, February 22, for its fifteenth day, on George Washington's birthday. The day began with prayer from Rev. Dr. Byron Sunderland of First Presbyterian Church. There commenced yet another debate on limiting the length of speeches. Exasperated, Kentucky's James Guthrie suggested: "Perhaps some of us had better take the benefit of the prayers of the church on Sunday. Some of us wish to get our propositions to Congress at an early hour. Those who oppose us—those determined to defeat action, can speak on until the fourth of March. I hope such is not their intention."[42]

Pennsylvania's fifty-year-old former "Great Christian Governor" James Pollock was an old Whig and a devout Christian who served in Congress and shared the same boarding house with Lincoln. He appealed to his colleagues' faith: "Christian men! Remember that our great Savior was a Prince of Peace—that he came to conquer with peace, not with the sword. 'The Lord God omnipotent reigneth.'"[43] Under Lincoln he became head of the US mint and played a role in putting "In God We Trust" on currency.[44] At Willard Hall, he recalled:

> I labored for the election of Mr. Lincoln, but I never understood that hostility to slavery was the leading idea in the platform of his party. Pennsylvania had other interests—other reasons very powerful, for supporting him. There was the repeal of the Missouri Compromise—ruinous discriminations in the Tariff—the corruption of the Government—the villainous conduct of its high officers; these and other considerations gave Mr. Lincoln more strength in Pennsylvania than the slavery question.

And he asked pleadingly: "How can we do greater honor to this glorious day, which gave the immortal Washington to his country and to the world, than by marking it on the calendar as the day that secured the safety and perpetuity of the American Union?"[45]

Virginia's fifty-four-year-old John Brockenbrough was a moderate Unionist from the Shenandoah Valley who approached the Peace Conference with a "catholic spirit," saying "never despair of the republic." But he also believed in secession and that the "honor and interest" of Virginia "bind Virginia to the cotton states," and that if the North did not conciliate at the Peace Conference, Virginia "should secede at once."[46] In Willard Hall, he observed:

> It seems that we can agree upon everything but this question of slavery in the Territories. So far as that subject is concerned, Virginia has declared that she will accept the Crittenden resolutions. She and her southern sisters will stand upon and abide by them. If gentlemen will come up to this basis of adjustment with manly firmness, the electric wires will flash a thrill of joy to the hearts of the people this very hour. Why not come up to it like men?[47]

Complaining that "sentiments have been uttered here that grate harshly on the minds of Southern gentlemen," Brockenbrough recognized a "war of ideas" and an "irrepressible conflict." If the North insists that slavery is a sin, "the sum of all villanies, then we may as well separate. We cannot live together longer."[48]

Pennsylvania's congressman, forty-seven-year-old David Wilmot, had admitted to delegates that he was a lightning rod of controversy thanks to his long advocacy of the "Wilmot Proviso" banning slavery in former Mexican lands. He declared his "first allegiance is to the principles of truth and justice. Convince me that your propositions are right, that they are just and true, and I will accept them. I will sustain them to the end. If they are wrong—and I now believe them to be—I will never sustain them, and I will show my faith in God by leaving the consequences with Him." But he could not vote for the majority report as he did "not think it is right thus to bind posterity" and to "entrench slavery behind the Constitution."[49]

Virginia's James Seddon, always ready to pounce in defense of Southern slavery, responded with alacrity: "Slavery is with us a democratic and a social interest, a political institution, the grandest item of our prosperity. Can we in safety or justice sit quietly by and allow the North thus to array all the powers of the Government against us?"[50]

North Carolina's Daniel Barringer echoed Seddon: "We claim that every Southern man has the right to go into the Territories with his property, wherever these Territories may be. The Territories belong to both; to the South as well as to the North. We want equality. We have no wish to propagate slavery, but every man at the South does wish to insist upon his right to enter the Territories upon terms of perfect equality with the North, if he chooses to do so. He may not exercise the right, but he will not give it up."[51]

Anxious to seek consensus, Kentucky's Charles Morehead warned against piling amendments into the majority report, as Seddon wanted to further define slavery protections in the territories. "I know as certainly as that God rules in heaven, that unless we come to some satisfactory adjustment in this Conference, a convulsion will ensue such as the world has never seen," he quivered. "I think we can yet save the seceded States. But at least let us save Texas and Arkansas. As it is, black ruin sits nursing the earthquake which threatens to level this government to its foundations. Can you not feel it, while there is yet time to prepare for the shock? If this giant frenzy of disunion raises its crested head—if red battle stamps his foot, the North will feel the shock as severely as the South."[52]

THE SIXTEENTH DAY

After strongly rejecting a motion to add language on slavery protection, the delegates adjourned, reconvening on Saturday, February 23. The sixteenth day started with prayer from Rev. Dr. Clement Butler of Trinity Episcopal Church. A motion urging all states to "faithfully abide in the Union" was tabled by eleven to nine, with Rhode Island, Delaware, New Jersey, and Pennsylvania voting with the slave states.[53]

In the wake of that vote, Ohio's fifty-four-year-old jurist and railroad executive Reuben Hitchcock observed:

> Our differences exist, and I do not think they were occasioned by the success of the Republican Party in the last presidential election. The plotters against the Union have seized upon the occasion to accomplish their designs. By no fault of their own, several of the border states are placed in a very unfortunate position. They wish to remain in the Union, but their people insist that certain of their rights shall be previously secured; in other words, guaranteed. It is my firm belief that if the inauguration of President Lincoln was over, if his administration had been for a few months in operation, we should all be at peace. Now, we must act upon the facts as they are presented to us.[54]

In a more conciliatory vein, Tennessee's Robert Carruthers urged acceptance of the majority report's current language, citing the Bible.

> We read in sacred history that the Israelites were once so conscientious that they would not fight on Sunday. They were attacked and overthrown. They finally agreed to compromise the question of conscience so far as to fight in self-defense on Sunday. They were attacked then, and the enemy was overthrown. The report is not such as we could wish it might be, but, such as it is, we will accept it and stand by it. We will adopt it, and we ask the North to adopt it, in the true spirit of compromise.[55]

In likewise urging acceptance, Stephen Logan of Illinois explained, "There is a contest between the North and the remaining Southern States, and the latter have no better chance in that contest alone, than

Turkey had in the grasp of the rugged Russian Bear. The gentlemen from these states do not threaten. All they say is, 'If we cannot agree longer together, let us go in peace. We will fight only in self-defense.'"[56]

North Carolina's Morehead rejoiced to hear such sympathetic Northern voices, having been jeered at in his state legislature, where Secessionists were the majority. He had told them "repeatedly that if we could once get the ear of the North, the North would do us justice." In response, they cited much of the North's perceived celebration of John Brown's raid. Goodrich of Massachusetts replied by correcting the charge that his governor had honored Brown, whom he had in fact called "crazy," but for whose family he afterward attended a fund-raiser.[57]

Maryland's fifty-five-year-old Augustus Bradford was a Democrat Unionist who would serve as his state's wartime governor. He pledged: "Give us the report as it came from the committee, without substantial alteration, and there is no power on earth that can draw the State of Maryland out of the Union! Maryland has been called the heart of the Union. The day she leaves the Union, that heart is broken! I am now inclined to set my face against all amendments. I think that is the better course."[58]

Bradford said in the "populous section of the State where I reside, the universal cry is, 'For God's sake, settle these questions!' Why can we not settle them? The committee informs us that the members of which it is composed, were nearly unanimous upon all points except the territorial question. Will reasonable men not yield a little to each other in order to settle that?"[59]

Similarly, Ohio's Ewing pleaded conciliation: "Let a man be firm as a rock in battle, but conciliatory in council; especially in such a council as this, where the lives of millions may be concerned. There is a firmness which is but another name for imprudence—for rashness." He offered, "We may be right—the North may be right; but we should not hazard the existence of the Union by a determination to exercise that right at all events, when, by some slight concessions, we could save the Union."[60]

But Crowninshield of Massachusetts urged the South not to push too hard. "I am not insensible to the condition of the country," he said. "Neither are my colleagues, nor the constituents they represent. But you must not expect us here, in the worst emergency you can imagine, to forget or throw away the rights of our people. If we consent to support this amendment, it is as far as we can go. You ought not to ask us to go farther."[61]

Kentucky's James Clay, who owned many slaves and lived on the estate of his famous late father, was succinct: "Mr. President, in behalf of the South, I think I know what to say. If our differences are to be settled at all, we must have our property in our slaves in the Territories recognized; and when that property is constitutionally recognized, it must be constitutionally protected. Such, I know, are the sentiments of the people of Kentucky."[62]

Speaking for the North, Charles Allen of Massachusetts was just as emphatic: "We of the North stand where our fathers did, who resisted the Stamp Act; who threw overboard the tea in Boston harbor. We have been taught to resist the smallest beginnings of evil; that this is the true policy." He observed the "debates of this Conference, and those of the Convention of 1787, will stand in a strange contrast to each other."[63]

Typically a political realist, Salmon Chase warned his fellow delegates of the limits in their influence on the nation.

A majority of the people have adopted the opinion that under the Constitution slavery has not a legal existence in the Territories. The triumph of this opinion is not the result of any sudden impulse. A President has been elected, and a Government will soon be organized, whose duty it will be to respect and observe the opinions of the people. You are now seeking, by the adoption of a single section, to change these opinions and this policy. Do not deceive yourselves, gentlemen. You will never accomplish this result so easily. You are presenting such a subject for debate and excitement as the country never had before.[64]

Virginia's Seddon proposed an amendment requiring that presidential appointments in the territories receive a majority of US senators from slave states. For the first time, John Tyler extraordinarily set aside his presidential role in the Peace Conference to address the issue himself directly from the floor. He seemingly had reserved his political capital, carefully conserved in Willard Hall, until now.

Tyler admitted the proposal was "extraordinary," but explained "that policy is the best, which reduces within the narrowest limits the patronage to be exercised by the executive authority." He had "heard with pleasure the feelings expressed, the references made, to the Cotton States. I have scarcely heard an unkind word said against them. We have come here to cement the Union—to make that Union, of which gentlemen have so eloquently spoken, permanent, noble, and glorious in the future as it has been in the past—not to be content with it as a maimed and crippled Republic."[65]

Now with "eight flourishing States . . . practically lost to us," Tyler urged exerting "every power we possess to bring them all back to the fold," based on "every motive of interest or patriotism." He observed the powers of Europe would eagerly give much "for this favored section." And yet "we stand here higgling over these little differences which alone have caused our separation. Is it not better that we should rise to the level of the occasion, and meet the requisition of the times, instead of expending precious hours in the discussion of these miserable abstractions?"[66]

Seddon's proposal would preserve the "equilibrium, the balance of power, between the sections," Tyler asserted. "It enables each section to appoint its own officers, to protect its own interests, to regulate its own concerns. It is fair and equal in its operations. With it, no section can have any excuse for dissatisfaction. I pledge the united support of the South to the Union, if it is adopted." But despite Tyler's personal intervention, the proposal overwhelmingly failed by eleven to four, with only Maryland, Virginia, Kentucky, and Missouri supporting it. Perhaps it was at this hour that Tyler began, at least inwardly, to despair of the Peace Conference.[67]

MEETING WITH LINCOLN

Very early on that Saturday morning of February 23, unknown to most Peace Conference delegates except perhaps a few Republicans in the know, Abraham Lincoln had strode through the swinging doors of Willard's Hotel, where Senator Seward was awaiting him. New York Peace Delegate William Dodge vacated his room to make way for Lincoln, telling him: "Mr. Lincoln, the prayers of many hearts were with you before you started this journey, they accompanied you all the way here, and they will follow you as you enter in on this administration."[68]

Reports widely circulated that Lincoln had hurried to Washington ahead of schedule because "important measures before the Peace Conference made it expedient, if not necessary, to consult him about them before action should be taken," as one newspaper recounted, while admitting there were "many rumors in regard to this proceeding that we shall not place much reliance in." In fact, there's no evidence that Lincoln adjusted his schedule for the Peace Conference, and he had in fact hurried through Baltimore due to security concerns. But his arrival predictably caused a sensation at Willard's, where emotions were already charged.[69]

Later that morning, shortly after the session was called to order, James Seddon was approached by his slave. Lucius Chittenden described the slave as a "man scarcely darker than himself, his equal in deportment, his superior in figure and carriage," who "had made himself a favorite by his civil and respectful manner, and by general consent was the only person, not a member or officer, who had the entree to the sessions of the Conference." The servant handed Seddon a "scrap of paper, apparently torn from an envelope," at which Seddon glanced and then passed to Missouri's Waldo Johnson. The note announced: "Lincoln is in this hotel!" As news spread through Willard Hall, commissioners "gathered in groups to discuss it, and were too much absorbed to hear the repeated calls of the chairman to order," no event yet at the conference having "produced so much excitement."[70]

This excitement prevented exclusive focus on debate, as "members were not in a condition of mind to make speeches or to listen to them," as Chittenden later recalled. After a "hurried consultation" among Republicans, Logan of Illinois then announced that "Mr. Lincoln, the President-elect, has arrived in this city. I feel certain that the Conference would desire to treat him with the same measure of respect which it has extended to the present incumbent of that high office." He moved that the "President of this Convention be requested to call upon the President-elect of the United States, and inform him that its members would be pleased to wait upon him in a body at such time as will suit his convenience, and that this Convention be advised of the result."[71]

"This motion was fiercely opposed," Chittenden later remembered, never failing to notice such slights, although he did not record this opposition in his journal that day. He recalled cries of "No! No! Vote it down!" and "Lay it on the table!" amid barely whispered insults of "Railsplitter!" "Ignoramus!" and "Vulgar clown!" Ever decorous, President Tyler ruled that "the proposal was eminently proper; that the office, and not the individual, was to be considered; that he hoped that no Southern member would decline to treat the incoming President with the same respect and attention already extended to the present incumbent of that honorable and exalted office." The convention apparently mollified by Tyler's summons to propriety, Logan's motion then was unanimously adopted, at least officially, with delegates agreeing to adjourn and reconvene at 7:30 P.M.[72]

Lincoln's early morning, largely unexpected arrival in Washington had not lacked for drama. Rumors of assassination plots had plagued Washington. Chittenden, often at the center of intrigue, later told of having been summoned to Baltimore surreptitiously on Sunday, February 17. There local Republicans unveiled to him complex anti-Lincoln conspiracies. He returned to Washington and informed a Lincoln associate, who assured him that the president-elect's security had been safeguarded.[73] Under the protection of Pinkerton detectives, Lincoln slipped through Baltimore in the very late hours, unannounced, in a secluded sleeping car, changing trains under cover of darkness while clad in a shawl and knit cap. Critics mocked the subterfuge as unmanly. Chittenden, who was always alert to perceived conspiracy, later asserted that Waldo Johnson exclaimed, "How the devil did he get through Baltimore?" upon hearing from James Seddon of Lincoln's arrival. Seddon irritably replied, seemingly for the benefit of any eavesdroppers like Chittenden who sat nearby, "What would prevent his passing through Baltimore?"[74]

Perhaps also surprised by Lincoln's arrival, or at least its timing, Tyler declined to "call upon" Lincoln, as the motion stipulated, instead writing him a note, receiving word that Lincoln would be "pleased to receive the members of this body at nine o'clock this evening, or at any other time which may suit their convenience." As Chittenden later noted, Republican members of the Conference were "not pleased with the manner in which the chairman performed his duty," but raised no objection over a "mere matter of form."[75]

The intrepid Chittenden, as he later recorded, thought "it might prove of advantage to Mr. Lincoln to have some information in advance of the men who would meet him that evening," so he went to visit him ahead of the others, to advise "who would visit him out of respect, and who would come out of curiosity, or only to jeer and ridicule." In Lincoln's apartment upstairs he found a "tall, stooping figure, upon which his clothing hung loosely and ungracefully." His "kindly eyes looked out from under a cavernous, projecting brow, with a curiously mingled expression of sadness and humor." Lincoln's limbs were "long, and at first sight ungainly" but overshadowed by the "cordial grasp of his large hands, the cheery tones of his pleasant voice, the heartiness of his welcome, in the air and presence of the great-hearted man." Lincoln dominated the conversation, leaving Chittenden saying nothing he had planned, as Lincoln hoped for "opportunity of meeting so many representative men from different sections of the Union; the more unjust they were in their opinions of himself, the more he desired to make their acquaintance," to dissuade them that he was "an evil spirit, a goblin, the implacable enemy of Southern men and women." He especially hoped all the slave state delegates would be present, specifically mentioning William Rives of Virginia and Judge Thomas Ruffin of North Carolina as particularly influential, plus several whom he had known in Congress years before.[76]

Chittenden remembered the earlier peace delegates' visit to President Buchanan, when they had processed behind President Tyler. With their visit to Lincoln, they were arranged more as "straggling groups" meandering to the meeting space, as a "most unfriendly audience," many of whom "entertained for him sentiments of positive hatred." They discussed Lincoln as a "curiosity" as they would have "spoken of a clown with whose ignorant vulgarity they were to be amused." Lincoln received the delegates with no signs of having "made the slightest preparation," standing alone in one of Willard's public drawing rooms. Finding no organized protocol, Chittenden recalled he stood by Lincoln to introduce each delegate by name. Evidently few if any boycotted, curiosity getting the best of them, as the crowd was as large as it had been for Buchanan. Lincoln showed little evidence of exhaustion from his early morning arrival, or from his tense transit through Baltimore, preceded by ten days of cross-country travel and greeting crowds.[77]

According to a Washington newspaper, Lincoln had just returned from dinner at Senator Seward's house, after spending much of the day at Willard's receiving guests like General Winfield Scott and Senator Stephen Douglas. At 9:00 P.M. he met the Peace Conference delegates, who had "formed in procession in the hall where they meet and proceeded to the reception parlor," with President Tyler and Salmon Chase having "led the van." Chase introduced Tyler to Lincoln, who "received him with all the respect due his position." Chase then "presented" each delegate to Lincoln, according to the newspaper.[78]

Delegates lined up around him in a circle after each was introduced, with Lincoln trying to give each a unique and sometimes playful greeting. To Kentucky's James Clay, he said, "Your name is all the endorsement you require," adding, "From my boyhood the name of Henry Clay has been an inspiration to me." To western Virginia's George Summers, he enthused: "You cannot be a Disunionist, unless your nature has changed since we met in Congress!" He asked of a Tennessean, "Does liberty still thrive in the mountains of Tennessee?"[79]

The urbane William Rives was a former US senator, minister to France, and a renowned statesman whom Lincoln had quoted in a speech twenty-two years before. Lincoln now fulsomely exclaimed: "You are a smaller man than I supposed—I mean in person: everyone is acquainted with the greatness of your intellect. It is, indeed, pleasant to meet one who has so honorably represented his country in Congress and abroad." Rives, as he recalled, replied, "I feel a small man in your presence," later saying of the encounter, "This piece of Western free and easy compliment passed off among his admirers for first rate Parisian cleverness and tact."[80]

Rives archly told Lincoln that "the clouds that hang over [the nation] are very dark. I have no longer the courage of my younger days. I can do little—you can do much. Everything now depends upon you." Lincoln replied, "I cannot agree to that," saying his course was "as plain as a turnpike road. It is marked out by the Constitution. I am in no doubt which way to go. Suppose now we all stop discussing and try the experiment of obedience to the Constitution and the laws. Don't you think it would work?"[81]

Virginia's George Summers replied to Lincoln, "Yes, it will work. If the Constitution is your light, I will follow it with you, and the people of the South will go with us." Then a more confrontational James Seddon interjected: "It is not of your professions we complain. It is of your sins of omission—of your failure to enforce the laws—to suppress your John Browns and your Garrisons, who preach insurrection and make war upon our property!"[82]

Lincoln tartly responded to Seddon: "I believe John Brown was hung and Mr. Garrison imprisoned. You cannot justly charge the North with disobedience to statutes or with failing to enforce them. You have made some which were very offensive, but they have been enforced, notwithstanding." Seddon retorted: "You do not enforce the laws. You refuse to execute the statute for the return of fugitive slaves. Your leading men openly declare that they will not assist the marshals to capture or return slaves."[83]

Not backing down, Lincoln told Seddon: "You are wrong in your facts again. Your slaves have been returned, yes, from the shadow of Faneuil Hall in the heart of Boston. Our people do not like the work, I know. They will do what the law commands, but they will not volunteer to act as tip-staves or bum-bailiffs. The instinct is natural to the race. Is it not true of the South? Would you join in the pursuit of a fugitive slave if you could avoid it? Is such the work of gentlemen?"[84]

Seddon leveled more charges at Lincoln: "Your press is incendiary! It advocates servile insurrection, and advises our slaves to cut their masters' throats. You do not suppress your newspapers. You encourage their violence."[85]

"I beg your pardon, Mr. Seddon," replied Mr. Lincoln. "I intend no offense, but I will not suffer such a statement to pass unchallenged, because it is not true. No Northern newspaper, not the most ultra, has advocated a slave insurrection or advised the slaves to cut their masters' throats. A gentleman of your intelligence should not make such assertions. We do maintain the freedom of the press—we deem it necessary to a free government. Are we peculiar in that respect? Is not the same doctrine held in the South?"[86]

In a loud voice, New York's William Dodge, recently and willingly dislodged from his Willard's room by Lincoln, now declared to the president: "It is for you, sir, to say whether the whole nation shall be plunged into bankruptcy; whether the grass shall grow in the streets of our commercial cities." Lincoln good-naturedly replied, "Then I say it shall not. If it depends upon me, the grass will not grow anywhere except in the fields and the meadows."[87]

Dodge then concluded: "Then you will yield to the just demands of the South. You will leave her to control her own institutions. You will admit slave states into the Union on the same conditions as free states. You will not go to war on account of slavery!"[88]

Lincoln somberly replied:

I do not know that I understand your meaning, Mr. Dodge, nor do I know what my acts or my opinions may be in the future, beyond this. If I shall ever come to the great office of President of the United States, I shall take an oath. I shall swear that I will faithfully execute the office of President of the United States, of all the United States, and that I will, to the best of my ability, preserve, protect, and defend the Constitution of the United States. This is a great and solemn duty. With the support of the people and the assistance of the Almighty I shall undertake to perform it. I have full faith that I shall perform it. It is not the Constitution as I would like to have it, but as it is, that is to be defended. The Constitution will not be preserved and defended until it is enforced and obeyed in every part of every one of the United States. It must be so respected, obeyed, enforced, and defended, let the grass grow where it may.[89]

Crittenden recalled that Lincoln's words about his constitutional duties stilled the crowd, with Republicans pleased, while "some of the more ardent southerners silently left the room," exasperated not to find the "entertainment to which they were invited," while some more conservative Southerners were intrigued and remained. In response to one question, Lincoln was pointed: "In a choice of evils, war may not always be the worst. Still I would do all in my power to avert it, except to neglect a Constitutional duty. As to slavery, it must be content with what it has. The voice of the civilized world is against it; it is opposed to its growth or extension. Freedom is the natural condition of the human race, in which the Almighty intended men to live. Those who fight the purposes of the Almighty will not succeed. They always have been, they always will be, beaten."[90]

Lincoln was evasive with questions from other Southerners. According to Chittenden, Rives of Virginia afterward commented:

He has been both misjudged and misunderstood by the Southern people. . . . They have looked upon him as an ignorant, self-willed man, incapable of independent judgment, full of prejudices, willing to be used as a tool by more able men. This is all wrong. He will be the head of his administration, and he will do his own thinking. He seems to have studied the Constitution, to have adopted it as his guide. I do not see that much fault can be found with the views he has expressed this evening. He is probably not so great a statesman as Mr. Madison, he may not have the will-power of General Jackson. He may combine the qualities of both. His will not be a weak administration.[91]

The next day, Rives wrote of Lincoln: "He seemed to be good-natured and well-intentioned, but utterly unimpressed with the gravity of the crisis and the magnitude of his duties. . . . He seems to think of nothing but jokes and stories. I fear, therefore, we are to expect but little from his influence with the convention."[92]

Undeterred by exhaustion, and possibly fueled by adrenaline, after the peace commissioners left him Lincoln received prominent citizens. Then he was told the hotel lobby was "filed with ladies, who desired to pay their respects," to which he "very readily consented." The ladies then "passed in review, each being introduced by the gentleman who accompanied her," with Lincoln undergoing the "new ordeal with much good humor." The evening not yet over, President Buchanan's cabinet paid their respects at 10:00 P.M.

The next morning, a Sunday, Seward met Lincoln at Willard's and they together departed from its Fourteenth Street entrance at 10:30 A.M. and walked the half mile to St. John's Episcopal Church, entering "unobtrusively" and sitting together in Seward's pew. Lincoln went largely unnoticed, even by Reverend Dr. Pyne, until the very end of the service. His sermon quoted 1 Corinthians 7:31, saying, "And they that use this world, as not abusing it: for the fashion of this world passeth away. KJV" And Dr. Pyne made "several allusions to the present state of the country, and to the change in the Administration which was about to take place." It was noticed Lincoln had "black whiskers and hair well-trimmed, and was pronounced by such as recognized him as a different man entirely from the hard-looking pictorial representations of him," with "some of the ladies" saying "in fact he is almost good-looking."[93]

Lincoln's arrival at Willard's and his encounters with the peace delegates left a formidable impression upon friends and adversaries, certainly adding urgency to their final proceedings. But Lincoln had made no openly direct comment on their deliberations nor did he offer any specific commitments. Seemingly like the rest of the nation, he would wait to see what happened.

EIGHT
AGREEMENT AND REJECTION

Mr. President, if General Washington occupied the seat
that you will soon fill, and it had been as necessary to
talk to him as we have to you to save such a Union as
this, I for one should talk to him as we have to you.

—James Guthrie to Abraham Lincoln

Still absorbing the impact of their Saturday encounter with president-
elect Lincoln, Peace Conference delegates reconvened at 10:00 A.M.
Monday, February 25. It was the start of their final three days together.
Rev. Dr. John Smith of Fourth Presbyterian Church opened with
prayer.

A Washington newspaper that morning carried the schedule for the
presidential inauguration on March 4. The order of the procession was
led by former US presidents, the Republican Association, the judiciary,
the clergy, foreign ministers, the diplomatic corps, current and former
cabinet members, and then the Peace Congress, followed by heads of

bureaus and state governors, military officers, and veterans starting with the Revolution, of whom a few oldsters still survived.[1]

But would the Peace Congress even still be in Washington on March 4? Given their animosity toward Lincoln, at least by many delegates, would they participate in his inauguration? The inauguration's details were described at great length in many newspapers, as though it would be just another normal inauguration. But this year's would be the first when states had quit the Union, when more were threatening, when civil war was on the worried minds of many, and when even the inauguration itself needed to be secured against threats of terror and coup. The Peace Congress was listed as participating, as though a normal part of the civic pageant. But these delegates were only there because of an unprecedented national crisis, for which they were summoned to somehow, miraculously, resolve. There were only a few days left to achieve this miracle.

Some were still hopeful. Another Washington newspaper reported that based on Saturday's voting, it was clear that the majority report of Kentucky's James Guthrie would prevail. Although it was acceptable to Virginia's William Rives and George Summers, James Seddon and President Tyler would reject it. "We have not expected that the convention would adopt anything that Messrs Tyler and Seddon would vote for, as their sympathies are notoriously with the cause of secessions," it snipped. Even if Virginia rejected the compromise, they would stand alone with "anti-compromise Republican Party delegations," it surmised. "We feel assured that the Virginia convention now in session in Richmond will frankly and cordially accept it." Predicting the convention may protract until "sometime tomorrow," it still pronounced that the "public may rest assured, we apprehend, that the threatening cloud is thus rapidly passing off the horizon of the country's future."[2]

That Monday morning at Willard's, delegates made various further attempts to amend the majority report, prompting Kentucky's James Guthrie to warn, "If we begin to adopt these amendments no one can tell where they will carry us." One amendment from Virginia's James Seddon aimed to further "secure slavery from all interference" by Congress in the territories. Guthrie pronounced it "unnecessary"; it was defeated fourteen to six, with Maryland, Virginia, North Carolina, Tennessee, Kentucky, and Missouri in the minority. Seddon also tried unsuccessfully to require Virginia's consent, and not just Maryland's, to any abolition of slavery in Washington, DC. And he tried to further specify the protection of slave property on the high seas.[3]

"We claim that our property in slaves shall be recognized by the Union just like any other property—that no unjust or improper distinction shall be made," Seddon said. "When we trust it to the perils of the seas, we wish to have it protected by the Federal Government."[4]

North Carolina's Ruffin spoke against Seddon's proposal, warning it might bind the United States to war, and the "ordinary course of national diplomacy" was sufficient. Seddon reiterated: "I think slave property upon every ground is as well entitled to the national protection as any other species of property."[5]

Delineating the differences between the North and South, North Carolina's Barringer said the former saw slavery as "an abnormal condition" that "cannot exist anywhere until it is established or authorized by law," while the latter asserts slavery "always, everywhere, exists until it is prohibited by law" as a "natural right" and a "normal condition." He admitted this "normal condition was not confined to a single race" but "extends to all races." He called Seddon's amendment "highly important to the South," explaining, "we say that slaves are both persons and property," and "we fear the established policy of the government will be changed by the party now coming into power."[6]

Seddon's amendment failed, with only Virginia, Tennessee, North Carolina, and Missouri supporting it. But he tried additionally another amendment adding to the Constitution the words "master and slave," clearly "in plain English language, so that the dangerous delusion so prevalent at the North, that the Constitution does not recognize slavery, may be thoroughly and forever removed; so that the Constitution shall, beyond any question, recognize the relation of master and slave; a duplex relation—a relation of person and property." He declared, "Put this into the Constitution, and you take the shortest and the most effective means of settling the question, and of promoting peace and tranquility. You strike the axe to the very root of bitterness, whence has sprung all our trouble, all our difficulties." Only Virginia, North Carolina, and Missouri voted for the amendment.[7]

New York's William Noyes warned that the majority report, by prohibiting any congressional action against slavery, would revive the slave trade in Washington, DC, which Congress banned in the Compromise of 1850. "It imposes upon the soil of the District the right of holding, retaining, and taking away the slaves by the owner himself, his agent or assignee," he explained. Vermont's Hiland Hall successfully proposed amending the majority report to constitutionally codify the slave trade ban in the federal capital, with a positive vote of eleven states to ten.[8]

Connecticut's Charles McCurdy similarly proposed language specifying the right of non-slave states to ban the slave trade, which passed by eleven to ten. Exasperated, Guthrie of Kentucky declared that "if this class of amendments is to be adopted, I cannot go on, with respect to myself or the Convention. I feel now, since this amendment is adopted, that my mission here is ended." After a motion to reconsider, McCurdy's proposal was rejected seven to fourteen. But another amendment protecting free states from slaves' "right of transit . . . without its consent" passed ten to eight.[9]

When North Carolina's David Reid tried to insert "Persons of the African race shall not be deemed citizens, or permitted to exercise the right of suffrage, in the election of federal officers," Guthrie exclaimed, "This is worse than ever, and it comes from the South too." Reid promptly withdrew his amendment.[10]

Baldwin of Massachusetts tried to remove the prohibition on Congress taxing slaves at a rate higher than other property, but only Maine, Massachusetts, and Connecticut supported him.[11] In response to another amendment, Seddon of Virginia warned that "an owner should be free to determine for himself the question whether he will part with his property upon receiving suitable compensation," while the proposal would let Congress decide, he complained. Seddon added: "The North denies the right of property in slaves, and would deny compensation also, unless compelled to make it under the Constitution. The North holding slavery to be unjust and unrighteous, would desire to abolish the institution without paying for it."[12]

Guthrie of Kentucky became indignant over continued proposed amendments to the majority report. "I feel that my mission here is ended, and that I may as well withdraw from the Conference," he averred. "I seem to be unable to impress gentlemen with the necessity of accomplishing anything. The report of the committee is not satisfactory to the South; it is even doubtful whether they will adopt it; certainly they will not, if it is cut to pieces by amendments. I may be compelled to sacrifice my property, or go with the secessionists. At my time of life, I do not wish to do either."[13]

The delegates adjourned until 7:30 P.M. that evening, when they debated how the prohibition on the importation of slaves might affect relations with seceded states. Missouri's John Coalter urged leaving the issue to Congress. A St. Louis newspaper, cited in Washington, had editorialized against him as someone who has "been sent to Washington to demand concessions and present the 'ultimatum' of Missouri to the North," but he should "please take notice that he has been repudiated at home. He represents nobody, and will do well to present his own ultimatum, and leave as speedily as possible," having "received the smallest vote on the secession ticket, proving that even his own party is disgusted with him." Indeed, "Mr. Coalter had better go back to South Carolina, and remain there. The members of the Peace Convention will do well to take notice that the Commissioners from Missouri have been repudiated by the state."[14]

But Coalter, who was pro-slavery and pro-Union, was seemingly undeterred. "We certainly do not wish to adopt a provision which will cut off the traffic in slaves between the Gulf States and the others," he assumed. "The negroes are a portion of the families of Southern men" and "regarded as such in all the transactions of life." Their families "may

227

at times become separated," with a "portion of them" now in the seceded states, and a "portion farther North," as often during one "season of the year the planter, with his family and slaves, lives upon the plantation in the Gulf States; and at another season, removes with his family and slaves to a plantation farther North." Coalter reasoned: "We do not wish to obstruct a relation or proceeding of this kind," which was "not a mere matter of dollars and cents" but involved the "happiness of families," and the "blacks themselves are interested in it."[15]

Seddon of Virginia, who opposed resurrection of the international slave trade, still didn't like "legislating in the Constitution," so he proposed saying "Congress shall have power to prohibit" the slave trade and to strike out the words that the slave trade was "forever prohibited." Charles Allen of Massachusetts argued against, saying: "This is a question which I would not leave to Congress. We know how immensely profitable this trade is—that fortunes are made by a single successful voyage. Don't let such an inducement to corruption creep into our Constitution." Doniphan of Missouri agreed: "I am opposed to the foreign slave-trade in every form. I would not even make a treaty with a nation or a State that would permit it. If the seceded States are to be regarded out of the Union, I would not treat with them; I would not invest Congress with such a dangerous power. Nothing will suit me but an unqualified prohibition of this trade in the Constitution itself."[16]

Morehead of Kentucky proposed new language on the slave trade saying: "The foreign slave-trade is hereby forever prohibited; and it shall be the duty of Congress to pass laws to prevent the importation of slaves into the United States and their Territories, from places beyond the limits thereof." His Kentucky colleague, Wickliffe, proposed adding to it the words "or coolies, or persons held to service or labor." He explained: "We are aware that certain countries which are much exercised over the criminality of slavery and the slave-trade, have recently adopted a system, the horrors of which are not surpassed by those of the middle passage. I refer to the importation of coolies and other persons from China and the East.

In my judgment, this is the slave-trade in one of its worst forms. I think if we prevent the importation of slaves at all, the provision ought to be made to cover such a case." Morehead accepted this addition, and the proposal passed eleven to eight, with free states voting no out of concern that the slave trade could revive without specific constitutional ban.[17]

Pennsylvania's longtime anti-slavery crusader Congressman David Wilmot complained that the majority report offered federal compensation to owners of fugitive slaves protected illegally but not to victims of "mobs and riotous assemblies in the slave States." He proposed similar compensation for "deprivation, by violence, of . . . rights secured by this Constitution." Guthrie warned this law "encourages seditious speeches at the South." William Stephens of Tennessee also was opposed, saying: "We have come here to arrange old difficulties, not to make new ones. Adopt this, and you lay the foundation stone of disunion. It is an encouragement to seditious speeches and purposes." It was rejected fourteen to seven.[18]

Orth of Indiana moved that fugitive slaves whose owners are compensated by the federal government should be considered free. J. Dixon Roman of Maryland objected: "This is nothing but an inducement to mobs and riots. Pass this provision, and no fugitive slave will ever again be returned from a free State. There will always be abolitionists enough to pay for a slave, and this payment will set the slave free, and will constitute the only penalty for this violence." He added:

If the peace of this country is to be hereafter established on a permanent basis, and the Union is to be preserved, you, gentlemen of the North, must recognize our rights, and cease to interfere with them. You have nothing to do with this question of slavery. It is an institution of our own. If it is a crime, we are responsible for it, and will bear the responsibility. We have never interfered with your institutions. You must now let us alone.

Orth's motion was rejected eleven to ten.[19]

THE EIGHTEENTH DAY

The exhausted delegates adjourned at 2:00 A.M. and reconvened at 11:00 A.M. on Tuesday, February 26, the conference's eighteenth day. A Washington newspaper reported that day that the "excitement" of the previous day "was far greater than on any previous occasion." "Anti-compromisers" led by New York's David Field strove against final action, while "extreme demands" were made by diehards like James Seddon to make compromise unpalatable. Guthrie of Kentucky became "excited to the point of starting to leave the hall," since "anti-compromisers" were "trifling" with more responsible delegates, but he was "persuaded to remain and subsequently again took his leading part in disposing of the business before them." When adjourned for dinner, the "friends of compromise were nearly all hopeless of being able to accomplish any final result whatever; as, under their rules, the minority, if determined, could prevent a final vote from being taken," by proposing constant amendments "to kill time." After reassembling, the majority "made up their minds to sit all night," but they finished the day's work at 1:30 A.M. The "friends of compromise have a clear majority," the newspaper was confident.[20]

That Tuesday morning, Connecticut noted that its last vote was mistakenly recorded no, which was the decisive vote. They requested reconsideration on Orth's amendment freeing fugitive slaves whose owners are compensated. So debate was renewed.

Morehead of Kentucky objected to Orth's proposal: "Our slaves would escape, you would rescue and pay for them, and that would be the end of them. Why not leave it to Congress to pass the necessary laws upon this subject? The adoption of this amendment would destroy all hope that our labors would be acceptable to the South." Rives of Virginia also denounced it as a "most comprehensive scheme of emancipation." Morehead predicted:

> We know from past experience what the Abolitionists of the free States would do under such a provision as this in the Constitution. There will

be an underground railroad line along every principal route of travel. There will be depots all along these lines. Canoes will be furnished to ferry negroes over the Potomac and Ohio. John Brown & Co. will stand ready to kill the master the very moment he crosses the line in pursuit of his slave. What officer at the North will dare to arrest the slave when John Brown pikes are stacked up in every little village? If arrested, there will be organizations formed to rescue him, and you may as well let the [negro] go free at once. You are opening up the greatest scheme of emancipation ever devised.[21]

Orth's proposal was amended to read: "And the acceptance of such payment shall preclude the owner from further claim to said fugitive." It passed 17–3, with only Virginia, Missouri, and Indiana opposed.[22]

A proposal rejecting secession and declaring the Union indissoluble was supported by Wilmot of Pennsylvania: "I think it high time that the Constitution was made unequivocal upon this subject of secession."[23]

Responding to Wilmot, Rodman Price of New Jersey bewailed "an element in this conference which, from the first day of our session, has opposed any action." He claimed the conference's policy had been to "distract and divide our counsels, to put off everything, to prevent all action." He admitted: "We all agree to the principle contained in this amendment; but if we adopt it and make it a part of the Constitution, we could never, under it, bring back the seceded States." And he pleaded: "Do not let us sit here like the great Belshazzar till the handwriting appears on the wall. Let us set our faces against delay. Let us put down with an indignant rebuke every attempt to demoralize our action or destroy its effect."[24]

Benjamin Howard of Maryland agreed that "there is no right of secession," but the "right of revolution always exists." He warned: "Virginia has hung her flag at half-mast as a signal of distress. If Virginia secedes our State will go with her, hand in hand, with Providence as our guide. This is not intended as a threat. GOD forbid! It is a truth which we cannot and ought not to conceal."[25]

Rives of Virginia complained, "While we are talking about abstractions, we are wasting our time." He urged moving to the "practical matters involved in the report, and its adoption." Noyes of New York noted the "slave power has now had possession of the government in all for more than fifty years. A President has been elected belonging to the opposing party. For that cause alone, and without claiming or assigning any other, the slave States, under the powerful protection of Virginia, have come here for guarantees." He asked of the South: "If you have a right to guarantees to quiet your apprehensions, have we not a right to insist that secession shall be put down and condemned by an explicit clause of the Constitution?"[26]

Rejecting Noyes's argument, the proposal declaring the Union indissoluble was voted down, eleven to ten.[27] Baldwin of Connecticut proposed a convention of the states, which was rejected thirteen to eight.[28] Virginia's Seddon proposed his state's version of the Crittenden Compromise, which failed sixteen to four.[29] Kentucky's Clay then offered the Crittenden package "pure and undefiled," which was rejected fourteen to five.[30]

After the flurry of doomed counter proposals, Salmon Chase then spoke. "I do not approve the confident pledges made here of favorable action by the people of either section, or of any state, upon whatever propositions may receive the sanction of this Conference," he declared. Chase denied that the recent election of Lincoln was merely a "sudden impulse" or that local questions had superseded national ones:

> I believe, and the belief amounts to absolute conviction, that the election must be regarded as the triumph of principles cherished in the hearts of the people of the free States. These principles, it is true, were originally asserted by a small party only. But, after years of discussion, they have, by their own value, their own intrinsic soundness, obtained the deliberate and unalterable sanction of the people's judgment.[31]

"You profess to be satisfied with slavery, as it is and where it is," Chase continued.

You think the institution just and beneficial. The very able gentleman from Virginia (Mr. Seddon), who commands the respect of all by the frankness and sincerity of his speech, has said that he believes slavery to be the condition in which the African is to be educated up to freedom. He does not believe in perpetual slavery. He believes the time will come when the slave, through the beneficent influences of the circumstances which surround him, will rise in intelligence, capacity, and character, to the dignity of a freeman, and will be free.[32]

But Chase insisted: "We cannot agree with you, and therefore do not propose to allow slavery where we are responsible for it, outside of your State limits, and under National jurisdiction. But we do not mean to interfere with it at all within State limits. So far as we are concerned, you can work out your experiment there in peace. We shall rejoice if no evil comes from it to you or yours."[33]

Chase urged a national convention, realistically pointing out that the two-thirds majority needed in Congress for the proposals emerging from the Peace Congress were unattainable. When Lincoln would assume his presidential duties and "undertakes to enforce the laws, and secession or revolution resists, what then? War! Civil war!" He pleaded:

Let us not rush headlong into that unfathomable gulf. Let us not tempt this unutterable woe. We offer you a plain and honorable mode of adjusting all difficulties. It is a mode which, we believe, will receive the sanction of the people. We pledge ourselves here that we will do all in our power to obtain their sanction for it. Is it too much to ask you, gentlemen of the South, to meet us on this honorable and practicable ground? Will you not, at least, concede this to the country?[34]

Chase's motion for a national convention was rejected eleven to nine.[35]

As the delegates finally moved toward voting on the majority report, Robert Carruthers of Tennessee promised: "I only desire to say for my State that if you will give us these propositions, Tennessee will adopt them, and it will sink secession beyond any hope of resurrection."[36]

Stockton of New Jersey, an old commodore who almost spoke as if from another age, resorted to classical analogies:

> In the days of Rome, Curtius threw himself into the chasm when told by the oracle that the sacrifice of his life would save his country. Alas! Is there no Curtius here? The alternative is a dreadful one to contemplate if we cannot adopt these propositions and secure peace. It is useless to attempt to dwarf this movement of the South by the name of treason. Call it by what name you will, it is a revolution, and this is a right which the people of this country have derived in common from their ancestors.[37]

A vote ensued on the majority report's first section: a constitutional amendment reinstating the old Missouri Compromise latitude 36°30′ boundary between free and slave territory. The majority were negative, eleven to eight. Four free states and four slave states supported it, with the rest opposed. The shocking result created confusion, bringing the conference to a temporary halt "for some minutes," leading to a call for reconsideration.[38]

Francis Granger of New York implored "those gentlemen from the slave States especially, who have by their votes defeated the compromise we have labored so long and so earnestly to secure, to take a little time for consideration." He then spoke for history:

> When, perchance, the rude hand of violence shall here have seized upon the monuments and archives of our country's history; when all the monuments of art that time and treasure may here have gathered, shall be destroyed; when these proud domes shall totter to their fall, and the rank grass wave around their moldering columns; when the very name of Washington, instead of stirring the blood to patriotic action, shall be a byword and a reproach—then will this people feel what was the value of the Union.[39]

By fourteen to five, the conference voted to reconsider and adjourn for an evening session, where Wickliffe of Kentucky said, "it is certain that the vote had better not be taken this evening." So the delegates next met at 10:00 A.M. on Wednesday, February 27, the nineteenth day of their proceedings.[40]

THE NINETEENTH DAY

The lobbying and conversations were intense in the gaslit parlors and corridors of Willard's Hotel that February night. Proponents for the Resolutions Committee's proposals argued that both the Union and peace depended on their ratification. Few were enthusiastic for them, but what was the alternative?

A Washington newspaper reported that on that tense evening when the Peace Congress seemed on the verge of collapse, several peace delegates "urgently appealed to Lincoln to interpose for a settlement of the pending difficulties," in an "interview lasting several hours." Likely this meeting is the same that Kentucky's Charles Morehead recalled later on two separate occasions.[41]

One year later, on February 23, 1862, Morehead was on parole from incarceration for his perceived support for the rebellion. The one-time Kentucky governor whom former First Lady Julia Tyler during the Peace Conference had hailed as the "handsomest man," recalled a conversation with Lincoln "several days" after Lincoln's arrival in Washington, likely that evening after the failed vote. He was accompanied by fellow Peace Commissioners William Rives and George Summers of Virginia, Alexander Doniphan of Missouri, and James Guthrie of Kentucky. "I ventured to express to him my sense of the dreadful impending danger, and entreated him and implored him to avert it," as he described at great length to Senator John Crittenden.

I said to him that he held the destiny of more than thirty millions of people in his hands; that if he acted the part of a wise statesman, in

235

avoiding a collision, he would occupy a place in the future of his country second only to Washington; but, on the other hand, if he adopted a policy which would lead to war, that the history of his administration would be written in blood, and all the waters of the Atlantic and Pacific Oceans could not wash it from his hands; that the true and wise policy was to withdraw the troops from Fort Sumter and give satisfactory guarantees to the eight remaining slaveholding states, and that the seven seceded states would not at once, but ultimately, by the mere force of gravitation, come back, and we should have a safer and firmer bond of union than ever. Mr. Rives pressed the same idea, when Mr. Lincoln said he would withdraw the troops if Virginia would stay in the Union.[42]

Late in 1862 Morehead had escaped the United States for abroad, fearing renewed arrest. He recalled his Lincoln meeting during a speech in Liverpool, England. As he remembered, fellow Peace Commissioner Stephen Logan of Illinois had told him Lincoln had desired a meeting, recalling their days together in Congress. Morehead had been on "very intimate terms" with Lincoln during their time in Congress together. It was agreed who else would attend, and they met at 9:00 P.M. Lincoln received them "very kindly," and asked about the "settled enmity" against him in the South. The peace commissioners sat about him in a semicircle. Morehead assured him there was no "personal enmity," and he appealed to him to give these guarantees which were demanded by the Southern men in that Peace Conference, "representing to him that it was in his power." Lincoln replied he was willing to give a constitutional guarantee protecting slavery in the South but his "whole life was dedicated to opposition to its extension," and he would not "betray" his party platform. They denied the government had the power to prohibit slavery in the territories but insisted slavery was unsuitable to them anyway, making the "laws of nature a stronger prohibition." He replied he was firmly "committed" on that issue.[43]

Morehead recalled his campaigning against Lincoln for president, mobilizing "all the zeal and energy of which I was master," but now accepting his election while urging "deference is due to the opinions of those who constitute the majority," since Lincoln was elected by a minority. Lincoln "rather briskly" said, "If he was a minority President he was not the first, and that at all events he had obtained more votes than could muster for any other man." Alexander Doniphan then suggested Lincoln could be passive toward secession, grant guarantees to the South, or resort to coercion. Morehead remembered appealing to Lincoln as he "never appealed to any other man and never expect to do again" by praying against coercion, through which the "history of the administration would be written in blood and all the waters of the Atlantic Ocean could never wash it from his hands."[44]

Lincoln, as Morehead recalled, was seated, a "long lanky man," with elbows on knees and hands on face, "in an attitude of listening, and when he would speak he would drop his hands and raise his head." Recalling a courtroom anecdote, Lincoln suggested they wanted him to "guvin' it up" before the case was even tried. Morehead replied, "Mr. President, it might be you would be 'guvin' it up' but hadn't better 'guv it up' without bloodshed than drench this land with blood, and then have to 'guv it up'?" Asking Lincoln to set his "jests" aside, after Lincoln told of an Aesop's fable regarding an elephant who agreed to be disarmed of his tusk only to be clubbed to death, Morehead warned of the "injury to the cause of humanity" if Lincoln permitted a "fratricidal war."[45]

According to Morehead, stately former senator Rives then stood up, "dignity and eloquence that I have seldom heard surpassed in the course of my life," appealing to Lincoln, calling himself a "very old man" for whom there had never "been a throb of his heart that was not in favor of the perpetuation of the Union . . . and that all his efforts had been exerted in endeavoring to procure such guarantees as would perpetuate it." But Rives also "with a trembling voice" told Lincoln he agreed with Morehead about the "horrors of this anticipated war," and that if Lincoln did resort to coercion Virginia would "leave the Union and join the seceding States." Rives pledged that "old as I am, and dearly as I have loved this Union, in that event I go, with all my heart and soul!" Lincoln "jumped up from his big chair, as Mr. Rives was standing, advanced one step toward him and said: 'Mr. Rives, Mr. Rives, if Virginia will stay in I will withdraw the troops from Fort Sumter.'" Rives replied, "Do that, and give us guarantees, and I can only promise you that whatever influence I have shall be exerted to promote the Union, and to restore it to what it was."[46]

Before the peace commissioners departed, Lincoln asked: "Well gentlemen, I have been wondering very much whether, if Mr. Douglas or Mr. Bell had been elected President, if you would have dared to talk to him as freely as you have to me." James Guthrie replied, "Mr. President, if General Washington occupied the seat that you will soon fill, and it had been as necessary to talk to him as we have to you to save such a Union as this, I for one should talk to him as we have to you."[47]

Immediately that next morning, Wednesday, February 27, their nineteenth day in session, the delegates again voted. This time the proposal passed but only by nine to eight, with Virginia and North Carolina voting against with Northern states.[48] A key switch was Lincoln's friend, Logan of Illinois, which placed that state in the yes column, while Kansas and New York were too divided to vote. Indiana decided not to vote. Missouri shifted from against to abstain, seeing the proposals as a "sort of shapeless mass," as Doniphan later reported, but deciding they "should go before the country for what they are worth."[49]

Some believed Lincoln had interceded, possibly through his friend Logan. But another Illinois Peace Delegate, John Palmer, later recalled that Lincoln had "expected nothing from the proceedings of the convention, and advised us to deal as liberally as possible with the subject of slavery." Lincoln had also "pointed out to us the impossibility of restoring the Union without a struggle, in which we concurred." And he had warned that "whatever I may think of the merit of the various propositions suggested, I should regard any concession in the face of a menace, as the destruction of the government itself, and a consent on all hands that our system should be brought down to a level with the disorganized state of affairs in Mexico." Lincoln further averred that the results ultimately were "in the hands of the people." Palmer himself voted for the propositions, somewhat apologetically, telling Lincoln "that I would have to go into the army, in order to prove, after voting for the proposed amendments to the constitution, that I was a sincere anti-slavery man."[50]

The second part of the majority report required a majority of slave state senators to approve new territory, which passed eleven to eight. Delegates then voted on the third part, prohibiting congressional interference with slavery, which passed twelve to seven. The fourth section affirmed fugitive slave laws, and passed fifteen to four. Delegates then affirmed the fifth section banning importation of slaves by sixteen to five. The next section then protected all the above amendments from revocation except by unanimity of the states, which passed eleven to nine. By twelve to seven, the seventh section guaranteeing federal compensation for fugitive slaves was passed. Salmon Chase asked for a vote on the whole package together, which President Tyler ruled out of order.[51]

THE CLOSING

As the Peace Conference closed, its expenses were reported as $735, excluding printing costs, which the City of Washington was pledged to pay. Each participating state was apportioned $35. The Willard Brothers, owners of the hotel, were thanked for their "liberal and generous tender, free of charge, of the use of the Hall and the lights." The city was also thanked for posting police to guard Willard Hall from "intrusion." President Tyler was thanked for the "dignified and impartial manner in which he has presided over the deliberations of this body."[52]

President Tyler then bade his farewell, "before we separate never in this world to meet again," saying he was "much pleased that the resolution you have just adopted gives me an opportunity of uttering a few words of congratulation." Responding to Virginia's call, Tyler knew they would perform with "patriotism and intelligence," and he had "not been disappointed." He believed the "blessing of God will follow and rest upon the result of your labors, and that such result will bring to our country that quiet and peace which every patriotic heart so earnestly desires."[53]

"I go to finish the work you have assigned me," Tyler pledged, "of presenting your recommendations to the two Houses of Congress, and to ask those bodies to lay your proposals of amendment before the people of the American Union." Admitting the proposals were not "in all respects what I could have desired," preferring what Virginia's legislature proposed (essentially the Crittenden Compromise), "still it is my duty to give them my official approval and support."[54]

Probably what was crafted there in the Peace Conference was the "best that under all the circumstances could be expected," he surmised. "So far as in me lies, therefore, I shall recommend its adoption." He asked God to "protect our country and the Union of these States, which was committed to us as the blood-bought legacy of our heroic ancestors!"[55]

General Winfield Scott ordered a 100-gun salute in homage to the concluded Peace Conference and its delegates. He offered what would be nearly the final applause for their hard-fought and much-watched work, in which the nation had invested much hope but had instead almost immediately crumbled, with almost no constituency to back it.[56]

The next day, Vice President Breckinridge was presiding over the US Senate when he received a brief communication from President Tyler: "I am instructed, as the presiding officer of the Convention, composed of Commissioners appointed by twenty-one States, now in session in this city, to deliberate upon the present unhappy condition of the country, to present to your honorable body the accompanying request and proposed amendment." It was to be Tyler's last exertion on behalf of the Peace Congress's proposals.[57]

Rather than stay in Washington any longer to advocate the Peace Conference proposals, Tyler hastily entrained to Richmond to immediately take his seat at the Virginia secession convention. On the evening of February 28, he denounced those same proposals he had pledged to support before. What a Northern paper called a Secessionist "motley" crowd gathered outside his Richmond hotel to "serenade" him. There he dismissed the Peace Congress as a "worthless affair," with the South having nothing for which to hope from Republicans. According to a Richmond newspaper report, he confessed before a crowd of "thousands" that "their mission had resulted in nothing which could provide any hope to the South," resulting in a report that was a "miserable, rickety affair, which afforded no guarantee of safety, or security, and was not worthy of acceptance." Tyler was joined by his fellow Peace Delegate James Seddon, who even more strongly derided the Peace Congress as a "delusion, a shame, and insult, and an offense to the South." But if the Southern commissioners had been "more strongly backed up by public sentiment at home, had there been exhibited a positive determination to have ample security for the future or secede at once, Virginia could have got all she wanted," Seddon conjectured.[58]

A Cincinnati newspaper announced Tyler had "gone home to howl against the doings of the Conference," while a Kansas newspaper said Tyler was "constitutionally a traitor, and could not be otherwise if he should try." An Ohio newspaper called him a "dirty scoundrel." An Indiana newspaper thought him an "old and petty trickster."[59]

Two weeks later, Tyler explained himself more fully to the Virginia Convention, where he was a delegate. Suffering from illness, perhaps accentuated by his exertions related to the Peace Congress over the previous two months, he was sometimes barely audible. With limited energy, he spaced his speech to the Virginia Convention over two days.[60] The seventy-one-year-old former president reminded his fellow Virginians of his long public service, that started at age twenty-one, "having scarcely put on the toga virilis," when he was "cheered on his way by the approving smiles of those who had elected him." After that the "pathway of his life was lighted up by gracious smiles," and achieving the "highest public stations," leaving public service sixteen years ago, "prosperous and happy." He had left that happiness only when summoned to address the national crisis, which he had first foreseen thirty years ago, "when the dark cloud which now overspreads the hemisphere just rose above the horizon, no bigger than a man's hand. It was the cloud of Abolitionism."[61]

These fanatical sectionalists had declared to the South: "You are miserable slaveholders, and we cannot partake with you in the feast of peace and religion." Tyler confessed that when he ponders this "race of hungry, artful Catalines, who have misled the northern mind solely for their own aggrandizement, my blood becomes so heated in my veins as to scald and burn them in its rapid flow." He had hoped to restore the Union at the Peace Conference, but instead he found that "many had come with no olive branch in their hands . . . nothing to give—nothing to yield . . . would not yield one iota—not an 'i' dotted nor a 't' crossed."[62]

The final package from the Peace Congress was "passed by a minority of that Convention—a measure which was defeated by a majority the night before, but which was afterwards passed by a minority, upon a reconsideration the next day, of nine to eight," so "of what value and consequence, then, is it?" He doubted that the cotton states would have returned to the Union by its promises, and it was "still idler to presume that three-fourths of the States could ever be gotten to adopt them." He regretted that Lincoln failed to recognize the "right of the people of any of these states to seek their happiness under any other government than that inaugurated by himself, of a sectional majority." Tyler expressed hope that some Northern states might join the new Confederacy in their own quest for freedom. And he extolled the global economic power of Southern cotton. He asked of Virginia: "You have to choose your association. Will you find it among the ice bergs of the North or the cotton fields of the South?" Then he concluded by hailing his beloved state: "I have entire confidence that her proud crest will yet be seen waving in that great procession of states that go up to the temple to make their vows to maintain their liberties, 'peaceably if they can, forcibly if they must.'"[63]

Well before his March 13 speech to the Virginia Convention, Tyler's rejection of the Peace Conference was well known, starting with his speech to the crowds outside Richmond's Exchange Hotel on February 28.

THE PROPOSITIONS IN CONGRESS

The Peace Conference propositions, as transmitted by Tyler, arrived almost immediately after its adjournment in the US Senate, where Vice President Breckinridge obligingly read Tyler's message on February 27. Senator Crittenden urged its referral to a committee of five, which included himself and Senator Seward. One senator joked the Senate should take action by three-fourths vote the next day. The idea of a committee at least was approved twenty-six to twenty-one, with one senator denouncing as an "unnecessary consumption of time," while still voting for the committee.

In the committee's report the next day, Seward and one other senator offered a minority report, urging a national convention instead of the Peace Conference measures. Senator Robert Hunter of Virginia argued the propositions would put the Southern states in a "far worse position" than under the current Constitution and Dred Scott decision, which protected taking slaves into the territories without restriction. Crittenden, who had adopted the Peace Conference ideas over his own, declared in the Senate, "I want to save the country and adjust our present difficulties," drawing applause. Senator James Mason of Virginia admitted the Peace Conference had "gotten together the best mode of adjustment which would satisfy their judgment, but which I am sure will not satisfy the judgment of the southern states." Republican Senator Edward Baker of Oregon, a Lincoln friend who would lose his life on the battlefield later in the year, explained his support for the Peace Congress: "I will not shut my eyes to the fact that 20 states appeal to us; I will not shut my eye to the fact that there is imminent danger of permanent dissolution . . . [or] that the Republican Party is . . . not yet . . . an actual majority; I do not believe it is possible for one third of the people to coerce the opinions of two thirds." Senator James Green of Missouri argued against, complaining he could not travel through free states with his servants, which was a "disgrace," and declaring if not corrected, "we must divide, we will divide." The Peace Conference proposals were voted down in the US Senate on the afternoon of March 4 by twenty-eight to seven, with die-hard Republicans joining zealous Southerners, and with several prominent senators not even present.[64]

A New York newspaper reported on March 2 that the "recommendations of the Peace Conference seem to meet with little favor in the U. S. Senate from either side," with Senator Seward having offered a substitute proposal. Another paper denounced it as "wishy washy twaddle." The newspaper sighed: "And so the Senate adjourns, without having done anything more than talk."[65]

On the evening of March 4, US Congressman John McClernand, a Unionist Democrat from Illinois, tried to bring the Peace Conference proposals before the House of Representatives by moving to suspend the regular House rules, which became a test vote. "It is not a peace congress at all," responded abolitionist Republican Owen Lovejoy of Illinois, an ordained Congregationalist minister, who insisted: "There is no such body known to this house." Lacking a quorum, one congressman playfully asked the House sergeant at arms to arrest missing congressmen from South Carolina not seen since December, provoking laughter. Another riposted that he'd not noticed the "slightest detriment due by their absence." Another remarked, "We have saved this Union so often that I am afraid we shall save it to death." Still another pronounced he was "utterly opposed to any such wishy-washy settlement of our national difficulties." A Southern congressman, Democrat Thomas Hindman of Arkansas, who would soon be a Confederate army general, derided it as "unworthy of the vote of any southern man." One congressman explained he supported having a vote on the Peace Conference just to "have the pleasure of killing it." Another congressman voted to allow a vote, while expressing his "abhorrence of these insidious propositions, conceived in fraud and born of cowardice." Pennsylvania abolitionist Republican Thaddeus Stevens objected to the Peace Conference propositions "on behalf of John Tyler, who does not want them in," eliciting laughter. The vote to suspend the rules received a vote of ninety-three to sixty-seven, failing to reach the needed two-thirds, so there was no debate on the Peace Conference in the House. Die-hard Republicans voted with hard-core Southern Democrats in opposition. Conciliatory Republicans, like Charles Francis Adams of Massachusetts, voted with Unionist Democrats, like Daniel Sickles of New York, in favor of con-sideration. "This vote divides the Republican Party and sounds its death knell," Congressman McClernand immediately responded with clear frustration. He would soon serve as a US Army general in the impending war. The demise of the Peace Congress proposals in the US Congress effectively left them no politically viable clear path forward, although theoretically states could have ratified the amendments individually.[66]

RESPONSES FROM THE STATES

At the Missouri secession convention on March 5, Peace Delegate Alexander Doniphan reported to delegates, at their insistence. He explained that "we have no other cause for the difficulties that now agi-tate and disturb the country save the question of negro slavery," as the country is otherwise a "prosperous" and "free and happy people," feeding "starving millions of the world from overflowing granaries and cloth[ing] the naked with its cotton." The national "revolution" had culminated in the recent election of a "sectional party." To restore nationality over sec-tionality, Doniphan said the Peace Conference settled on amendments that "should settle this question now and forever." Missouri had initially voted against the "shapeless mass," preferring to leave the Constitution as it was. Doniphan had decided to vote in his own delegation, desir-ing "acknowledgement of the right in slave property." "Minorities" need "specific enactment" for their protection, as "majorities can always find sufficient provisions in the Constitution to create banks or a tariff." The one goal was to remove slavery "entirely from the arena of politics, and give such guarantees to slaveholding states that are now to remain, and induce the states that are now out eventually to come back." Doniphan explained that Missouri had first voted against the majority report at the Peace Conference, but after the reconsideration was "perfectly willing that this proposition should go to the country (not with her sanction) and therefore by the unanimous consent of her whole delegation she declined" to vote, allowing the proposals to pass.[67]

Doniphan's colleague John Coalter further explained to the Missouri Convention that Missouri's delegation had acquiesced to the majority report resolutions, "not believing them to amount to anything, but still holding that it was the best they could get." He added: "We felt the condition of the country was such that peace was needed in order to bring about any good and valuable results." And he recalled telling Northerners, "If you abhor slavery, how long before you abhor slaveholders? This, we represented to them, was the very point which had roused the southern mind." Coalter expressed regret that Congress had "not sanctioned" the propositions, so "what will now be adopted, God only knows." He concluded, "I do not know that any good will result from the action of the Peace Congress," though there was "frankness and candor from every part of the Union."[68]

Some of the Southern peace delegates earnestly fought for the Peace Congress proposals in their respective states, despite their seeming political death. Against the efforts of Tyler and Seddon, Peace Delegate and former US senator William Rives touted the proposals at the Virginia Convention in a March 8 speech. A Washington newspaper mocked his efforts, complaining he had "done nothing but agitate the slavery question for the last six months; that this very speech begins and ends with [negroes] . . . and that he is now proposing to stir the whole thing from the bottom, and in every part of the country, by insisting upon amendments of the Constitution, to secure certain abstract rights of slaveholders within territories, admitted to be of no practical importance." The newspaper claimed that in contrast, Republicans were not guilty of similar agitation "considering that they have done nothing, and proposed nothing, in respect to slavery, since the election of Mr. Lincoln, and that, if they could have had their own way, not a word would have been said on the subject in Washington last winter, either at the Capitol or at the dancing Hall at Willard's Hotel, where the 'negro' in his various aspects, was discussed and adjusted by the Peace Conference."[69]

Various Unionists in the upper South still occasionally grasped the Peace Congress's ideas as among the few remaining slender straws for hope about the Union. Unionists in Ashe County, North Carolina, affirmed the Peace Congress at a March 13 meeting, to little effect.[70] More common were remarks such as those by a delegate to the Tennessee secession convention in April, who observed: "The Peace Conference sat a month in Washington and employed every effort to win to reason the stubborn fanaticism of the party that sustains the President, all in vain. His Congressional majorities treated all reasonable efforts of adjustment with silence or contempt."[71] Secessionists were contemptuous of the Peace Congress, whose failure validated their cause. A South Carolina newspaper sputtered: the "Peace Conference at Washington came from Virginia . . . [but was] spurned and spit upon by the North, and now poor old Virginia is still upon her knees begging the Black Republicans for God's sake to give them some excuse to remain in fellowship with them," which should cause the "blush of shame to mantle the cheeks of every true Virginian."[72]

Two weeks after war had begun with the April 12 Confederate firing on Fort Sumter, Peace Delegate Robert Caruthers of Tennessee, a former US congressman, told a Nashville newspaper that the "dreaded state of things, which I so much feared, ever since my association with the Northern men in the Peace Conference, is now upon us." He had when in Washington in "my devotion to the Union, hoped almost against hope, that something might turn up to save it from 'final disruption, and restore' it to its integrity as a whole. But I now have no such expectation. All prospect of saving or restoring it is gone." The choice was now starkly between fraternity with the South or subservience to the North. He asked: "Can any man hesitate which of the two positions to choose?" During the war Caruthers was elected as Tennessee's governor by Confederates but never took office due to federal occupation.[73]

Reflecting much of Northern opinion by late April, a Vermont newspaper editorialized:

> There is no further occasion to talk of Crittenden resolutions, of Virginia Peace Conferences, of peaceable secession, of re-constructions of the government, and such like matters, which for months have distracted the minds of some who have meant well for their country which have been held up by others merely as blinds to keep out of sight as far as possible their own schemes for the destruction of the national government, till they should have gathered consistency and power enough to ensure success to their own premeditated treason.[74]

So, after being the focus of so much hope and anxiety, the Peace Congress and its proposed constitutional amendments to avert disunion and civil war died a largely unmourned death in the late winter and spring of 1861. They were spurned by many in both the North and South, as the impending war rushed forward, swamping all else in its path.

EPILOGUE
LEGACY

Thus ended the great American Civil War, which must upon
the whole be considered the noblest and least avoidable of all
the great mass conflicts of which till then there was record.

—Winston Churchill

On March 4 president-elect Abraham Lincoln rode in an open carriage with outgoing President James Buchanan down Pennsylvania Avenue toward the US Capitol. The street was lined by crowds—and by troops, including sharpshooters and artillery, on orders of General Winfield Scott, anxious to ensure a peaceful inauguration. Aged General John Wool, a peace delegate from New York, stood sentinel at a battery of artillery. It was a typically brisk, windy March day in Washington, DC. The incoming and the outgoing presidents chatted amicably. Buchanan looked old and tired yet relieved. Reputedly he said to Lincoln: "My dear sir, if you are as happy in entering the White House as I shall feel on returning to Wheatland, you are a happy man indeed." Lincoln replied pleasantly but without unctuous flattery: "Mr. President, I cannot say that I shall enter it with much pleasure, but I assure you that I shall do

249

what I can to maintain the high standards set by my illustrious predecessors who have occupied it." General Scott, in his own carriage, rode
on streets parallel to the presidential entourage, examining security precautions. The day of official events proceeded like clockwork, doubtless
to Scott's satisfaction.[1]

Buchanan had always been a gracious host, and he presided over
his administration's closing days with dignity, hosting farewell receptions and meals for friends and officials. He must have been gravely
disappointed by the Peace Congress's rejection by its own creator, his
predecessor and longtime associate John Tyler, and the dead-end it met
in Congress. In his final hours of power and the following day, he continued to receive reports from besieged Fort Sumter, which he forwarded
to Lincoln. He left Washington the next day, never to return. He was
received by friendly crowds in Baltimore, and at home in Lancaster,
Pennsylvania, where he found a sort of peace at his bucolic estate outside town. He worried about his legacy. After the war began, he started
receiving threats based on his perceived pro-Southern policies. The local
Masonic order posted guards for his protection. Buchanan chafed at the
especially Republican attacks on his record, but supported the war effort,
which he claimed should be "sustained at all hazards." He called Lincoln
an "honest and patriotic man." When Confederate forces came near
his home during the Gettysburg campaign of 1863, he refused to leave,
although he sent his niece Harriet Lane to Philadelphia, explaining: "I
have schooled my mind to meet the inevitable evils of life with Christian
fortitude." In 1865, he was finally received into the Presbyterian church
"on his experimental evidence of piety" at age seventy-four. He died in
1868 at his beloved home, having published an apologia for his policies
of 1861. But he was still not vindicated.[2]

Harriet Lane, Buchanan's devoted niece, married at age thirty-six
while her uncle still lived. After his death she endured the tragedy of
losing both her children and her husband. As a wealthy widow she
often spent time in Washington, DC, endowing the National Gallery of
Art with her paintings, endowing a pediatric facility at Johns Hopkins

University, and endowing the soon-to-be-built National Cathedral and a boy's school to become St. Alban's. The cathedral dean and the Episcopal bishop of Washington conducted her funeral in 1903.

A lifelong Episcopalian like Lane, John Tyler had even less time to worry about his legacy than did her uncle. His and his family's devotion to the new Confederacy was complete. On March 5 his oldest grand-daughter had helped raise the new Confederate flag over the Capitol in Montgomery, Alabama.[3] Just five days after the firing on Fort Sumter, he voted with the majority at the Virginia Convention for secession on April 17, which Virginia's voters ratified in May. He had told the convention after their vote that there had never been a more "just and holy effort for the maintenance of liberty and independence," but he may not "survive to witness the consummation of the work begun that day." His expecta-tion was correct. Before the vote, he had written his wife, Julia: "These are dark times, dearest, and I think only of you and our little ones. But I trust in that same Providence that protected our fathers. These rascals who hold power leave us no alternative. I shall vote secession, and prefer to encounter any hazard to degrading Virginia." He admonished her to live as "frugally as possible" as "trying times are before us."[4] Tyler also realized the "battle at Charleston" had "aroused the whole North," and "they will break upon the South with an immense force."[5]

After Virginia's secession, a mob in Philadelphia threatened Tyler's son, an outspoken Secessionist who had condemned the Peace Conference as a plan to "demoralize the people of the southern section." He was forced to flee to Richmond, where he worked for the Confederacy. "I am truly sorry he went so far astray from his line of duty," commented former president Buchanan when hearing the news of the younger Tyler, who had helped him gain his presidential nomination. The sentiment must have applied doubly to the father.[6] After the war, Buchanan sent the impoverished son $1,000, which the son declined.[7]

In June 1861 the older Tyler was elected to the Provisional Confederate Congress, now meeting in Richmond. In July he toasted the Confederate victory at the Battle of Bull Run. On July 4 at historic Jamestown,

Virginia, where English-speaking America first began, near his estate, he bemusedly told Confederate soldiers he was still young enough to fight. When his mother-in-law suggested Julia Tyler's return to New York for safety, he assured her that their home on the James River "will be far safer than Staten Island."[8] In November, he was elected to the newly formed Confederate US House of Representatives, for which he would take office in January 1862. But instead he suddenly took ill and died while staying at the Exchange Hotel in Richmond, where he had famously denounced the Peace Congress ten months earlier. Fellow Peace Delegate William Rives was among the last to visit, and Tyler's wife was present, having come to him due to a fearful premonition. "Perhaps it is best," were his last words. Tyler lay in state in the Virginia Capitol, his body draped by the Confederate stars and bars. His funeral took place across the street at St. Paul's Episcopal Church, where the bishop presided. Confederate President Jefferson Davis was in attendance.[9]

Tyler's friend, former Virginia governor Henry Wise, had visited Tyler during his final hours. He pronounced that Tyler was a "firm believer in the atonement of the Son of God, and in the efficacy of His blood to wash away every stain of moral sin." He had been "by faith and by heirship a member of the Episcopal Church of Christ, and never doubted Divine Revelation."[10]

During the war Tyler's beloved Sherwood Forest was spoiled but not destroyed by occupying federal troops. Initially the estate had federal guards in 1862, thanks to appeals from Julia's mother in New York through fellow New Yorker and Peace Delegate General John Wool. When a slave escaped with some of Julia's clothing, Julia complained to the local federal commander that such an escapade if unpunished might "produce a restless feeling among the rest of my negroes who are in fact blessed in being situated above every want with very moderate effort on their own part."[11]

After gaining a pass in late 1862, Julia took six of her seven children to her mother in New York. She returned home with two of them in 1863, finding the "negroes are well disposed and in order."[12] Numerous Tylers served the Confederacy, and one of John Tyler's grandsons by his first wife died in combat. Julia raged against her pro-Union New York brother while also being "utterly ashamed" of her native state. She complained of the federal blockade against the South, which was part of General Scott's "Anaconda" plan to squeeze the rebellion: "Even our river boat would be fired at and taken, if that impudent war steamer, lying off Newport News could get the chance."[13] She was referring to the *Pocahontas*, their bright blue "royal barge" with matching blue satin cushions whose slave oarsmen wore matching uniforms with bows and arrows stitched in their collars, designed by Julia herself. The Tylers during happy years of peace had plied the river under its canopy, visiting neighbors at venerable plantations that once had housed peers of the Founding Fathers. Their beautiful boat disappeared during the war.[14] Early in the war the Tylers also lost their vacation home farther down the river near federal fortress Monroe, prompting Julia to complain: "Was there ever such a savage wicked war?"[15]

Julia spent part of 1863 in Richmond, getting close to the first Confederate couple Jefferson and Varina Davis, the latter of whom noted Julia "positively did not look one day over twenty" and was "so fresh, agreeable, graceful, and exquisitely dressed."[16] She escaped again to see her mother in late 1863, this time more daringly on a blockade runner, also shipping several bales of cotton for a nice profit. During her absence in 1864, federal forces composed of black troops raided Sherwood Forest, capturing her plantation manager, a relative. Julia pleaded to President Lincoln: "By the memory of my husband, and what you must be assured would have been his course in your place, had your wife appealed to him, remove these causes of anxious suspense."[17]

Sherwood Forest was turned over by federal forces to several slaves. The main house, shorn of its valuables, temporarily became a school for whites and blacks. Meanwhile, hours after Lincoln's assassination in 1865, several men broke into Julia's Staten Island family home demanding her "rebel" flag. The incident made the newspapers. With Jefferson Davis imprisoned after the Confederate collapse, his destitute wife, Varina, wrote her friend Julia for help: "I sometimes wonder if God does not mean to wake me from a terrific dream of desolation and penury." Julia sent her clothing.

Julia met First Lady Julia Grant at the White House in 1872, having moved to Georgetown in the District of Columbia the year before. Julia Tyler's portrait as First Lady was displayed in the White House. She socialized with Republicans, scandalizing her son, and looked for spiritual solace after the death of her daughter. After experimenting with spiritualism, she found comfort in Roman Catholicism, whose schools for her children had impressed her. A bishop presided over her induction into the church. She insisted on re-baptism even after being discouraged by the church against it, since the church recognized her Episcopal baptism. For her, Catholicism was the "best and truest religion," and the "other sects" like "ships at sea without anchor or rudder, though until one comes to understand this one is not to blame for continuing with them."[18]

She gained a federal pension as former First Lady in 1881, already having a small pension as the widow of a War of 1812 veteran. Mostly she resided comfortably in Richmond, across the street from a Catholic church where she devoutly practiced her faith. In 1888 she died after a stroke while at the Exchange Hotel, where her husband had died twenty-six years before.

Thanks to a significant inheritance from her New York mother, Julia's final years were relatively comfortable, certainly compared to many Southern luminaries impoverished by the war. But she no longer lived royally with scores of slaves, a blue carriage with liveried coachmen, or a river barge with uniformed oarsmen. The universe her husband had sought to preserve had been governed by a planter aristocracy who espoused Republican principles laced with classical rhetoric and depending on a permanent caste of enslaved blacks; it was no more. Always a defiant apologist for her husband and the Southern cause, Julia Tyler still grudgingly reconciled to the new order as she lived in New York and Washington, dined with former adversaries, and abandoned the illusion that the slaves at Sherwood Forest had been content in their servitude. Almost all of them had fled during the war.

The Tylers embodied the old order whose last political hurrah was the Washington Peace Conference. The leading participants summoned all the wisdom they could from long lives, often dating to the eighteenth century. They often cited the patriotic sentiments of the Founding Fathers, whom some of them had personally known. Many of them could personally recall the disasters of the War of 1812, in which some of them had fought, particularly the burning of Washington itself by the invading British. For decades many of them had helped orchestrate the great compromises that at least delayed division and civil war. But their creativity had run dry, and the old stratagems no longer worked. The Founders had assumed or at least hoped, as Lincoln emphasized, that slavery would eventually end. So, too, at least initially, had the subsequent generation, including John Tyler.

But as these sons of the Founders aged, this vision faded. They instead realized that the South's wealth and racial stratification deeply depended on slavery. They saw no plausible alternatives. Nor did they fully understand the political revolution of the 1850s that resulted in the creation and triumph of the Republican Party and Lincoln. Their primary response was to fear and resist it.

This fading old generation had hoped the Peace Conference could broker the grand accommodations of the past. But the new generation, which included many Republican delegates from the North, largely thought like Indiana governor Oliver Morton, who explained to Lincoln why his state sent delegates: "It was not that I expected any positive good to come of it, but to prevent positive evil."[19] After its culmination, Lincoln's secretaries later judged the Peace Congress proposals to be "as worthless as Dead Sea fruit."[20] But Kentucky Senator John Crittenden perceptively judged that the Peace Congress, by investing the upper South's hopes in a potential accommodation, had crucially delayed secession for states like Virginia and helped prevent secession by border states like his own. The Peace Conference also arguably allowed a cooling period that facilitated the peaceful count of the electoral vote in Congress and Lincoln's inauguration.

The debates of the Peace Congress focused nearly exclusively on slavery, and their rhetoric encapsulates the national division that led to civil war. Lincoln's meetings with the full Peace Congress, and later with select delegates urging his active conciliation, illustrate the political iron of the new president that persuaded the old generation that the accommodationist era of James Buchanan was decisively over.

Unintentionally, the clergy who prayed each day at the Peace Conference better represented the future than did the old men before whom they delivered their invocations. They were nearly all steadfastly pro-Union and anti-slavery, and would remain so throughout the war. America's great denominations had divided over slavery, but the clergy of Washington, DC—reputedly a divided city and even Southern city—had emphatically chosen for the new order.

The debates at the Peace Congress also confirmed the unbridgeable chasm between the North and South that was politically insoluble. The South, for its protection from the new Republican anti-slavery ascendancy, demanded permanent, ironclad, irrevocable constitutional protections for slavery. Such protections the Founding Fathers had never given; the Constitution was almost completely silent about slavery. The South believed that their domestic order, even their very lives, required a national agreement to end all debate over slavery, putting the most incendiary of all controversies to bed forever. A newly Republican north could not agree without repudiating the Founders' hopes, as they understood them, that slavery was ultimately incongruous with American democracy.

Winston Churchill would call the "great American Civil War" the "noblest and least avoidable of all the great mass conflicts of which till then there was record." The Peace Congress seems to prove him right.[21]

ACKNOWLEDGMENTS

This book would not be possible without generous help from the staff, directors, and supporters of the Institute on Religion and Democracy, whose work has helped me to appreciate even more the role of religion in shaping American history and political life. I am also grateful to the always helpful staff of the Newspaper and Current Periodical Reading Room at the Library of Congress. Finally, I'm most grateful to the supportive and encouraging editors at Thomas Nelson, particularly to former editor Joel Miller, who inspired the subject of this book.

NOTES

ONE: CRISIS

1. Robert Gunderson, *Old Gentlemen's Convention: The Washington Peace Conference of 1861* (Madison: University of Wisconsin Press, 1961), 43; Frederick V. McNair, *Astronomical, Magnetic, and Meteorological Observations Made During the Year 1891 [and 1892] at the United States Naval Observatory* (Washington, DC: United States Naval Observatory), 467; Margaret Leech, *Reveille in Washington: 1860–1865* (New York: New York Review of Books, ITY: Simon Publications, 2001), Kindle location 860.
2. "The Commissioners' Convention," *National Intelligencer*, February 4, 1861, 3.
3. Gerhard Peters and John T. Woolley, The American Presidency Project, "James Buchanan: Fourth Annual Message to Congress on the State of the Union, December 3, 1860," http://www.presidency.ucsb.edu/ws/?pid=29501.
4. Ibid.
5. Robert Seager II, *And Tyler Too: A Biography of John & Julia Gardiner Tyler* (New York: McGraw Hill, 1963), 446.
6. Lyon Gardiner Tyler, *Letters and Times of the Tylers* (Richmond: Whittet & Shepperson, 1885), 578; "The National Crisis," *Richmond Daily Dispatch*, January 18, 1861, 1.
7. "The Virginia Resolutions," *Daily National Intelligencer*, January 22, 1861, issue 15, 116, col. C; "From Richmond," *Alexandria Gazette*, January 21, 1861, 3.
8. Tyler, *Letters and Times of the Tylers*, 581; "Virginia's Call for a

Conference," *Newark Advocate*, February 1, 1861, issue 27, col. B; "The Virginia Mediation," *Daily National Intelligencer*, January 25, 1861, issue 15, 120, col. A, 3.

9. "Virginia Legislature," *Daily National Intelligencer*, January 21, 1861, issue 15, 115, col. F.

10. "The Virginia Resolutions," *Daily National Intelligencer*, January 22, 1861, col. C, 3.

11. Seager, *And Tyler Too*, 450–51.

12. "Ex-President Tyler's Report," *Daily National Intelligencer*, February 4, 1861, issue 15, 128, col A, 2.

13. "Celebration at Jamestown," *Southern Literary Messenger*, vol. 24, issue 6 (Richmond: T.W. White, June 1857), 455.

14. Seager, *And Tyler Too*, 400–01; "Correspondence between the President and Mr. Tyler," *Daily Constitutionalist* (Augusta, GA), February 6, 1861, vol. 16, issue 31, 2.

15. Philip Shriver Klein, *President James Buchanan* (Newtown, CT: American Political Biography Press, 1995), 100.

16. James Buchanan, *Mr. Buchanan's Administration On the Eve of the Rebellion, [1866]* (New York: D. Appleton and Company, 1866), 15.

17. James Buchanan, *The Works of James Buchanan*, vol. 6 (Philadelphia & London: J. B. Lippincott Co., 1908–1911), 16.

18. Klein, *President James Buchanan*, 334.

19. Ibid., 349–50.

20. "The President's Reception," *The Daily Exchange* (Baltimore), January 2, 1861, 1.

21. "The President's Levee," *The Constitution* (Washington, DC), January 17, 1861, vol. 2, issue 235, 3.

22. "Important from Washington," *Augusta Chronicle*, January 17, 1861, vol. 25, issue 14, 3.

23. "Ex-President Tyler's Report," *Daily National Intelligencer*, February 4, 1861, issue 15, 128, col. A, 2.

24. Ibid.

25. Tyler, *Letters and Times of the Tylers*, 596.

26. James Buchanan, *The Works of James Buchanan*, vol. 12 (Philadelphia & London: J. B. Lippincott Co., 1908–1911), 187.

27. "Ex-President Tyler's Report," *Daily National Intelligencer*; "From Washington," *Daily Dispatch* (Richmond, VA), January 29, 1861, 3; "Washington News," *Augusta Chronicle*, January 29, 1861, vol. 25, issue 24, 1.

28. "Letter from Ex-President Tyler," *New York Herald*, January 18, 1861, col. E, 2.

29. Texas became the seventh seceded state on February 1, 1861.

30. State Legislature of New York, *Journal of the Assembly of the State of New York (84th Session)* (Albany: Charles Van Benthuysen, 1861), 158.

31. "The Massachusetts Delegation and Senator Sumner," *Evening Star*, February 1, 1861, 2.

32. Gunderson, *Old Gentlemen's Convention*, 74–75.

33. Ibid., 74–78.

34. Lucius Chittenden, *Recollections of President Lincoln and His Administration* (New York: Harper & Brothers, 1891), 20.

35. Gunderson, *Old Gentlemen's Convention*, 10.

36. "The Peace Congress," *Daily National Intelligencer*, February 11, 1861, issue 15, 134, col. B, 3.

37. "Antecedents of the Delegates," *Evening Star*, February 6, 1861, 1.

38. "The Peace Convention," *Evening Star*, February 6, 1861, 2; Chittenden, *Recollections of President Lincoln*, 23.

39. Sara Agnes Rice Pryor, *Reminiscences of Peace and War* (New York: Macmillan Company, 1905), 47.

40. Dewey Wallace, ed., *Capital Witness* (Franklin, TN: Plumbline Media, 2011), 105–07; "Willard's Hall, Where the Peace Convention Is Now Held in Washington," *Frank Leslie's Illustrated Newspaper*, February 16, 1861, 4; "A Notable Church," *Evening Star*, May 18, 1893, 7.

41. "The Peace Convention," *New York Herald*, February 9, 1861, 10; "The Fine Portrait," *Evening Star*, February 9, 1861, 3.

42. "The Revolution," *New York Herald*, February 5, 1861, col. A, 1.

43. "The Peace Convention," *Vermont Chronicle*, February 12, 1861, 26, issue 7, col. G.

44. Nathaniel Hawthorne, *Complete Works of Nathaniel Hawthorne* (Boston: Houghton Mifflin & Company, 1896), 340–41.

45. William Howard Russell, *The Civil War in America* (Boston: Gardner A. Fuller, 1861), 8.

46. George Templeton Strong, *Diary of the Civil War* (Seattle: University of Washington Press, 1988), 393; John D. Wright, "George Templeton Strong," *The Routledge Encyclopedia of Civil War Era Biographies* (New York: Routledge, 2013), 566.

47. Michael Burlingame, ed., *Lincoln's Journalist: John Hay's Anonymous Writings for the Press, 1860–1864* (Carbondale: Southern Illinois University Press, 1998), 49–50.

48. "Conference Convention," *Daily National Intelligencer*, March 1, 1861, 3.

49. Rachel Shelden, *Washington Brotherhood* (Chapel Hill: University of North Carolina Press, 2013), 104, 177–78.

50. Kirkland Ruffin Saunders, "Perhaps Westover Church and Its Environ" (Richmond, VA: W. M. Brown, 1937), 79.

51. Oliver Chitwood, *John Tyler: Champion of the Old South* (Newtown, CT: American Political Biography Press, 1990), 434–35.

52. Edward Crapol, *John Tyler: Accidental President* (Chapel Hill: University of North Carolina Press, 2012), 33.

53. "First Lady Biography: Julia Tyler," National First Ladies' Library, http://www.firstladies.org/biographies/firstladies.aspx?biography=11; Chitwood, *John Tyler*, 403–04.

54. Chitwood, *John Tyler*, 252–54.

55. Tyler, *Letters and Times of the Tylers*, 590.

56. Ibid., 596; Shelden, *Washington Brotherhood*, 182.

57. "The Peace Congress," February 11, 1861, 3.

58. Ibid.; Shelden, *Washington Brotherhood*, 178; Leech, *Reveille in Washington*, Kindle location 351.

59. "Ex-President Tyler's Report," *Daily National Intelligencer*, February 4, 1861, 2.

60. "John Tyler," *Portsmouth Journal of Literature and Politics* (February 9, 1861), 2.

61. "The Sectional Troubles," *Fayetteville Observer*, February 14, 1861, issue 996, col. D.

62. Gunderson, *Old Gentlemen's Convention*, 10; "Virginia News," *Alexandria Gazette*, February 18, 1861, 2.

63. Tyler, *Letters and Times of the Tylers*, 596.

64. L. E. Chittenden, *A Report of the Debates and Proceedings in the Secret Sessions of the Conference Convention, For Proposing Amendments to the Constitution of the United States, Held at Washington, D.C., in February, a.d. 1861* (New York: D. Appleton & Company, 1864), second day, 17.

65. Crapol, *Accidental President*, 6, 38, 235.

66. Ibid., 47–48.

67. Ibid., 51–53, 59–60.

68. Seager, *And Tyler Too*, 394.

69. Crapol, *Accidental President*, 61, 249–50.

70. Seager, *And Tyler Too*, 430.

71. Ibid., 429, 431.

72. Crapol, *Accidental President*, 61, 64–65.

73. Seager, *And Tyler Too*, 440.

74. Ibid., 434, 435–37.

75. Ibid., 432.

76. Crapol, *Accidental President*, 257; Seager, *And Tyler Too*, 444–45.

77. "Letter from Ex-President Tyler," *New York Herald*, January 18, 1861, 2.

78. Chittenden, *Report of the Debates*, second day, 14–17.

79. "The Peace Congress," *Daily Dispatch* (Richmond, VA), February 7, 1861, 1.

80. "Ex-President Tyler's Address," *Evening Star*, February 6, 1861, 2; "The Washington Conference," *Newark Advocate*, February 8, 1861, issue 28, col. G.

81. "Mr. John Tyler, Jr.," *Freedom's Champion*, January 5, 1861, col. A.

82. Robert Cook, *Civil War Senator* (Baton Rouge: Louisiana State University Press, 2011), 129; Gunderson, *Old Gentlemen's Convention*, 11.

83. "The Peace Convention," *Vermont Chronicle*, February 12, 1861, 26.

84. "The Prospect," *Evening Star*, February 7, 1861, 2.

85. "The Revolution," *New York Herald*, February 4, 1861, col. A.

86. "The True State of the Question," *Liberator*, February 15, 1861, 26.

87. "Hon. John Tyler, Virginia," *Columbus Daily Enquirer*, February 8, 1861, 3.

TWO: THE FEDERAL CITY

1. "Washington's Birthday," *Philadelphia Inquirer*, February 18, 1861, 4.

2. Robert Gunderson, *Old Gentlemen's Convention* (Madison: University of Wisconsin Press, 1961), 54.

3. "The Secession Troubles Celebration," *Philadelphia Inquirer*, February 23, 1861, 1.

4. "The Celebration in Washington," *New York Herald*, February 23, 1861, 10, col. C.

5. "Local News," *Evening Star*, February 22, 1861, 3.

6. John Nicolay and John Hay, *Abraham Lincoln: A History*, vol. 2 (New York: The Century Company, 1890), 149–51.

7. Horatio King, *Turning on the Light* (Philadelphia: J. B. Lippincott Company, 1895), 52.

8. "House of Representatives," *Daily National Intelligencer*, February 12, 1861, 2.

9. Philip Klein, *President James Buchanan: A Biography* (Newtown, CT: American Political Biography Press, 1995), 236, 242.

10. "The Secession Troubles Celebration," *Philadelphia Inquirer*; "The Celebration in Washington," *New York Herald*, February 23, 1861, 10, col. C.

11. "Local News," *Evening Star*, February 23, 1861, 3.

12. Ibid.

13. "Washington's Birthday," *Daily National Intelligencer*, February 25, 1861, 3.

14. "The Secession Troubles Celebration," *Philadelphia Inquirer*.

15. King, *Turning on the Light*, 54.

16. "General Scott's Views," *Philadelphia Inquirer*, January 19, 1861, 5.

17. Anthony Trollope, *North America* (New York: Harper & Brothers, 1862), 312.

18. Ibid., 305–09.

19. Sara Agnes Rice Pryor, *Reminiscences of Peace and War* (New York: Macmillan Company, 1905), 4.

20. Ibid., 9.

21. Trollope, *North America*, 309.

22. Ibid., 315–17.

23. Ibid., 315.

24. Ibid., 311.

25. Pryor, *Reminiscences*, 6.

26. Trollope, *North America*, 317.

27. Ibid., 318.

28. Edward Crapol, *John Tyler: The Accidental President* (Chapel Hill: University of North Carolina Press, 2012), 260.

29. Trollope, *North America*, 314.

30. Ibid., 312.

31. Ibid., 319.

32. John DeFerrari, "Center Market's Chaotic Exuberance," *Streets of Washington* (blog), May 24, 2010, http://www.streetsofwashington.com /2010/05/center-markets-chaotic-exuberance.html.

33. Pryor, *Reminiscences*, 42–43.

34. W. B. Bryan, *History of the National Capital* (New York: Macmillan Company, 1916), 433.

35. George William Bagby, "Washington City," *Atlantic Monthly*, January 1861, 1–8.

36. "Miss Charlotte Cushman," *Evening Star*, February 9, 1861, 3.

37. "Theater," *Evening Star*, February 12, 1861, 2.

38. "Theater," *Evening Star*, February 15, 1861, 3.

39. "Theater," *Evening Star*, February 16, 1861, 3.

40. "The Concert and Presentation Last Night," *Evening Star*, February 15, 1861, 3.

41. "Lecture," *Evening Star*, February 9, 1861, 3.
42. Smithsonian, *Annual Report of the Board of Regents of the Smithsonian Institution, 1861* (Washington, DC: Government Printing Office, 1862), 54.
43. Rachel Shelden, *Washington Brotherhood* (Chapel Hill: University of North Carolina Press, 2013), 181.
44. "Lent," *Evening Star*, February 13, 1861, 3; "Center Market," *Evening Star*, February 26, 3.
45. "We Understand," *Evening Star*, February 11, 1861, 3.
46. "Capitol," *Evening Star*, February 11, 1861, 3.
47. "Methodist Church, Ninth Street," *Evening Star*, February 18, 1861, 3.
48. "Melancholy Suicide of a Naval Officer," *Evening Star*, February 9, 1861, 3.
49. "A Difficulty," *Evening Star*, February 16, 1861, 3.
50. "President's Levee," *Evening Star*, February 13, 1861, 3.
51. Pryor, *Reminiscences*, 53.
52. Lyon Gardiner Tyler, *Letters and Times of the Tylers* (Richmond: Whittet & Shepperson, 1885), 596.
53. Ibid., 597.
54. Oliver Perry Chitwood, *John Tyler: Champion of the Old South*, rev. ed. (Newtown, CT: American Political Biography Press, 1990), 441.
55. Gunderson, *Old Gentlemen's Convention*, 58.
56. Robert Seager II, *And Tyler Too* (New York: McGraw Hill, 1963), 451, 454; Tyler, *Letters and Times of the Tylers*, 612–13.
57. Worthington Chauncey Ford, ed. *Letters of Henry Adams* (Cambridge, MA: Riverside Press, 1930), February 8 and 13, 1861, 86–89.
58. "Affairs at Washington," *Salem Register*, February 18, 1861, 2.
59. Shelden, *Washington Brotherhood*, 182.
60. William J. Cooper Jr., *Jefferson Davis, American* (New York: Vintage, 2001), 343.
61. Ernest Ferguson, *Freedom Rising* (New York: Vintage, 2005), 37.
62. Lynda Lasswell Crist, ed., *The Papers of Jefferson Davis*, vol. 7 (Baton Rouge: Louisiana State Press, 1992), 18–23; Transcribed from the Cong. Globe, 36th Cong., 2d Sess., 487 (1861).
63. Cooper, *Jefferson Davis, American*, 5–8.
64. Ibid., 343–46; Joan Cashin, *First Lady of the Confederacy: Varina Davis's Civil War* (Cambridge: Harvard University Press, 2008), 95.
65. Shelden, *Washington Brotherhood*, 167.
66. Cashin, *First Lady*, 137–38.

67. Ibid., 93.

68. Shelden, *Washington Brotherhood*, 84, 168.

69. Cashin, *First Lady*, 77, 88.

70. "The Peace Congress," *New York Herald*, February 8, 1861, col. E.

71. "The Peace Convention," *Evening Star*, February 7, 1861, 3.

72. Pryor, *Reminiscences*, 7.

73. Frederick Blue, *Salmon Chase: A Life in Politics* (Kent, OH: Kent State University Press, 1987), 135.

74. Lucius Chittenden, *Recollections of President Lincoln and His Administration* (New York: Harper & Brothers Publishers, 1904), 32–35.

75. "The Peace Congress," *Evening Star*, February 8, 1861, 3.

THREE: Opening Debate

1. Robert Seager II, *And Tyler Too* (New York: McGraw Hill, 1963), 454.

2. L. E. Chittenden, *A Report of the Debates and Proceedings in the Secret Sessions of the Conference Convention, For Proposing Amendments to the Constitution of the United States, Held at Washington, D.C., in February, a.d. 1861* (New York: D. Appleton & Company, 1864), first day, 11.

3. Ibid., first day, 12.

4. Robert Gunderson, "William Rives and the 'Old Gentlemen's Convention,'" *Journal of Southern History* 104 (November 1956): 467.

5. Robert Gunderson, *Old Gentlemen's Convention: The Washington Peace Conference of 1861* (Madison: University of Wisconsin Press, 1981), 71.

6. "Our Richmond Correspondence," *Philadelphia Inquirer*, January 23, 1861, 2.

7. Lucius Chittenden, *Recollections of President Lincoln and His Administration* (New York: Harper & Brothers Publishers, 1904), 51–52.

8. Roy W. Curry, "James A. Seddon: A Southern Prototype," *Virginia Magazine of History and Biography*, April 1955, 125, 128, 131–32, 134.

9. Ibid., 130, 134.

10. John Beauchamp Jones, *A Rebel War Clerk's Diary at the Confederate States Capital* (Philadelphia: J. B. Lippincott & Co., 1866), 312.

11. Chittenden, *Report of the Debates and Proceedings*, first day, 12.

12. Chittenden, *Recollections of President Lincoln*, 24.

13. Chittenden, *Report of the Debates and Proceedings*, third day, 20.

14. Chittenden, *Recollections of Lincoln*, 23–24; Chittenden, *Report of the Debates and Proceedings*, third day, 18.

15. "The Washington Peace Conference," *The Caledonian*, February 15, 1861, 2.

16. Chittenden, *Recollections of Lincoln*, 25–26.

17. Chittenden, *Report of the Debates and Proceedings*, introduction, 4, 7.

18. "Spirit of Washington Letters," *Daily Cleveland Herald*, February 7, 1861, issue 32, col. B.

19. "The Washington Peace Congress," *New York Herald*, February 7, col. C; Chittenden, *Report of the Debates and Proceedings*, third day, 21.

20. Chittenden, *Report of the Debates and Proceedings*, third day, 22.

21. Ibid., fourth day, 21, 26.

22. Ibid., fifth day, 28–29; sixth day, 30.

23. Lindsey Apple, *The Family Legacy of Henry Clay* (Lexington: The University Press of Kentucky, 2011), 101–04.

24. "Death of the Hon. John C. Wright," *Daily National Intelligencer*, February 14, col D; Chittenden, *Report of the Debates and Proceedings*, seventh day, 31, eighth day, 32–33.

25. Chittenden, *Report of the Debates and Proceedings*, eighth day, 35.

26. Ibid., 33–40; "History of the Diocese," Episcopal Diocese of Washington, http://www.edow.org/about/the-diocese/about-the-diocese/history.

27. "A Bad Appointment," *Cincinnati Daily Enquirer*, February 15, 1861, 2.

28. "The New Consignment to the Border Sepulcher," *Cincinnati Daily Press*, February 16, 1861, 2.

29. "The New Commissioner from Ohio," *Nashville Union and American*, February 17, 1861, 2.

30. Gunderson, *Old Gentlemen's Convention*, 61.

31. Frederick Blue, *Salmon P. Chase: A Life in Politics* (Kent, OH: Kent State University Press, 1987), 5.

32. Ibid., 7.

33. Ibid., 16–17, 24–26, 74–75.

34. Ibid., 12–13.

35. Ibid., 28–32.

36. Salmon P. Chase, *The Address and Reply, on the Presentation of a Testimonial to S. P. Chase, by the Colored People of Cincinnati* (Ithaca: Cornel University Library, 1845), 12, 18, 35.

37. Ibid., 22, 35.

38. Blue, *Salmon P. Chase*, 127.

39. John Weiss, *Life and Correspondence of Theodore Parker*, vol. 2 (New York: D. Appleton & Company, 1864), 519–20.

40. Blue, *Salmon P. Chase*, 128.

41. Doris Kearns Goodwin, *Team of Rivals* (New York: Simon and Schuster, 2005), 115.

42. Blue, *Salmon P. Chase*, 134; John Niven, *Salmon Chase: A Biography* (New York: Oxford University Press, 1995), 231.

43. "The Washington Peace Conference," *New York Herald*, February 7, col. C; "Spirit of Washington Letters," *Daily Cleveland Herald*, February 7, 1861, issue 32, col. B.

44. Gunderson, *Old Gentlemen's Convention*, 56.

45. "The Washington Peace Congress," *New York Herald*, February 7, 1861, col. C; "The Report of the Committee," *Evening Star*, February 15, 1861, 2.

46. "The Peace Congress," *Evening Star*, February 9, 1861, 2.

47. "The Peace Conference," *New York Herald*, February 11, 1861, col. B; "The Peace Convention," *New York Herald*, February 9, 1861, 10, col. C.

48. "The Peace Convention," *Augusta Chronicle*, February 10, 1861, 2.

49. "The Peace Conference," *Augusta Chronicle*, February 14, 1861, 2; "Union Meeting in Baltimore," *Sandusky Register*, January 11, 1861, 2; "Washington," *Providence Evening Press*, January 11, 1861, 2.

50. Bernard Steiner, *Life of Reverdy Johnson* (Baltimore: The Norman Remington Co., 1914), 27–28.

51. Ibid., 32.

52. Ibid., 39.

53. Ibid., 18.

54. Ibid., 42–43.

55. "Address of Reverdy Johnson," *Sacramento Daily Union*, September 15, 1861, 8.

56. Steiner, *Life of Reverdy Johnson*, 42–43.

57. "A Strong Description," *Charleston Mercury*, February 11, 1861, 1.

58. "The Peace Convention," *New York Herald*, February 9, 1861, col. C.

59. "The Feeling of the Tariff Question," *New York Herald*, February 17, 1861, 1.

60. "Washington News," *Cleveland Morning Leader*, February 18, 1861, 4.

61. "The Vote in Virginia," *Cleveland Morning Leader*, February 14, 1861, 2.

62. "The Action of the Border States," *Gazette and Sentinel*, February 16, 1861, 2.

63. "Affairs at Washington," *Salem Register*, February 18, 1861, 2.

64. Chittenden, *Report of the Debates and Proceedings*, ninth day, 41.

65. Ibid., 42.

66. Ibid., 42–43.

67. "The Peace Conference," *Nashville Union and American*, February 15, 1861, 2.

68. Seager, *And Tyler Too*, 456.

69. Argument of Roger S. Baldwin of New Haven before the Supreme Court of the United States in the Case of the United States, Appellants, vs. Cinque, and Others, Africans of the Amistad, New York, S.W. Benedict, 1841, 4, http://avalon.law.yale.edu/19th_century/amistad_001.asp4.

70. Samuel Dutton, *An Address at the Funeral of Honorable Roger Sherman Baldwin* (New Haven: Thomas J. Stafford, 1863), 13.

71. Ibid., 8–10, 23.

72. Ibid., 15–16, 26.

73. Ibid., 27–28.

74. Ibid., 19–20.

75. Chittenden, *Report of the Debates and Proceedings*, ninth day, 45–47; Dutton, *An Address at the Funeral*, 20.

76. Chittenden, *Report of the Debates and Proceedings*, ninth day, 47–48.

77. Ibid., 53–54.

78. "The Peace Conference at Washington," *Daily Nashville Patriot*, February 18, 1861, 2.

79. "Report of the Peace Conference," *Cleveland Morning Leader*, February 18, 1861, 3; "An Executive Dinner," *The National Republican*, February 16, 1861, 3.

80. "Report of the Committee of the Peace Conference," *The Daily Dispatch*, February 16, 1861, 3.

FOUR: The Clergy and Churches

1. L. E. Chittenden, *A Report of the Debates and Proceedings in the Secret Sessions of the Conference Convention, For Proposing Amendments to the Constitution of the United States, Held at Washington, D.C., in February,* a.d. *1861* (New York: D. Appleton & Company, 1864), 17.

2. Rev. Charles Hall, *A Sermon Preached to the Opening of the Eighty-First Convention of the Diocese of Maryland, May 25, 1864* (Washington, DC: McGill & Witherow, 1864), 7.

3. Stetson Conn, *Washington's Epiphany, Church and Parish* (Washington, DC: Church of the Epiphany, 1976), 1–14.

4. Ibid., 24.

5. Ibid., 25; "Rev. Dr. C. H. Hall Dead," *New York Times*, September 13, 1895, 4.

6. "City Statistics," *Evening Star*, January 3, 1859, 3; Conn, *Washington's Epiphany*, 27–32; "Musical," *Evening Star*, March 18, 1859, 3.

7. Conn, *Washington's Epiphany*, 40.

8. Ibid., 39.

9. "Religious Services by the Military," *The National Republican*, May 13, 1861, 3; "Religious," *Evening Star*, May 14, 1861, 2.

10. Conn, *Washington's Epiphany*, 35–38; Richard Grimmett, *St. John's Church, Lafayette Square: The History and Heritage of the Church of the Presidents, Washington, DC* (Minneapolis: Mill City Press, 2009), 274–75.

11. "Route of March," *The National Republican*, March 6, 1862, 3; "Married in Church," *Evening Star*, September 24, 1861, 3.

12. Conn, *Washington's Epiphany*, 39.

13. Rev. Charles H. Hall, *A Mournful Easter: A Discourse Delivered to the Church of the Epiphany* (Washington, DC: Gideon & Pearson, 1865), 11.

14. Ibid., 14.

15. Ibid., 15.

16. "Rev. Dr. C. H. Hall Dead," *New York Times*, September 13, 1895, 4; "Dr. Hall's Pastorate Here," *The Washington Post*, September 14, 1895, 6.

17. Grimmett, *St. John's Church, Lafayette Square*, 153–54.

18. "Gen. Scott's Religion," *New York Times*, October 14, 1852, 2.

19. "Latest Intelligence," *New York Times*, February 28, 1853, 4.

20. "The Sickles Trial," *New York Times*, April 13, 1859, 8.

21. Grimmett, *St. John's Church, Lafayette Square*, 39–44.

22. Ibid., 44, 63, 154.

23. "Obsequies of the Lamented Col. Ellsworth," *The National Republican*, May 27, 1861, 3.

24. John Niven, ed., *Salmon P. Chase Papers* (Kent, Ohio: Kent State University Press, 1994), 165, 232, 246.

25. Clement Moore Butler, *Life Is a Tale that Is Told* (Washington, DC: C. Alexander, 1850), 12, 14–15.

26. Jens Christian Roseland, *American Lutheran Biographies* (Milwaukee: A Houtkamp & Son, 1890), 129–30.

27. Merrill Edwards Gates, ed., *Men of Mark in America: Ideals of American Life*, vol.1 (Washington, DC: Men of Mark Publishing Company, 1906), 186–87.

28. J. George Butler, *Courageous Trustfulness: Twentieth Pastoral Anniversary, July 4, 1869, St. Paul's Lutheran Church* (Washington, DC: Judd & Detweiler, 1869), 1–16.

29. Homer Calkin, *Castings from the Foundry Mold* (Nashville: Parthenon Press, 1968), 91, 93.

30. Ibid., 125–30.

31. "The Gettysburg Address, as reported 150 years ago," *Akron Beacon Journal*, November 19, 2013, http://www.ohio.com/editorial/the-gettysburg-address-as-reported-150-years-ago-1.445985.

32. Ibid.

33. "In the Name of Jehovah Our Banner We Raise," Hymnary.org, http://www.hymnary.org/person/Stockton_TH1?sort=desc&order=Texts+by+T.+H.+Stockton+%2811%29.

34. Alexander Clark, *Memory's Tribute to the Life, Character and Work of the Rev. Thos. H. Stockton* (New York: S.R. Wells, 1869), 1–30.

35. Ibid.

36. Harvey W. Crew, et. al, "Centennial History of the City of Washington D.C.," *Washington D.C. Genealogy Trails*, http://genealogytrails.com/washdc/books/cenhistchp16.html.

37. John C. Smith, *Jehovah-Jireh. A discourse commemorative of the twenty-seventh anniversary of the organization of the Fourth Presbyterian Church, Washington, D. C., delivered on Sabbath, 25th November, 1855* (Washington, DC: Thomas McGill, 1855), 16, 31, 51–52; Joseph Thomas Kelly, "Rev. John C. Smith, D. D., and Other Pioneer Presbyterian Ministers of Washington," Records of the Columbia Historical Society, vol. 24 (Washington, DC: Historical Society of Washington, D.C., 1922), 127–28.

38. Kelly, "Rev. John C. Smith, D.D.," Records of the Columbia Historical Society. Smith, Jehovah-Jireh, 50.

39. Ibid., 46–47.

40. Ibid., 16, 33, 35–36, 38.

41. Ibid., 118–35.

42. Crew, et. al, "Centennial History of the City of Washington D.C."

43. Dedicated to Elizabeth Stone (no author listed), *The National Presbyterian Church: The First 200 Years 1795–1995* (Washington, DC: National Presbyterian Church, 1996), 11.

44. "Death List of a Day," *New York Times*, July 1, 1901, l; "The Rev. Dr. Byron Sunderland," 7.

45. Rev. Sullivan Weston, *Sermons by the Rev. Mr. Weston, and the Rev. Byron Sunderland, Preached in the Hall of Representatives, Sunday, April 28th, 1861* (Washington: Henry Polkinhorn, Printer, 1861), 15, 17.

46. Ibid., 17–18.

47. Ibid., 22.

48. John Remsburg, *Abraham Lincoln: Was He a Christian?* (New York: Truth Seeker Company, 1893), 29.

49. Ida M. Tarbell, *The Life of Abraham Lincoln*, vol. 1 (New York: S. S. McClure Company, 1895), 124–25.

50. "News from Washington," *New York Times*, May 1, 1863, 3.

51. Allen C. Guelzo, *Abraham Lincoln: Redeemer President* (New York: W. B. Eerdmans Publishing, 2002), 321.

52. Ronald C. White Jr., *Lincoln's Greatest Speech: The Second Inaugural* (New York: Simon and Schuster, 2006), 139.

53. Noah Brooks, *Lincoln Observed: The Civil War Dispatches of Noah Brooks*, ed. Michael Burlingame (Baltimore: Johns Hopkins University Press, 1998), 13–14.

54. Marquis Adolphe de Chambrun, *Impressions of Lincoln and the Civil War: A Foreigner's Account* (New York: Random House, 1952), 114.

55. "President Buchanan," *Wheeling Daily Intelligencer*, April 28, 1857, 2.

56. "How a Chaplain is Elected," *True American* (Steubenville, OH), January 21, 1857, 2.

57. Grant R. Brodrecht, *Our Country: Northern Evangelicals and the Union During the Civil War* (doctoral dissertation, Notre Dame, 2008), 67.

58. "White House Funeral Sermon for President Lincoln," Abraham Lincoln Online, http://www.abrahamlincolnonline.org/lincoln/speeches/gurley.htm.

59. Crew, et. al, "Centennial History of the City of Washington D.C."; Peter Lumpkins, "Professor G. W. Samson: An Historic Baptist View on Wines," *SBC Tomorrow* (blog), January 21, 2008, http://peterlumpkins.typepad.com /peter_lumpkins/2008/01/professor-g-w-s-1.html.

60. James L. Haley, *Sam Houston* (Norman, OK: University of Oklahoma Press, 2004), 314.

61. Bruce Gourley, "Baptists and the American Civil War: September 26, 1861," Baptists and the American Civil War, http://www.civilwarbaptists.com/this dayinhistory/1861-september-26/.

62. "Rev. Dr. J. J. Bullock," *Raftsman's Journal*, April 13, 1864, 1; Bradley J. Longfield, *The Presbyterian Controversy: Fundamentalists, Modernists, and Moderates* (New York: Oxford University Press, 1991), 31.

63. "Meeting in Baltimore for the Benefit of Presbyterian Ministers," *The Daily Dispatch* (Richmond), December 11, 1865, 1.

64. William H. Averill, *A History of the First Presbyterian Church, Frankfort, Kentucky* (Cincinnatti: Monfort & Co., 1902), 72–73.

65. William Birney, *James G. Birney and His Times* (New York: D. Appleton and Company, 1890), 181–82.

66. "The Presbyterian General Assemblies," *Frank Leslie's Sunday Magazine* 24 (1888), 113.

67. Gourley, "The Baptists and the American Civil War."

68. Mitchell Snay, *Gospel of Disunion* (Chapel Hill: University of North Carolina Press, 1993), 123.

69. C. C. Goen, *Broken Churches, Broken Nation* (Macon, GA: Mercer University Press, 1997), 60.

70. Ibid., 77.

71. Ibid., 75.

72. Ibid., 76–77.

73. Ibid., 176.

74. Ibid., 136.

75. Ibid., 165.

76. Jack Maddex, "From Theocracy to Spirituality: The Southern Presbyterian Reversal on Church and State," *The Counsel of Chalcedon* (June–July 1998), 35.

77. Goen, *Broken Churches*, 83–85.

78. Peter Cartwright, *Autobiography of Peter Cartwright: The Backwoods Preacher*, ed. W. P. Strickland (New York: Carlton & Porter, 1857), 286–87.

79. Goen, *Broken Churches*, 95–97.

80. *Abridgment of the Debates of Congress, from 1789 to 1856*, vol. 7 (New York: D. Appleton and Company, 1857), 409, no author.

81. "Religious," *Evening Star*, June 13, 1860, 3.

FIVE: THE COMPROMISE

1. "Origin of the Peace Conference," *Staunton Spectator*, February 19, 1861, 2.

2. "Latest News," *The Democratic Press* (Eaton, Preble County, Ohio), February 21, 1861, 2.

3. "The Peace Conference at Washington," *Daily Nashville Patriot*, February 18, 1861, 2.

4. "Letter from Washington," *Nashville Union and American*, February 23, 1861, 2.

5. "The Peace Conference," *Vermont Phoenix*, February 21, 1861, 2.

6. "Affairs of the Nation," *New York Times*, February 19, 1861, 1.

7. "The Peace Convention," *Evening Star*, February 18, 1861, 2.

8. L. E. Chittenden, *A Report of the Debates and Proceedings in the Secret*

Sessions of the Conference Convention, For Proposing Amendments to the Constitution of the United States, Held at Washington, D.C., in February, a.d. 1861 (New York: D. Appleton & Company, 1864), 57.

9. "Summary," *Memphis Daily Appeal*, February 24, 1861, 2.

10. "The Peace Conference," *Evening Star* (Washington, DC), February 18, 1861, 3.

11. Chittenden, *A Report of the Debates and Proceedings*, 61.

12. Ibid., 62.

13. Ibid.

14. Ibid., 64.

15. Ibid., 65.

16. Ibid., 67.

17. Ibid., 59–67.

18. "The Peace Conference," *Evening Star*, February 18, 1861, 3.

19. Chittenden, *A Report of the Debates and Proceedings*, 68.

20. Ibid.

21. Ibid.

22. Ibid., 69.

23. Ibid.

24. Ibid.

25. "A National Convention," *Nashville Union and American*, February 23, 1861, 2.

26. Chittenden, *A Report of the Debates and Proceedings*, 68.

27. Ibid.

28. *In Memoriam, Maj. Gen. Samuel Ryan Curtis, Died December 26, 1866* (Keokuk, Iowa, Rees' Job Office, 1867), 18.

29. James Chace, *Mexico under Fire, Being the Diary of Samuel Ryan Curtis, 3rd Ohio Volunteer Regiment, during the American Military Occupation of Northern Mexico, 1846–1847* (Fort Worth: Texas Christian University Press, 1994), 133.

30. "The Peace Conference," *Evening Star*, February 18, 1861, 3.

31. Chittenden, *A Report of the Debates and Proceedings*, 72–73.

32. Ibid.

33. Ibid.

34. Ibid.

35. Ibid., 75–76.

36. Ibid., 76–79.

37. Ibid., 80–82.

38. Ibid., 83–85.

39. Ibid., 86–88.

40. Ibid., 88–89.

41. Ibid., 90.

42. Ibid., 90–91.

43. Ibid., 91–92.

44. Ibid., 92–93.

45. Ibid., 93.

46. Ibid., 94.

47. Ibid.

48. Ibid., 94–95.

49. Ibid., 95.

50. Ibid., 96–97.

51. Ibid., 98.

52. George Sewall Boutwell, *Address of Hon. George S. Boutwell: To the People of Berlin* (Boston: Abner Forbes, 1850), 29–30.

53. George Sewall Boutwell, *Reminiscences of Sixty Years in Public Affairs* (New York: McClure, Phillips & Co., 1902), 269–70.

54. Ibid., 269–70.

55. Ibid., 272.

56. "Affairs of the Nation," *New York Times*, February 18, 1861, 1.

57. Boutwell, *Reminiscences of Sixty Years*, 278.

58. Ibid., 278–79.

59. Ibid.,280.

60. Ibid., 281.

61. Chittenden, *A Report of the Debates and Proceedings*, 98–102.

62. Boutwell, *Reminiscences of Sixty Years*, 268–73.

63. Chittenden, *A Report of the Debates and Proceedings*, 102–04.

64. Ibid., 103–04.

65. Ibid., 104.

66. Ibid., 105.

67. Ibid., 105–06.

68. Ibid., 107–08.

69. "Letter from Washington," *Nashville Union and American*, February 22, 1861, 2.

70. "Proceedings of the Peace Conference," *New York Times*, Monday, February 18, 1861, 1.

71. Ibid.

72. "Items Telegraphed from Washington," *Evening Star* (Washington, DC), February 19, 1861, 3.
73. Chittenden, *A Report of the Debates and Proceedings*, 110.
74. Ibid., 110–11.
75. Ibid., 112.
76. Ibid., 113–14.
77. Ibid., 114.
78. Ibid., 114–16.
79. Ibid., 118–19.
80. Ibid., 120.
81. Ibid., 120–21.
82. Ibid., 122–23.
83. Ibid., 124.
84. Ibid.
85. Ibid., 124–27.
86. Ibid., 127–28.
87. Ibid., 128.
88. Ibid., 129.
89. Ibid., 131.
90. Ibid., 129–32.
91. Barclay Rives, *William Cabell Rives: A Country to Serve* (New York: Atelerix, 2014), 54, 190–200.
92. Chittenden, *A Report of the Debates and Proceedings*, 133.
93. Ibid., 133.
94. Ibid., 133–35.
95. Ibid., 135.
96. Ibid., 135–36.
97. Ibid., 136–37.
98. Ibid., 137–38.
99. Ibid., 138.
100. Ibid., 138–39.
101. Ibid., 139–40.
102. Ibid., 140.
103. Ibid., 142.
104. Ibid., 142–43.
105. Ibid., 143.
106. Ibid., 143–44.

107. "The 'Peace Conference,'" *Semi Weekly Standard* (Raleigh, NC), February 23, 1861, 3.

108. Chittenden, *A Report of the Debates and Proceedings*, 144–45.

109. Ibid., 146.

110. Ibid., 146–47.

111. Ibid., 149.

112. Ibid., 55.

113. Ibid., 150.

114. Ibid., 151.

115. Ibid., 152–53.

116. Ibid., 153.

117. Ibid., 153–54.

118. Ibid., 154–55.

119. Ibid., 155.

120. Ibid., 156.

121. "Virginia Placed in a False Position," *National Republican* (Washington, DC), February 22, 1861, 2.

122. "Progress of the Peace Congress," *Holmes County Republican* (OH), February 21, 1861, 2.

123. "Forebodings of Mr. Tyler," *Nashville Union and American*, February 23, 1861, 2.

124. "Indianapolis Correspondence," *The Plymouth Weekly Democrat* (Plymouth, IN), February 21, 1861, 2.

125. "The Peace Conference," *Vermont Phoenix* (Brattleboro, VT), February 21, 1861, 2.

126. "The Sharp Practice of the Border States," *Cincinnati Daily Press* (Cincinnati, OH), February 21, 1861, 2.

127. "Wheeling," *Daily Intelligencer* (Wheeling, WV), February 19, 1861, 2.

SIX: SECURING THE CAPITOL

1. US House of Representatives, Reports of the Select Committee of Five, on the Following Subjects By United States Congress. House Select Committee of Five (Washington, DC: US Government Printing Office, 1861), 54–61.

2. Margaret Leech, *Reveille in Washington* (New York: Harper and Collins 20011), Kindle location 468.

3. Cong. Globe, 37th Cong., 2d Sess., 326 (1861).

4. Lucius Chittenden, *Recollections of President Lincoln and His Administration* (New York: Harper & Brothers Publishers, 1904), 37.

5. Ibid., 38–39.

6. Ibid., 38.

7. Ibid., 41.

8. "The Votes Counted," *The National Republican*, February 14, 1861, 3.

9. Chittenden, *Recollections of President Lincoln*, 41.

10. "The Votes Counted," *The National Republican*, February 14, 1861, 3.

11. Chittenden, *Recollections of President Lincoln*, 41.

12. Ibid., 42.

13. Ibid., 43.

14. Ibid.

15. Ibid.

16. Ibid., 44.

17. Ibid.

18. Ibid., 45.

19. Ibid., 46.

20. Ibid.

21. "House," *The National Republican* (Washington, DC), February 14, 1861, 2.

22. Walter Stahr, *Seward: Lincoln's Indispensable Man* (New York: Simon and Schuster, 2012), 236.

23. John Taylor, *William Henry Seward: Lincoln's Right Hand* (New York: HarperCollins, 1991), 136.

24. "Counting the Votes," *Evening Star*, February 13, 1861, 3.

25. "Affairs of the Nation," *New York Times*, February 15, 1861, 1.

26. "Strange Indeed," *Clearfield Republican*, February 20, 1861, 2.

27. "Counting the Votes," *Burlington Free Press*, February 15, 1861, 2.

28. Brian Wolley, "Lincoln's Whistle-Stop Trip to Washington," Smithsonian .com, February 9, 2011, http://www.smithsonianmag.com/history/lincolns -whistle-stop-trip-to-washington-161974/.

29. Don Fehrenbacher, ed., *Abraham Lincoln, Speeches, Letters, Miscellaneous Writings, Presidential Messages and Proclamations* (Washington, DC: Library of Congress, 1989), 197–206.

30. Ibid.

31. Roger Launius, *Alexander William Doniphan: Portrait of a Missouri Moderate* (Columbia, MO: Univeristy of Missouri Press), 239, 249.

32. Frederic Culmer, "A Snapshot of Alexander W. Doniphan, 1808–1887," *Missouri Historical Review*, 38:1 (October 1943), 29.

33. Ibid.

34. Ibid.

35. Abraham Lincoln, "1861: Address at Buffalo, New York, February 16, 1861," *The Writings of Abraham Lincoln*, vol. 5, Classic Reader (website), http://www .classicreader.com/book/3766/99/.

36. Ibid.

37. Culmer, "A Snapshot of Alexander W. Doniphan, 1808–1887," 29.

38. Kimberly Harper, "Alexander William Doniphan," The State Historical Society of Missouri, http://shs.umsystem.edu/historicmissourians/name/d /doniphan/index.html.

39. George Boutwell, *Reminiscences of Sixty Years in Public Affairs* (New York: McClure, Phillips & Co., 1902), 271.

40. Stahr, *Seward: Lincoln's Indispensable Man*, 224, 226.

41. Robert Gunderson, *Old Gentlemen's Convention* (Madison, WI: Greenwood Press, 1981), 51.

42. John Bigelow, *Retrospections of an Active Life*, vol. 1 (New York: Baker & Taylor, 1909), 355.

43. Gunderson, *Old Gentlemen's Convention*, 52.

44. William Davis, *A Government of Our Own* (New York: Simon & Schuster, 1994), 71–77.

45. David Gardiner Tyler, *Letters and Times of the Tylers* (New York: Whittet & Shepperson, 1885), 597.

46. "The Southern Confederacy," *The National Republican* (Washington, DC), February 11, 1861, 3.

47. Joan Cashin, *First Lady of the Confederacy Varina Davis's Civil War* (Cambridge: Harvard University Press, 2008), 102; William Cooper, *Jefferson Davis: American* (New York: Vintage, 2001), 347–48; Davis, *A Government of Our Own*, 128.

48. Cooper, *Jefferson Davis: American*, 349–52.

49. "Inauguration Day in Dixie," *Presidential History Geeks* (blog), February 18, 2011, http://potus-geeks.livejournal.com/95311.html.

50. Davis, *A Government of Our Own*, 158–61.

51. Jefferson Davis, "Jefferson Davis' First Inaugural Address," The Papers of Jefferson Davis, http://jeffersondavis.rice.edu/Content.aspx?id=88.

52. Ibid.

53. Davis, *A Government of Our Own*, 165–67.

54. "The Contrast," *Nashville Union and American*, February 21, 1861, 2.

55. Mary Chesnut, *Mary Chesnut's Civil War*, ed. C. Vann Woodward (New Haven: Yale University Press, 1983), 7–8.

56. Cooper, *Jefferson Davis: American*, 357–58.

57. Cashin, *First Lady of the Confederacy*, 104.

58. Cooper, *Jefferson Davis: American*, 358; Davis, *A Government of Our Own*, 274.

59. "From the Ledger," *The National Republican* (Washington, DC), February 4, 1861, 2.

60. Davis, *A Government of Our Own*, 275.

61. Robert Gunderson, "William C. Rives and the 'Old Gentlemen's Convention,'" *The Journal of Southern History* (November 1956), 469–70.

62. Ibid.

63. Tyler, *Letters and Times of the Tylers*, 619–21.

64. "The Peace Convention," *Daily Nashville Patriot*, February 16, 1861, 2.

65. "The Virginia Convention," Evening Star, February 16, 1861, 2.

66. "The Virginia State Convention," *New York Times*, February 27, 1861, 1.

67. Ibid.

68. "Virginia Placed in a False Position," *The National Republican* (Washington, DC), February 22, 1861, 2.

69. Tyler, *Letters and Times of the Tylers*, 634.

70. Ibid., 611–14.

71. Ibid.

72. "From Washington," *The Daily Dispatch* (Richmond, VA), February 18, 1861, 3.

73. Tyler, *Letters and Times of the Tylers*, 611–14.

74. "From Washington," *The Daily Dispatch*, February 27, 1861, 1.

75. Tyler, *Letters and Times of the Tylers*, 613.

76. Ibid.

SEVEN: LINCOLN'S ARRIVAL

1. "The Peace Convention," *Evening Star*, February 20, 1861, 2.

2. L. E. Chittenden, *A Report of the Debates and Proceedings in the Secret Sessions of the Conference Convention, For Proposing Amendments to the Constitution of the United States, Held at Washington, D.C., in February, a.d. 1861* (New York: D. Appleton & Company, 1864), 160.

3. "Obituary Sketch of Charles J. McCurdy," Memorials of Connecticut Judges and Attorneys As Printed in the Connecticut Reports 60:593–602, http://www.cslib.org/memorials/mccurdyc.htm.

4. Ibid.; Chittenden, *A Report of the Debates and Proceedings*, 160.

5. Chittenden, *A Report of the Debates and Proceedings*, 161.

6. The Lincoln Institute, "David Dudley Field (1805–1894)," Mr. Lincoln In New York (website), http://www.mrlincolnandnewyork.org/content_inside .asp?ID=56&subjectID=3.

7. Henry Field, *The Life of David Dudley Field* (New York: Charles Scribner's Sons, 1898), x.

8. Chittenden, *A Report of the Debates and Proceedings*, 162.

9. Ibid., 164.

10. Ibid., 166.

11. Ibid., 170.

12. Ibid., 170–71.

13. Ibid., 171.

14. Ibid., 172–74.

15. Ibid., 175–76.

16. Ibid., 177–80.

17. Ibid., 181–83.

18. Ibid., 183–85.

19. Ibid., 185–87.

20. Ibid., 189.

21. Ibid., 189–90.

22. Ibid., 191–92.

23. Ibid., 192.

24. Ibid., 194–95.

25. "Highly Important from Washington," *New York Times*, February 21, 1861, http://www.nytimes.com/1861/02/21/news/highly-important-washington -peace-conference-its-deliberations-passage-tariff.html.

26. Chittenden, *A Report of the Debates and Proceedings*, 199–200.

27. Ibid., 201–02.

28. Ibid., 202.

29. "Progress of the Peace Conference," *Holmes County Republican* (Millersburg, Holmes County, OH), February 21, 1861, 2.

30. "The Peace Conference," *Daily Intelligencer*, February 25, 1861, 3; Chittenden, *A Report of the Debates and Proceedings*, 207.

31. Chittenden, *A Report of the Debates and Proceedings*, 205.

32. Ibid., 213.

33. Ibid., 214–15.

34. Ibid., 215–16.

35. Ibid., 216–39, 249.

36. Ibid., 252.

37. Ibid., 244–55.

38. Ibid., 257–59.

39. Ibid., 263–65.

40. Ibid., 264–69.

41. Ibid., 264–69.

42. Ibid., 274.

43. Ibid., 275–78.

44. "James Pollock Biography," James Pollock In God We Trust Museum, http://jamespollockmuseum.com/james-pollock-bio/.

45. Chittenden, *A Report of the Debates and Proceedings*, 277–78.

46. Robert G. Gunderson, "William Rives and the 'Old Gentlemen's Convention,'" *The Journal of Southern History*, 22:4 (November 1956), 464–65.

47. Chittenden, *A Report of the Debates and Proceedings*, 279–83.

48. Ibid., 279–83.

49. Ibid., 284–85.

50. Ibid., 285.

51. Ibid., 294–95.

52. Ibid., 296–97.

53. Ibid., 300–01.

54. Ibid., 302.

55. Ibid., 304–05.

56. Ibid., 305–06.

57. Ibid., 306, 315–16.

58. Ibid., 307.

59. Ibid.

60. Ibid., 314.

61. Ibid., 318–19.

62. Ibid., 320–21.

63. Ibid., 322.

64. Ibid., 327.

65. Ibid., 330–31.

66. Ibid., 331–32.

67. Ibid., 329–34.

68. Harold Holzer, *Lincoln President-Elect: Abraham Lincoln and the Great Secession Winter 1860–1861* (New York: Simon & Schuster, 2008), 406.

69. "Mr. Lincoln in Washington," *Daily Intelligencer* (Wheeling, WV), February 25, 1861, 2.

70. Lucius Chittenden, *Recollections of President Lincoln and His Administration* (New York: Harper & Brothers Publishers, 1904), 66.

71. Ibid., 65–67; Chittenden, *A Report of the Debates and Proceedings*, 336.

72. Chittenden, *Recollections of President Lincoln*, 67.

73. Ibid., 58–64.

74. Ibid., 66.

75. Ibid., 68.

76. Ibid., 68–69.

77. Ibid., 70–71.

78. "Local News," *Evening Star*, February 25, 1861, 3.

79. Chittenden, *Recollections of President Lincoln*, 70–72.

80. Barclay Rives, *William Cabell Rives: A Country to Serve* (New York: Atelerix, 2014), 3, 269.

81. Chittenden, *Recollections of President Lincoln*, 73.

82. Ibid.

83. Ibid.

84. Ibid., 74.

85. Ibid.

86. Ibid.

87. Ibid., 74–75.

88. Ibid., 75.

89. Ibid.

90. Ibid., 75–76.

91. Ibid., 77.

92. Rives, *William Cabell Rives*, 2.

93. "Local News," *Evening Star*, February 25, 1861, 3; "Mr. Lincoln Yesterday," *The National Republican* (Washington, DC), February 25, 1861, 3.

EIGHT: AGREEMENT AND REJECTION

1. "The Inauguration of the President Elect," *The National Republican* (Washington, DC), February 25, 1861, 2.

2. "The Question Virtually Settled," *Evening Star*, February 25, 1861, 2.

3. L. E. Chittenden, *A Report of the Debates and Proceedings in the Secret Sessions of the Conference Convention, For Proposing Amendments to the Constitution of the United States, Held at Washington, D.C., in February, a.d. 1861* (New York: D. Appleton & Company, 1864), 348, 350–52.

4. Ibid., 352.

5. Ibid., 352–53.

6. Ibid., 353–54.

7. Ibid., 356–58.

8. Ibid., 358–60.

9. Ibid., 360–62, 372.

10. Ibid., 361.

11. Ibid., 363.

12. Ibid., 366.

13. Ibid., 369.

14. "The St. Louis Democrat," *The National Republican* (Washington, DC), February 25, 1861, 2.

15. Chittenden, *A Report of the Debates and Proceedings*, 376–77.

16. Ibid., 377–78.

17. Ibid., 378–79.

18. Ibid., 381–83.

19. Ibid., 385–87.

20. "The Peace Convention," *Evening Star*, February 26, 1861, 2.

21. Chittenden, *A Report of the Debates and Proceedings*, 394.

22. Ibid., 395.

23. Ibid., 399.

24. Ibid., 400–01.

25. Ibid., 405–06.

26. Ibid., 407–08.

27. Ibid., 409.

28. Ibid., 411–17.

29. Ibid., 418–21.

30. Ibid., 421–24.

31. Ibid., 428.

32. Ibid., 430.

33. Ibid.

34. Ibid., 433.

35. Ibid., 433.

36. Ibid., 436.

37. Ibid., 436–37.

38. Ibid., 438.

39. Ibid., 438–39.

40. Ibid., 439.

41. "Items Telegraphed from Washington," *Evening Star*, February 28, 1861, 2.

42. Mrs. Chapman Coleman, *The Life of John J. Crittenden*, vol. 2 (Philadelphia: J. B. Lippincott & Co., 1873), 337–38.

43. Charles M. Segal, *Conversations with Lincoln* (Piscataway, NJ: Transaction Publishers, 2002), 86–87.

44. Ibid., 87–88.

45. Ibid., 88–89.

46. Ibid., 90.

47. "Important Statement of Ex-Governor of Kentucky," *Liverpool Mercury* (Britain), October 13, 1862, 3.

48. Chittenden, *A Report of the Debates and Proceedings*, 441.

49. "Missouri Convention," *Missouri Republican*, March 6, 1861, 3.

50. John Palmer, *Personal Recollections of John M. Palmer* (Cincinnati: R. Clarke Co., 1901), 84, 88–89.

51. Chittenden, *A Report of the Debates and Proceedings*, 442–46.

52. Ibid., 450–51.

53. Ibid., 451–52.

54. Ibid.

55. Ibid.

56. "A Salute of One Hundred Guns," *Evening Star*, February 28, 1861, 3.

57. Chittenden, *A Report of the Debates and Proceedings*, 471.

58. "Latest News, by Telegraph," *Keowee Courier* (Pickens Court House, SC), March 9, 1861, 2; "News Summary," *Detroit Free Press*, March 1, 1861, 1.

59. "The Country," *The Daily Press* (Cincinnatti), March 9, 1861, 2; "News Summary," *White Cloud Kansas Chief*, March 21, 1861 2; "The Guernsey Times," *The Spirit of Democracy* (Woodsfield, OH), March 13, 1861, 2; "Final Action of the Peace Conference," *Vincennes Gazette*, March 9, 1861

60. Oliver Perry Chitwood, *John Tyler: Champion of the Old South* (Newtown, CT: American Political Biography Press, 1990) i, 452.

61. Lyon Gardiner Tyler, *Letters and Times of the Tylers, Volume II*, (Richmond, VA: Whittet & Shepperdson, 1885), 623–27.

62. Ibid., 628–29.

63. Ibid., 629–32.

64. Cong. Globe, 37th Cong., 2d Sess. 1254–55, 1269–70, 13–1317, 1405 (1861).

65. "Mottoes of the Day," *New-York Daily Tribune*, March 2, 1861, 4.

66. Cong. Globe, 37th Cong., 2d Sess. 1331–33 (1861).

67. "Missouri Convention," *Missouri Republican* (St. Louis), March 6, 1861, 25.

68. Ibid.

69. "Mr. Rives's Speech," *The National Republican* (Washington, DC), April 6, 1861, 2.

70. "Union Meeting in Ashe," *Weekly Standard* (Raleigh, NC), April 3, 1861, 2.

71. "Substance of the Remarks of Hon. F.K. Zollicoffer," *Daily Nashville Patriot*, April 16, 1861, 2.

72. "A Pregnant Fact," *Keowee Courier* (Pickens Court House, SC), April 13, 1861, 2.

73. "Letter from Judge Robt L. Caruthers," *Nashville Union and American*, April 30, 1861, 2.

74. "The Rebellion," *Burlington Free Press* (Burlington, VT), April 19, 1861, 2.

Epilogue

1. Philip Klein, *President James Buchanan: A Biography* (Newtown, CT: American Political Biography Press, 1995), 402.

2. Ibid., 408–409, 420, 423, 427.

3. Robert Seager II, *And Tyler Too* (New York: McGraw Hill, 1963), 460.

4. Oliver Perry Chitwood, *John Tyler: Champion of the Old South* (Newtown, CT: American Political Biography Press, 1990), 454–55.

5. Seager, *And Tyler Too*, 463.

6. Ibid., 464–65.

7. Ibid., 517.

8. Lyon Gardiner Tyler, *Letters and Times of the Tylers* (Richmond, VA: Whittet & Shepperson, 1885), 644.

9. Chitwood, *John Tyler: Champion of the Old South*, 464–65.

10. Tyler, *Letters and Times of the Tylers*, 667.

11. Seager, *And Tyler Too*, 475–76.

12. Ibid., 478.

13. Ibid., 466.

14. Ibid., 285.

15. Tyler, *Letters and Times of the Tylers*, 649.

16. Seager, *And Tyler Too*, 481.

17. Ibid., 490.

18. Ibid., 539.

19. Maury Klein, *Days of Defiance: Sumter, Secession, and the Coming of the Civil War* (New York: Vintage Books, 1999), 253.

20. John Hay and John Nicolay, *Abraham Lincoln*, vol. 3 (New York: Century Co., 1917), 323.

21. Winston Churchill, *History of the English Speaking Peoples* (New York: Greenwich House, 1991), 430.

INDEX

W–X

Wadsworth, James, 12

War of 1812, x, xi, xv, 6, 13, 35, 44,
136, 140, 141, 254, 255

Washington, DC
churches in. *See individual churches
by name*
controversial Washington's birthday
parade in, xi–xii, 30–34
during the days of the Peace
Conference (description), 36–43
largest church building at the time
in, 102
population as of 1860, 36

Washington, George, xi, 15, 18, 30, 32,
35, 39, 40, 43, 122, 157, 207

Washington, Martha, 40

Webster, Daniel, 24, 63, 93

Wesley, John, 98

Westover Episcopal Church (VA), 17

Whig(s), 12, 19, 35, 62, 68, 70, 144,
147, 174, 179, 188, 200, 207

White, Thomas, 198

White House, x, xi, xii, xiii, 5, 6, 8, 14,
15, 16, 17, 18, 19, 20, 24, 31, 32, 33,
36, 37, 38, 40, 51, 53, 57, 61, 87, 90,
91, 92, 93, 94, 97, 102, 105, 109,
127, 163, 178, 186, 190, 249, 254
first First Lady to dance publicly in
the, 19
funerals at the, 90, 91, 93, 109
Trollope on the, 37
visit of the Peace Conference delegates, xi, 51–53

"White House of the Confederacy," 57

Wickliffe, Charles, 13, 58–59, 63, 77, 82,
86, 120, 140, 200, 203, 204, 228, 235

Willard, Henry, 15, 16, 239

Willard Hall, 11–17, 26, 29, 53, 55, 58,
63, 64, 76, 77, 84, 87, 89, 102, 104,
128, 147, 180, 193, 195, 207, 208,
213, 239
the delegates at, 11–17

Willard's Hotel (Washington, DC), ix,
x, xiii, 1, 13, 14, 15–17, 20, 31, 37,
41, 69, 93, 95, 97, 102, 104, 109,
127, 163, 164, 169–70, 178, 214,
217, 219, 221, 222, 224, 235, 247
cost of lodging and food at, 17
history of, 15–16
site of the 1861 Peace Conference, ix
Templeton's criticism of, 16

William and Mary College, 18, 34

Wilmot, David, 12, 208, 229, 231

Wirt, William, 66

Wisconsin, 11

Wise, Henry, 252

Wolcott, Christopher, 64–65, 70

Wood, John, 12

Wool, John, 44, 249, 252

Wright, John C., 55, 62–65, 70, 85

Y–Z

"Yankee Doodle" 44

Young Men's Bible Association, 66

Young Men's Temperance Society, 66

ABOUT THE AUTHOR

Mark Tooley is president of the Institute on Religion and Democracy, where he has worked since 1994 and prior to which he was employed by the Central Intelligence Agency. He is a lifelong resident of Northern Virginia and student of history. His articles on history, religion, and politics have appeared in many publications. Tooley's last book was *Methodism and Politics in the Twentieth Century*.